... and
...ions, including *Granta*,
... the *New York Times Book Review*.

'Elena Lappin can absorb new languages like a sponge absorbing water: a useful gift, since a life begun in Russia soon swept her from country to country, and she could live comfortably in each of them. But in which could she go that one step further, and find her true self as the writer she knew herself to be? This book is her story of her search for that special language. It is a captivating book, so sparkly with vitality, humour and genuine charm that English readers have to love it – and feel lucky. Because the language Lappin finally homed in on is theirs!' Diana Athill

'Lappin presents a thoughtful migrant's memoir that will speak to all those of us who find their lives suspended between nations, cultures, languages; between past and present selves; between rival identities and loyalties; to all those who live with a hyphen at the centre of their life stories. Which is to say, to nearly everyone' Dan Vyleta, Giller Prize-shortlisted author of *The Crooked Maid* and the bestselling *Smoke*

'Her supple prose is infused by warmth, tenderness and ebullience ... An uplifting story' Amanda Craig, *Observer*

'This intriguing memoir throws a unique light on the fortunes of a young woman – her travels, her cultural inheritance and, most of all, her languages. Elena Lappin's tale is an archetype of post-war political upheaval, her travels and migrations a reflection of world events ... [a] remarkable memoir' Anne Garvey, *Jewish Chronicle*

'This beautiful exploration of what it means to be European in the twenty-first century has never been more necessary ... In characteristically elegant prose, Lappin takes readers on a brave personal journey as she uncovers painful family secrets set against a backdrop of political cruelty and perpetual motion. Her warmth, humanity and above all understanding of the need for communication shimmer throughout, making this a book full of optimism, deeply resonant with today's world of global dislocation' Anne Sebba

'Elena Lappin is a marvellous writer. Her riveting memoir describes living in five languages and as many countries. The family relationships and the political upheavals which so often shape them are complex, yet her writing is as readable and warm as a letter from a friend' Vesna Goldsworthy, author of *Gorsky*

Also by Elena Lappin

Foreign Brides
The Nose

WHAT LANGUAGE DO I DREAM IN?

My Family's Secret History

ELENA LAPPIN

virago

VIRAGO

First published in Great Britain in 2016 by Virago Press
This paperback edition published in 2017 by Virago Press

1 3 5 7 9 10 8 6 4 2

Copyright © Elena Lappin 2016

The moral right of the author has been asserted.

A CIP catalogue record for this book
is available from the British Library.

ISBN 978-1-84408-578-1

Typeset in Bembo by M Rules
Printed and bound in Great Britain by
Clays Ltd, St Ives plc

Papers used by Virago are from well-managed forests
and other responsible sources.

Virago Press
An imprint of
Little, Brown Book Group
Carmelite House
50 Victoria Embankment
London EC4Y 0DZ

An Hachette UK Company
www.hachette.co.uk

www.virago.co.uk

For Maxim, my little brother

O Memory, where is now my youth,
Who used to say that life was truth?

Thomas Hardy, 'Memory and I'

The history of mankind is the instant
between two strides taken by a
traveller.

Franz Kafka

Kolik jazyků umíš, tolikrát jsi člověkem.
You have as many lives as the number
of languages you speak.

Czech proverb

Prologue

In July 2015 my father and I set out for a rare walk near my parents' apartment in Prague. They have lived in Germany since 1970, but for the last ten years or so they have been returning to this second home. My mother is content in either place, but my father is visibly happier in this city he has loved since he was a teenager.

Walking is very difficult for him now. He has a chronic pain in his back which is so severe he can only do a few steps at a time, leaning on his cane. Without it he still looks youthful, elegant and full of life. But when the pain gets the better of him he shows his real age – eighty-four – while he catches his breath and waits for his energy to return. It always does.

In Hamburg, he spends most of his time at home, sleeping in front of the TV. But in Prague he finds daily excuses for small errands he can run, places he can see, people he can visit. In Prague he is many years younger in spirit.

On this day – the eve of my return to London – my father announced: 'Let's go and buy those teaspoons you wanted. I know a shop.' A long time ago I had said I needed more teaspoons; he remembered.

We made our way there very slowly, down cobbled streets, across busy roads. We took a bus, then a tram. Then, not far from our destination, my father said he needed a break, so we stopped off at an outdoor café.

'Look,' he said, pointing upwards. 'This is the house.'

'Which house?'

'The one I lived in with my older brother and his wife when I first came here from Moscow.'

I knew, of course, that he had moved to Prague as a teenager in 1947 – his Czech still has a slight tinge of a Russian accent – but in all the years we lived there, when I was growing up, and later, when we came back for frequent visits, my father never mentioned his first Prague address. He always talked about those early times as if his history here had begun when he married my mother. But now he suddenly opened up.

'Look,' he said, pointing at a building across the street. 'That's where we bought our meat. And see that corner? We had a great tailor there. The day after I got here Grisha took me to buy two suits, because I had arrived with nothing.'

He looked around – at the traffic, the trams, the people ... Taking it all in, he said: 'It hasn't really changed that much, you know. The day I saw this street for the first time was the moment I fell in love with Prague. I saw civilisation for the first time in my life. At home we didn't even have an indoor toilet.'

Suddenly, he summoned the waiter and said he wanted to pay, *right now.* 'Let's go. I want to show you the apartment we lived in. It's actually on this corner.'

And so we went there, slowly. It was a very nice art deco apartment building, in good condition. A young woman walked out of the front door just as we arrived; my father squeezed past her as if he had every right to enter. Then he stood in front of the lift, hesitating.

'I'm not sure which floor it was,' he said, clearly annoyed with himself. 'I think . . . fourth. No, fifth. Yes, fifth.' Stepping out of the lift on the fifth floor, he smiled, very happily: 'There, that last door. That's it. That was ours.'

'What do you want to do now?' I said.

'I'll ring the bell and tell them I used to live here, of course. What else?'

'OK.'

The old man, my father, gathered up all his strength, and with a real twinkle in his eye walked up to a stranger's door and pressed their bell button. I took a photo of him standing there, slightly bent but still full of his strong character. He looked dignified, excited, but also a little sad. Or maybe the sadness was all mine.

No one answered. He rang again. Nothing.

He was disappointed. 'I really wanted to show you a slice of my youth,' he said. 'But never mind. Let's go and get those teaspoons.'

The lift door was still open. On the way down I asked a question about the apartment, what it was like. And what was Prague like, in 1947?

'Stop it,' he said brusquely. 'You *know* I don't want to talk about these things.'

The Phone Call

The phone rang in the middle of a noisy Sunday family dinner in the kitchen of my London home, one evening in February 2002. I had just finished serving the second course. My husband and three children were loudly debating several issues at once and laughing as they argued. My daughter and my middle son were in their teens, my oldest son in his early twenties. I was forty-seven.

I closed the door to the kitchen and went to pick up the phone in the dining room.

'Is this Lena?' said a very Russian-sounding man, in English.

'Yes. Who is this?'

'I am calling from Moscow. Are you in good health? I have to tell you something very upsetting. Please, sit down.'

'I'm OK. What is it? Please, speak Russian if you prefer.'

He did. His voice trembled with emotion. Most Russian voices do; this did not surprise me.

'Does the name Schneider mean anything to you?'

'No.'

'Really?' He seemed genuinely shocked.

'Schneider was the name of your real father. Your mother

was with another partner before your father. His name is Joseph. You are his daughter. She knew him as Schneider but his real family name was Minster. They were Americans living in Moscow. Your grandfather was once an undercover agent for the Soviet Union. He—'

The man on the phone suddenly lost his confidence. He was stumbling from one topic to another as he tried to tell me so much, very quickly. The strange thing was that I believed him. Without understanding why or how or even what was actually happening to me, I felt the truth of this story. Something clicked, fell into place.

'It took me so many years to find you, Lena. So many years.'

He was my uncle by marriage, the ex-husband of Joseph's sister. The reason why he had undertaken this search was that he had an only daughter who was a little younger than me, and who was living in the States. He wanted his daughter to know her family. He felt that this was very important.

'Your real father is living in New York. The entire family emigrated from the Soviet Union in 1973, as Jews. You have a half-brother by your father's second wife ... Also in New York.'

I felt the first pang of disappointment, and pain. Why wasn't this father looking for me? And why had my parents never told me?

The man on the phone (who finally introduced himself as V) said I should speak to my parents to verify his story. And did he have my permission to give Joseph my number? I agreed to both, and we hung up.

I didn't go straight back to the kitchen. I phoned my mother in Hamburg and told her about the phone call. She was silent. Silence – in conversation – is practically non-existent in our family. My parents are always talking, in expressive cadences, about everything under the sun. Except their secrets, apparently.

So I knew she was confirming the truth when she didn't say anything at all, and then: 'Let me speak to your father. I'll call you right back.'

The phone rang again.

'Lena? *Eto tvoy otec govorit.*'

A man with a much stronger voice than V's, speaking in Russian with a slight stutter. 'Lena? This is your father speaking.'

We had a surprisingly normal conversation, about where we both lived, what we do ... As if I didn't already have a father. In middle age, I was suddenly transported back into my infancy. What did I know? What did I not know?

A year earlier I had published my first novel, called *The Nose*. It was the story of a young American woman living in London, whose parents, especially her mother, had created an impenetrable wall of silence between themselves and their children. Only as an adult does my heroine almost accidentally stumble into uncovering and understanding the truth about her family. I thought I had invented and imagined it all. But perhaps I was writing about what I did not yet understand, but had lived with all my life.

Before we said goodbye I told Joseph that I was flying to New York in a week's time, on a journalism assignment. We arranged to meet. He sounded very excited.

Then I called my brother Maxim in Berlin. My father was visiting him, and while Maxim and I spoke I could hear his voice in the background, talking to my mother on his mobile. I quickly told Maxim what had just happened.

'Why are you so lucky?' he said, laughing. But then he was serious: 'Are you OK?'

'I am,' I said. 'Or maybe not. I don't know.'

My parents then both called, in quick succession. Each confirmed the truth of V's story.

'To be honest,' said my mother, 'I am relieved it's out.'

'I'm worried that I am going to lose you,' said my father.

No one except my brother seemed to be concerned about how this bombshell was affecting me. My parents were the core, I was the periphery. Whose story was this, really? And what was the story?

I rejoined my own family in the kitchen, and gave no sign of what had just occurred, how my life – and in some way theirs – had just been turned on its head. I knew this: my father would always be my father, whoever Joseph might become to me.

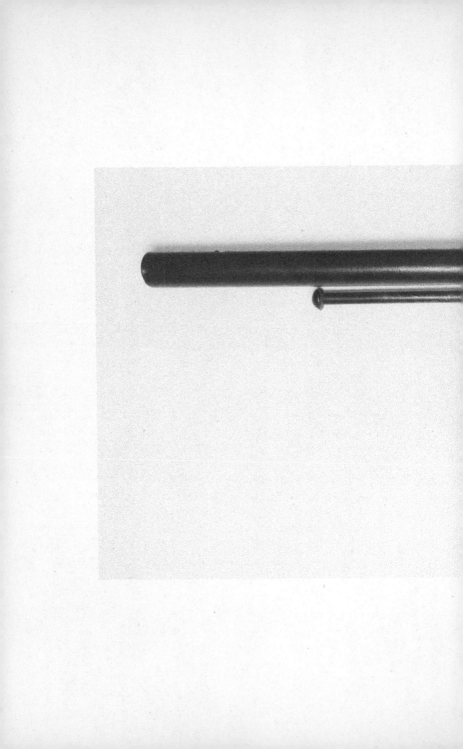

Chekhov's Gun on my Father's Wall

'If in the first act you have hung a pistol on the wall, then in the following one it should be fired,' Anton Chekhov famously wrote in 1889. The literary device known as Chekhov's gun posits that writers must be as disciplined about introducing crucial elements into their narratives as criminals planning a perfect murder. Nothing can be left to chance. Every detail exists for a reason, which must be revealed at just the right moment.

I grew up with the kind of gun Chekhov may have had in mind: a nineteenth-century Smith & Wesson revolver, hanging on the wall in the study of the man I knew as my father in Prague. Hooked on a nail above a sofa, it attracted everyone's attention as an unusual decoration. I loved to climb up and touch its heavy black metal grip, rusty brown barrel and casing. To me it always smelled as if it had just been fired, an aroma of dust and smoke – the latter imaginary, yet potent.

My father's home office was a place of enchantment for me, furnished in the latest 1960s style (blond rounded shapes, pastel colours) but dotted with objects that exuded history: a large antique armchair, softly upholstered and extravagantly set in black wood; an enormous oil painting in a heavy gilded frame, a portrait of an old man that could have been from the Rembrandt school – dark yet mysteriously illuminated. But this was borrowed history, the kind you can buy when you purchase an antique: other people's lives had been lived in their presence, in their own time. Only the gun on the wall was part of my father's own history, a real witness.

The family story, told and endlessly repeated to anyone who was interested (and even if they weren't), was that it was dug up, by accident, in the garden of my father's parents' home in Kuntsevo, a suburb of Moscow. No one knew how it had got there, or to whom it had originally belonged. The gun didn't fire any more, of course (would Chekhov make literary provision for a damaged weapon?), but it looked impressive. It had a kind of solid beauty, designed and crafted with a sense of unembellished aesthetics. My father was very attached to it, and so was I.

And I still am. The gun moved with us from Prague to Hamburg (having made its earlier journey to Prague from Russia), when we emigrated there in 1970. Its home is still my father's study, but for many years now it has no longer been a wall decoration. Instead, my father keeps it on a marble shelf above a radiator, in front of a framed photograph of his mother. She died when he was only five years old, in her early forties, and so looks forever young in this only portrait I have ever seen of her: strong dark eyes, centre-parted dark hair tied back in a no-nonsense manner. She has good, clear features, an open, unsmiling face, full lips; she looks stern and forbidding, perhaps a little hard, and even sad. She was the mother of six sons (two were from her first marriage), and had to be tough, practical, focused. Would she have mellowed, in the manner of all Jewish grandmothers? If she had lived and accompanied her sons into their adulthood would my father – her youngest – have become a different man?

I emailed him a photo of a similar gun I had found on the internet and asked if he thought they were the same make and period. He shot back in Czech, without missing a beat: 'I wish I had your problems!' My father has no interest in teasing out the poetic relevance of this or any other object. It wouldn't occur to him to wonder why he keeps the gun next to his mother's portrait, and surrounds it with antique menorahs. Confronted with the Chekhovian claim that the continued presence of this revolver in his life is, or ought to be, no accident, my father would reply, 'Of course it is. It's just an old gun. That's all.'

It was him, in fact, who found it. It had been buried in the garden for many years, but not too deep for a child digging for treasures. With the family mutt Tobik for company, he spent hours on his own when his much older brothers were too busy or too uninterested to pay attention to him. One day in the late 1930s his play yielded a real result. He couldn't believe his luck: this pistol was so old it could have witnessed the big revolution, several wars, and maybe even a romantic duel or two ... My father was allowed to keep it. When he left Russia while still a teenager (against his father's wishes) to join his brothers, who were already living in Prague, he didn't take much with him; but he took this gun. It must remind him of the things he never talks about: the home he grew up in, his early childhood.

My father's parents were both Jews, from different backgrounds. His father was from the Czech part of Carpathian Ruthenia, and ended up in Russia as a soldier of the Austro-Hungarian Army during the First World War. There, after being kept as a prisoner of war, he met his future wife, who was from the Ukraine. Their first years were spent in Kiev, where my father's older brothers were born. Later the family moved to Kuntsevo and I would not have any idea what their family life was like if I hadn't had several long telephone conversations with one of my father's brothers a few years before he died.

This uncle told me things I could never have imagined: the family kept all Jewish holidays, with special dishes used during Passover. But, most significantly, their home served as a house of prayer for local Jews during High Holidays, presumably in secret. My father is a deeply secular Jew, and never studied Hebrew nor had a bar mitzvah. But his Jewishness is an intrinsic part of his personality, and whenever he hears Jewish songs and prayers (in which he cannot participate) he always wells up and often cries. They touch and connect him with what he no longer consciously remembers: his home. When I told him what I learned from his brother he was actually surprised: he himself was not aware of all the traditions kept in his parents' house.

He was a child during the Second World War, and, like many people from areas near the front lines, spent those years in evacuation in Asiatic Russia. But his brothers joined the Czechoslovak corps of the Red Army, under General Svoboda. The war reconnected them with their father's Czech roots, and when it was over they all moved to Prague (still a Western democracy, until the communist putsch of 1948). My father learned Czech, but always retained Russian as his 'best' language. The high school he attended was a Russian gymnasium, originally created for the children of White Russian ex-pats, but after the war it was increasingly filled with young people who loved communism. As a teenager, my father was an ardent young communist. A relative who owned a tiny grocery shop in Prague, and later immigrated to Israel, remembered his passionate outrage in the 1940s: 'Your business will be expropriated when the revolution comes.' My father's love affair with communism turned out to be short-lived and ended badly (or perhaps rather well, depending on one's point of view) when he was denounced by a friend.

The gun has always been an essential item among the few familiar objects he surrounds himself with when he works at his desk or spends time in his study. Even now, in his eighties, when work as a translator and interpreter is rare, this room is still his personal domain, aesthetically very distinct from the spaces occupied by my mother. Hers are over-cluttered with items of dubious provenance and quality (she collects everything and is unable to throw anything away), whereas his minimalist office is sparsely arranged. On his oversized oak desk, which we found in one of the first apartments we moved into in Hamburg, is a sepia photograph of his father in a glass frame set in a heavy marble base. On its reverse side – he turns the frame around from time to time – is a cheerful colour snapshot of me, very suntanned and summery, aged about twenty, cuddling a fluffy teddy bear. On the walls, next to his floor-to-ceiling bookcases filled with dictionaries, are large portraits of my very beautiful mother when she was in her forties.

In her room, at the other end of their long-corridored Hamburg apartment, my mother displays photos of her own, much more numerous family: Armenian on her father's side, Russian Jewish on her mother's. There are many group photos of handsome, dark-haired relatives with deep gazes and smiling faces, women holding babies, mementoes of lives lived in a very different climate. My mother was born in Baku, Azerbaijan, where her parents met and shared some happy years. Their move from Baku to Moscow in 1938 was sudden, an escape from Stalin's purges among my grandfather's colleagues. Eventually Moscow became my mother's permanent base – until she met my father, and married and followed him to Prague.

My father is a translator by profession, from Czech into Russian. In later years, when we emigrated from Prague to Hamburg (after the Soviet invasion of Czechoslovakia in

1968), he also added German, which could not have been easy. The clatter of his typewriter was always a permanent acoustic backdrop, loud and pervasive. It was the sound of my father's authority in the house, not to be disturbed. I always did. I hated the invisible barrier between his work and our family life. I resented his absolute dedication. Today, I admire it, and envy it. My father was the quintessential freelancer, working from home – not an easy feat with two noisy kids constantly running around, often with many of their friends visiting and playing loud games. My mother was usually absent – she had a full-time job as a geographer–economist, a two-hour commute each way. She would leave the house early in the morning and return in the evening, every single day. She would braid my long hair while I was still asleep, saying softly, 'The other side!' when she needed me to turn over. When I got up, two hours later, my braids were perfect, ready for school with pretty silky bows firmly tied at each end.

My father took on any translations he could get. Having started with small technical ones, he eventually became a prominent literary translator and interpreter, earning a very good living. We had two cars, a Simca and a small Fiat, and a large, beautiful apartment. When we emigrated to Germany I watched my parents start all over again, at the age of forty, without knowing a word of their new language. I saw the same talents and absolute commitment to hard work take them from a rough beginning in a foreign country to, ultimately, another large apartment filled with paintings and some antiques. And two cars. The smoothness of this transition was what they expected of their children too.

Today, the ancient Smith & Wesson is the only object that has been physically present in all of my father's incarnations, and in some of mine. It has lived with him since his childhood in Russia, accompanied him through his high-school years and adulthood in Prague, and made the journey to Hamburg, where it remains. In mocking admiration of my obsession with the gun and its history, my father announced that I will inherit it, and that he is prepared to put it in writing. When that happens the gun will move to my home (my children love it too) and continue to be a tangible link in the chain of our family wanderings. I don't want to think about it, but I know that one day I will place it close to a portrait of my father. He believes in leaving the ghosts of the past alone, undisturbed, forgotten. He says forgetting is his peace of mind.

Contrary to Chekhov's maxim, this is a gun that will never be fired, no matter how many acts follow its original appearance. Regardless of its history prior to being unearthed in the Russian garden, its current power is in its silence and continued presence. To me, it seems to be saying, Be careful what you hide.

Cherries

There was a moment in my early childhood when I stood in a garden, by a wooden gate and fence, and stared with amazement at masses of enormous, almost-black cherries hanging from the branches of the trees. An older woman wearing a pale yellow dress handed me a few and said with pride, 'Our cherries.' I reached for them and can still taste their mellow sweetness, buried in firm, juicy red flesh which bled on my hands and trickled pinkly down my naked knee.

This happened in the same garden where my father unearthed the gun, on my only visit to his family home in Kuntsevo. The woman's name was Tyotya Sonia – Auntie Sonia; she was my father's stepmother. I never returned there and never saw her again. I don't remember anyone or anything else from this visit, although I had come with my mother and both her parents, and my father's father was also present. This detailed memory of the cherry garden has remained alive, effortlessly, as if I had been a much older child. It wasn't until I began to reconstruct my life with systematic attention to dates that it struck me: I was only two and a half at the time. It was August 1957. My mother had already decided to follow her future husband to Prague, so this was my last summer as a Russian child, on a visit to her future in-laws. I was being presented to them.

English has only one word for cherry, but in Russian there are two different words for this fruit, or rather its two main varieties: *chereshnya* and *vishnya*. Chekhov's famous play *The Cherry Orchard* is *Vishniovyi Sad* in Russian. 'Vishnya' is the heavier, darker kind of cherry, and it was this word Auntie Sonia used in my memory of our encounter. '*Nasha vishnya*,' she had said; my mother would later contemptuously describe her Russian to me as having a 'Yiddish-inflected, provincial accent'. There was a soft pride in Tyotya Sonia's voice; perhaps she was eager to impress this new family. I always crave cherries. Whenever I buy them – and they have to be the dark kind, the ones I think of as *vishnya* – I hope to relive that first rich taste. I hog them, and devour them all in one go.

Why has this memory stayed with me in such a pure form, unchanged, forever fresh? Perhaps because this was the only long outing I had been taken on at that age. We travelled to Kuntsevo by tram; the entire experience had the sheen and excitement of novelty for me. Whatever the reason, I am grateful for this first childhood memory: my very own cherry orchard is the only real link I have to my father's history, a sense of being there, in the place where he was born and where he grew up.

It is difficult to inherit the histories of those who raise us when they choose to hide them. Unlike my mother, my father hates being asked about what he remembers. He often says, 'I don't remember anything, and I don't try.' Maybe his past is a minefield he is afraid to step into. Only very occasionally, when not asked, will he begin to uncoil a film reel of vivid memories, which, surprisingly, don't seem to be buried under too many layers of enforced forgetting. I had always known that his mother died of a lung infection when he was five years old and that he doesn't remember her at all, except for seeing her corpse in the house before the funeral. But one day he suddenly told me how his mother pulled him on a sleigh in deep white snow, rushing to a doctor or hospital after he cut his hand on a rusty nail from a wooden container. He remembered the box and the nail, and his bleeding hand, and his mother, decisive and quick, facing the freezing wind. The sleigh tracks in the hard snow.

Kuntsevo had no meaning for me other than the name of my father's birthplace. The fenced garden I remember made me think of it as a rural place. But a house with a garden and cherry trees in 1950s Russia? At a time when my mother's parents lived in shared, communal apartments like most Muscovites? I needed to know more about this home, and what it was really like.

My father is a short, agile, dark-haired (now silver-haired) man, cinematically good-looking and a powerful presence. His expressive face has always been dominated by large spectacles in strong, elegant frames. He has penetrating, heavy-lidded brown eyes and a loud voice that he is unable – and unwilling – to modulate, whether he is speaking or clearing his throat. He alternates between being overbearing, and very funny and gentle. Growing up, I thought of him as a large man (in fact, he is only a little taller than my mother, who is tiny), and did not realise he was short until, as a teenager, I stormed out of the house after one of our frequent arguments and kept walking away, having just declared that I was leaving home. A few minutes into my dramatic march down the street I turned around and saw him in hot pursuit on the other side of the road, following me like a badly trained operative. He looked very upset and worried, and endearingly vulnerable. My father, I now saw, was a small man who was larger than life. I felt very secure and rooted in his love, and loved him, always, with a tinge of tender sadness, as if he needed my emotional protection more than I needed his. Of course I turned around and went back home on that grey Hamburg afternoon – until our next fight.

I grew up thinking that my birth was a moment of joy for my parents. For almost fifty years of my life I knew this, and my birth certificate confirms it: I was born in Moscow in 1954. My father is listed as Czech, my mother Armenian. In the Soviet Union, so-called nationality was legally determined by the father. So, according to this document, I am Czech. My father's Jewishness and my mother's half-Jewishness, on her mother's side, is completely (though unintentionally) concealed. If my father hadn't inherited his father's Czechoslovak citizenship his nationality would have been listed as Jew. Soviet identity papers appeared to be respectful of a person's national allegiance; in actual fact, they represented institutionalised racism, enabling the authorities to categorise everyone's nationality with ease, and for their own purposes. When Stalin conducted purges of Jewish doctors these were not abstract selections of people who were doctors by profession and Jewish by name or appearance or overt religion: it actually said so in their papers. There was a hierarchy of nationalities; to be listed as Russian was far preferable to being listed as Jew. Armenian was better than Jew but worse than Russian. Czech was sheer luxury, symbolising foreignness beyond the reach of the Soviet caste system but still within Russia's orbit of so-called friendly states – if only barely. It was explained to me that at the time of my birth my father was living in Prague, and my parents were waiting for official permission to marry, as he was a foreign national. When this finally came through my mother and I were allowed to travel to Prague and join him. Thus began my Czech childhood. My brother Maxim would soon become a part of it – he was born in Prague in 1960.

When I arrived in Prague with my mother, in 1958, I had a Soviet passport. In Czechoslovakia a Soviet passport – the

kind issued to Soviet citizens living abroad – was a handy one
to have: it allowed almost unrestricted travel to the West. At
the same time, paradoxically, travelling back to Moscow on
this Soviet passport was impossible without a special visa and
permit. This twisted logic of a communist state is hard to comprehend, yet at the time it made perfect sense: a Soviet citizen
living in Prague was considered almost a Westerner, and a subversive influence on those at home. For this reason, even – or
especially – family visits were inhumanely difficult, in either
direction. When my mother left my baby brother with her parents in Moscow while she was recuperating in Prague from a
gall-bladder operation, it turned out to be almost impossible to
get him back. Tearful visits to the Soviet Embassy proved use-
less; visas were granted with random wilfulness, with the aim
of humiliating the citizen. After nearly a year my grandfather
was allowed to visit us in Prague and bring the toddler back. I
still remember the day Maxim came home: everyone gathered
around his cot and rejoiced about this gift, finally returned to
us. I was excited to have my brother back, and found it hilarious
that he had forgotten his Czech and now spoke only Russian.
To this day, my brother owes his perfect Russian accent to his
enforced extended stay in Moscow at the age of almost two.
My grandparents were overjoyed to have him there to spoil and
cherish, my parents in agony about his open-ended absence,
and I somehow did not question it.

My brother is convinced that he was traumatised, and it is
interesting to me that he judges this incident from a modern
perspective, as if he had been 'abandoned'. Being six years
older, I have a much stronger awareness of the implications the
Iron Curtain imposed not just on the East European bloc but
on every single individual life of its citizens. It made everyone
feel like a pawn in the hands of an invisible evil giant. When
my mother decided to marry my father and move to Prague in

the 1950s, she was in fact severing herself from her roots and family, embarking on a lifetime of painful separations – not only for herself, but for her children too. Borders were not mere demarcations on the map: they were the fault lines of dormant personal tragedies, ready to erupt like earthquakes at any moment and destroy people's lives. Visits with our Moscow family, on either side of the border, were so rare and difficult to arrange that I could count the number of times I saw my grandparents since leaving Moscow on the fingers of one hand.

V's phone call in 2002 shocked me into thinking again about those years of my first separation from my Moscow roots. While my mother seemed quite relieved that the burden of lying to me about my biological father had been lifted, and understood my need to know and even write about it, my father's reaction was a different story. During a very brief period of family détente after V's phone call, he relented and opened up about some previously untold memories of becoming my father, his voice infused with love and a sudden shadow of uncertainty. He became deeply concerned about losing me. He listened to what I had to tell him about my new family – which, at the time, wasn't very much – and then said, 'I am afraid that you will be completely absorbed by them. You will leave us. I will lose you.' I felt less like a daughter than like a woman caught between two men. It was a very odd feeling. Suddenly I was loved by two fathers, with what appeared to be the same degree of tenderness. Yet despite my curiosity about the new father I knew that the only real father I could ever have was the man who had actually raised me.

I was aware that my parents' tolerance for my digging deep into the suppressed facts of our lives would not last long. It was too painful for them, too difficult to deal with, like a broken limb they had managed to heal and didn't want to test by exposing it to too much new strain. They didn't seem concerned about the effect all this was having on me. With the same skill and resilience that had allowed them to execute and sustain this successful operation for over five decades, they now managed to direct their attention back to themselves. Their patience for my efforts to really understand what happened proved short-lived. My father couldn't deal with it, and my mother gave in to his pressure, as she had always done.

One afternoon, not long after I had decided to write this memoir, I was sitting in my parents' kitchen in Hamburg, recording a conversation with my mother about her memories of my early childhood. In her eightieth year, she still looked beautiful, and some fifteen years younger than her age. I hear her vibrant young voice on the tape, along with munching noises as she enjoyed her afternoon snack of cornflakes and yoghurt after her long dog walk. She is talking about my memory of the cherry trees at my father's home when he enters the kitchen and realises what we are discussing. He explodes. It feels like getting caught in the planning of a doomed coup.

'But you don't even know what my book is really about,' I hear myself say on the tape, surprisingly calmly. 'It's about the languages in my life, and how I discover that English was actually there from the very beginning.'

'What English? What are you talking about?' He sounds genuinely surprised, and confused.

'My other grandparents spoke English at home, in Moscow. They—'

'What kind of nonsense is that? Why would they speak English? They were just regular Moscow Jews—'

'No they weren't,' I interrupt. 'They were Americans living in Moscow. You didn't know?'

It is obvious that he had no idea. I say to my mother (my turn to sound surprised), 'You didn't tell him?'

'No,' she admits. To my father, with some pain – or anger –
in her voice: 'You never wanted to know!'

At this point he exits the kitchen, overwhelmed by this new
information he doesn't know what to do with. The film he
wants to watch on TV has just started. It has to be more interesting, or easier to digest, than my life story.

My mother and I are alone again. After a brief silence, she
says, slowly, 'I didn't tell him because he never asked. But why
didn't he ask? I wonder ... ' Her voice trails off, but quickly
returns with new energy: 'I know why. He didn't want to
know much about you because knowing more would make
it harder for him to accept you as his own. He saw you as my
daughter, and therefore his. It was easier for him to imagine
you were just you, without any baggage.'

She said she understood my excitement about the peculiar
narrative twist in my life – my hidden native connection with
the English language, through this newly revealed American
family: 'You didn't know you had it, but it drew you back to
itself, like a charm.'

Obviously, my parents wouldn't have been able to maintain
this odd illusion that my birth resulted from a semi-immaculate
conception, 1950s Soviet-style, had they lived in Moscow
after they married. I would have grown up with my father as
a stepfather and my biological father as someone I would see
occasionally. But the move to Prague and my de facto adoption
was the equivalent of moving to another world; hence it was
possible for my mother to cut us both off from my real origins,
apparently irrevocably. 'We were a complete family,' she once
told me. She used the Russian word *polnotsennaya*, which means
'whole'. Whole and wholesome.

My father's resistance to my need to know the truth about
who I was, and indirectly about who my parents were, and to

write about it, was a serious obstacle for me initially. I had been conditioned, or had conditioned myself, to think of my parents as the people to whom I was not allowed to cause any pain. Their happiness was my responsibility. My happiness was more than my own feeling about my life: it was a way of making theirs easier.

My parents' oldest friend, Slava, in his nineties and still living in Prague, unexpectedly informed me that as a child I may have been fully aware of what I thought I never knew. He revealed to me that when I was a little girl, I confided in him that I had a secret. 'Really?' 'Yes. You told me, "Don't tell anyone, but I have another father."' This was said during a phone conversation, with my parents, whom he was visiting, laughing in the background. My mother quickly came to the phone and whispered in conspiratorial tones that Slava was drunk and I shouldn't listen to him: 'There is no way you could have remembered. He is making this up.' My father was out of earshot.

I was completely intrigued, and phoned Slava at his home on another day, when his being drunk could not be blamed for anything he said. We had a long conversation, during which I realised that he was the only witness to my early years in Prague who was not a family member. More than that: being of mixed Russian and Czech origin himself (not Jewish), he had also known my father's family and visited their home in Kuntsevo on several occasions. He could actually tell me what it looked like.

Slava had no trouble at all remembering what he had said on the phone. I questioned him carefully, aware that there is no such thing as a completely reliable witness, especially after almost five decades. Slava seemed incredibly lucid and happy to talk (perhaps his being married to a much younger wife was keeping his head clear). I made him retell the circumstances of that conversation we once had, to test how the revelation about my 'secret' would fit into the context. It did, perfectly. It happened on a visit of his to our apartment. Maxim was about three or four years old, so I would have been nine or ten. We were being noisy and naughty, as we always were, and probably being told to behave by our parents. Slava said, 'I told you to listen to your father. Then you turned to me and whispered: "I have a secret. He is not my real father. I have another father." I explained to you that your real father was the one who looked after you and raised you, and you had to listen to him, and you said yes.'

Then he said, 'You do know about your real father, right?' I told him I hadn't known, no, not until a few years ago. Slava was convinced I had to be aware of it as a child, 'because when you came from Moscow with your mother, you were not a baby'.

The time gap between the age when I shared this secret with him and the age of my arrival in Prague was not that large: only seven years at most. It makes perfect sense that I was aware of suddenly having a new father in a new country, and had not forgotten the old one. Not yet. Then I must have suppressed, blocked out or truly forgotten all about him.

Slava knew my father before he married my mother, and had been told by him that he was going to bring a Jewish wife from Moscow to live with him in Prague. This bride had a daughter – me. My father needed to have my past erased, to start with a clean slate, as a family with my mother. For a very young man in his twenties, this was a huge commitment, an act of love, a sign of a great ability to love, but also a daring feat of single-mindedly controlling the lives of not one but two human beings, directly, and of many others indirectly.

I asked Slava about the house in Kuntsevo. The town itself, it turned out, was more than an insignificant speck on the map of the Soviet Union: it was a suburb of Moscow with two distinct halves. In one, people had dachas and summer homes, and nice houses with gardens. In the other were the recreational dachas of Soviet functionaries, most famously Stalin's own guarded retreat, where he died in 1953 – a year before I was born. So my father's childhood was a tableau in the shadow of Stalin – literally.

The family home, said Slava, was an extremely nice house, 'very well appointed, with elegant furniture'. He remembers several beautifully hosted meals there. He described my father's father as a 'very impressive, smart man; we called him *knyaz kuntsevskyi* (the Lord of Kuntsevo), because he presided over such elegance'. I suddenly understood the significance of the large set of silver cutlery my parents still have, a wedding gift by my father's father. Yet I also understood much more. My father's innate ability to dress immaculately, to create a sense of aesthetic luxury in any home we have ever lived in, to fill his surroundings with beautiful objects and a richly equipped kitchen (he loves buying dishes, cutlery, glasses) – all this is the childhood home he still carries in him, yet claims not to remember.

And what do I have in me, what do I carry? I begin piecing my memories together, placing them where they belong, recognising where they didn't, against my father's resistance, against both my parents' lack of real interest, against their fears, against mine. My memories, like a bowl of cherries. Just for me.

Silver Spoon

I was born in Moscow on a freezing December morning, without any sign or prospect of the proverbial silver spoon in my mouth. Nevertheless, I was given a real one, by my great-grandmother. In keeping with the family passion for food it was a substantial, heavy soup spoon, rather than a dainty tea one. My name is engraved in elegant cursive Cyrillic letters on the front of its handle, and the date of my birth – '16.XII.54' – on the back. But it's not a name I have ever heard, or remember hearing, as my own: it reads *To Alyonushka*, a tender diminutive of Elena. Yet my mother confirms that I was indeed called Alyonushka, especially by my maternal grandmother Zelda. My beginnings seemed so purely Russian, and this baby name a perfect match for my early surroundings. But in fact there were many other ingredients in the ethnic mix that was my first home.

My mother was the only daughter of Yakov Cachmachcev and Zelda Perlstein. My grandmother never changed her last name. This was quite common for women in Soviet Russia, and not a sign of feminism – although my grandmother, born at the very beginning of the twentieth century, was in fact an emancipated woman par excellence. Despite her modest family background (her father had been a watchmaker and repairer), she had a university degree and an uninterrupted working life as an economist – uninterrupted by motherhood, war or any other obstacles she may have faced. However, I suspect that the real reason she remained a Perlstein was the odd acoustic complexity of her husband's last name. Cachmachcev was the Russified version of the original Armenian name Cachmachcan, which – as I found out one day from a Turkish bank teller in London – means 'lighter' in Turkish (*cakmak*), perhaps in imitation of the sound made when lighting a fire. Family historians on my mother's side have made much of this name and its origin (did our ancestors engage in some sort of gun or gunpowder manufacture or trade?), but all I can personally attest to is the impossibility of pronouncing it in any language without sounding like one is, indeed, spewing some kind of fire or triggering a mild explosion. When I am asked for my mother's maiden name as part of an identity or security check, there is always a pause after I pronounce it. I know that during this brief silence the employees are comparing the random sound they just heard with the letters on their computer screen, and that no matter how hard they try they can see no correlation. They always give up, very quickly and very politely, swallowing hard as they say, 'That's lovely, thank you.'

Named Raissa (Rachel) after her Jewish grandmother who had died only six months before her birth, my mother grew up surrounded by her lively, warm Armenian extended family. Gayane, her diminutive paternal grandmother, herself the mother of nine children, was the one who gave me the silver spoon. I touch it sometimes and imagine that moment, my lifetime ago, when she handed it with much love to her beloved granddaughter, congratulating her on my birth. There was a special bond between my mother and the only grandmother she had ever known. Love strengthens the fabric of memory. Her memories of Gayane are so rich that it's not hard for me to imagine her, almost as if I had known her myself. I have a real sense of the home she created in Baku with her dashing husband for their six sons and three daughters, an open house with parties and live music they made themselves every evening. She was full of laughter, had a superb soprano voice, and despite her Armenian background had a Russian high-school education. She spoke accent-free, educated Russian, along with French and German. When I was an infant she visited my mother a few times and rocked me. Having out-lived her husband and three of her children, she reached a ripe age despite many ailments, but did not live long enough for me to remember even a trace of her presence. Yet the spoon is still with me, and always will be, as a permanent reminder of her love, generous spirit and also, it must be said, exquisite taste: it is really a thing of classic beauty and elegance (unlike my great-grandmother herself who, my mother tells me, was lovely and cuddly rather than beautiful). The engraved words and numbers have the lightness and fluidity of an elegant pen on paper.

Baku was a natural place for the paths of my mother's parents to converge. Her mother had been born in Vladikavkaz, in Ossetia, a river town in the foothills of the Caucasus Mountains. Her parents had arrived there from Jewish shtetls, though my grandmother's own Jewish education and knowledge of Yiddish was close to non-existent. She studied economics at the University of Baku, in a city that was a colourful melting pot of ethnicities and religions: Muslim Azeris, Russians, Jews, Armenians. It was not too far from my grandfather's origi-nal family home in the ancient Armenian town of Guymri, north of the capital Yerevan. The tensions and conflicts would simmer and eventually erupt into bloody wars, but during my mother's early childhood Baku was the peaceful, lively, multi-lingual city she still loves. There is a building in Baku with her family name still carved on it, built by her uncles, at a time when they ran a successful business, a kind of department store. The affluence was short-lived; in 1918, during a period of massacres of Armenians, the family fled, leaving their homes behind and gradually selling everything they had in order to survive. My grandfather was forced to break off his university studies as the 'son of a capitalist'; he began working in a lowly position in a Soviet oil engineering company, but eventually, due to his supreme meticulousness and skills, moved up into management positions.

Zelda and Yakov were colleagues at the same company. They were friends, but for my grandmother the friendship wasn't changing fast enough into something more. Yakov was very attracted to women, and very attractive to women – and always would be, causing my grandmother many a jealous moment during their long life together, and fiery scenes of passionate arguments my mother doesn't like to remember. To kick-start this lifetime of passionate loving, my grandmother arranged for Yakov to meet her in an office. When he knocked on the door she said 'Come in,' and when he did he found her waiting for him, naked. The rest is family history – theirs, my mother's and, ultimately, mine.

My mother was Zelda's and Yakov's only child, a gorgeous, tomboyish little girl with long dark hair and very blue eyes. She was adored not only by her parents but also by every single member of her extended family – on the vast Armenian side, and the less numerous Jewish side. From her mother she inherited a loud, infectious laugh and a spirit of wilful independence; from her father, a passion for games and music (despite a complete lack of talent for the latter). From both, easygoing generosity and warmth of soul, and a magnetism that draws people to her, men and women, and makes her the delightful centre of attention. As in most Soviet families, my mother grew up living in very close quarters with her parents, often sharing a room in a communal apartment. Sometimes the three of them would lie in bed for hours, giggling and laughing, just because, at that very moment, it felt good to forget that their life was impossibly hard.

My mother describes her parents as extremely tolerant and understanding, never interfering in her life choices. She in turn never dreamt of being critical of them. When my brother or I argued with her, she would often say, with genuine astonishment, 'I would never say something critical to my parents. It just wouldn't be possible.'

Life in a dictatorship is a profoundly humiliating, dehumanising experience. There is no such thing as having your own, truly personal sphere where your individuality can flourish unconstrained. There is no aspect of your life that is not controlled by the arbitrary whims of the dictator and his inner power circle – whims whose only aim is to instil mortal fear in every citizen, of any age, gender or role in society, whether they support the regime or not. Laughter was not only about feeling joy; it was, more often, about feeling free – within the constraints.

As a new baby, my mother's first child, I must have been a ray of light during a dark time. Babies always are. I was born less than a year after Stalin's death in 1953. Growing up, the name Stalin symbolised a remote spectre of horrors, the darker precursor of the horrors I would have to live with myself. Yet the remoteness of Stalin's power and legacy was an illusion. My life would be profoundly influenced by the regime my parents and grandparents were born into.

But even in such dark times, chances are my great-grandmother had nothing more profound on her mind when she presented me with the spoon than this simple thought: we have a new child in the family – let's feed her and love her and help her grow up to be happy. They didn't fail.

My Birth

My mother was not married when she fell pregnant with me. She was a student of geography at Moscow University, close to the end of her degree. During one of her expeditions mapping out distant territories – before she was pregnant, in the early 1950s – she had witnessed a secret nuclear test explosion, the type of atomic mushroom the world associates with Hiroshima and Nagasaki.

When my mother's pregnancy became very visible, she was called in to the office of the director of student affairs (in other words, the person responsible for spotting and punishing any political misbehaviour among the student body). My mother was not only not married – though this, in itself, was not frowned upon in the Soviet Union – but also involved with a man whose own political status was precarious. She was nervous about the interview; it could have spelled the end of her studies and any subsequent professional career. In fact, it could have blackened her political report card for ever. The woman functionary did not ask, 'Are you planning to get married?' but rather, 'Who is the father?' My mother, in a flash of both inspiration and fear, replied, 'I am a single mother.'

This was not strictly true, but neither was it completely false. The apparatchik was satisfied with the answer, and there were no repercussions. My mother was able to complete her degree.

While she was still living at home with her parents, my mother may have had complete freedom to do as she liked (which she had obviously exercised), but she was also very much her parents' devoted daughter, not especially keen on distancing herself from the emotional safety of their cocoon. Her pregnancy was something everyone accepted: it just happened, the timing was neither good nor bad – it just was. This attitude of taking things as they came, getting on with whatever fate might serve up, planned or unplanned, wanted or not, was a kind of wisdom it took me many years to truly appreciate.

When the contractions began her mother took her to the maternity hospital by taxi, but once there she had to leave her. No one other than the patients and medical staff was allowed inside the hospital, not even visitors. The reason given for this strict procedure was 'hygiene', but the result was that, along with germs, the medical establishment isolated patients completely from their family and other support systems. This was especially tough on new mothers.

After she had been admitted and briefly examined, my mother was placed in the corner of a room behind a curtain, all alone. No one explained to her what was happening or what was about to happen, no one even talked to her. She coped with her progressing labour pains as best she could, but was slowly reaching a state of panic. No nurse came to see her all night, and no doctor either. In the early hours of the morning someone finally entered her room: a cleaner, who had come to mop the floor. My mother was elated to see her, and asked her: 'Nyanyechka, how long is this going to last?' The cleaner stopped mopping for a moment and looked at my mother. 'Is it your first?'

'Yes.'

'Well then it's going to take a looooooong time.'

Only in the very last stages did a gruff nurse attend to my mother, and a doctor appeared to check on her. There were no complications, but no joy either: no one could reach my mother to congratulate her for the entire week of her stay in hospital. After my healthy first cry I was shown to her, tightly wrapped in a blanket, Soviet-style. No part of my little body could really move. I had a lot of dark hair, and plump shoulders, for a newborn.

That week in the maternity hospital was a social eye-opener for my twenty-four-year-old mother. She shared a room with about a dozen working-class women, all of whom had given birth many times before, and never stopped cursing their men for getting them pregnant and causing them such pain and hardship. It was like a scene from a female hell. My mother lay there quietly, and I wonder, did she secretly agree with them?

In the Soviet Union, the most common form of contraception was abortion. Multiple abortions, in most cases. I have relatives who, even in later years – into the 1970s – had one abortion after another, with all the resulting complications: gynaecological problems, inability to have children in later years, other health issues. I have never asked my mother whether, in her circumstances, she ever considered this option. I'd rather not know.

When they brought me home I slept in a little zinc bathtub for the first week or two. According to Jewish superstition, one is not allowed to buy anything at all for a baby before the birth. My grandmother and mother gradually collected all the necessities, until nothing was missing. I still have the tiniest baby shirts my grandmother sewed for me, and my first little jacket. It is red and white, with thick cotton padding to keep me warm. The stitching has lasted to this day and shows no sign of disintegrating.

In my earliest baby photos my young mother often wears a white gauze mask over her face. She was fanatical about not exposing me to any germs, and rarely took me to visit people. According to her, I didn't have a single cold or even a runny nose until kindergarten age. I was not too keen on her breast milk, so her plentiful surplus went to our next-door neighbour's baby daughter Lara (my 'milk sister'). I still remember Lara as my first and only Russian childhood friend; later, when I visited from Prague, she came over to play and I felt self-conscious about my Russian. It didn't sound quite the same as hers, and I think she even corrected a mistake I made, which upset me.

I thought of my mother when, at about the same age, I was giving birth in Ottawa, Canada, to my first baby. My husband was with me. I could not imagine going through labour by myself; it seemed completely natural to share every moment of the experience. But in the same room, behind a curtain, was a woman who was alone, quietly suffering through her contractions without a partner's help. The midwives were always present, but the difference between her experience of childbirth and mine was obvious. I felt very lucky. I also thought of my mother, in a different way, during the birth of my second son, in Haifa, Israel. There I had a very dogmatic Russian midwife, obviously Soviet-trained, whose understanding of labour seemed to be stuck in the 1950s. She told me to lie on my back and wait. I argued that that was the worst thing I could do, and insisted on walking around or rocking on all fours to accelerate the process and reduce the pain, as I had learned to do in Canada. The midwife was outraged at my disobedience, and our relationship continued to deteriorate throughout the birth. As she gave me yet another anachronistic instruction when I was least able to take it, I lost my temper and slapped her. I am sorry I did, but it felt good – like slapping the horror that was the Soviet way of bringing new life into this world.

A Russian List of First Words

My grandfather was abroad during the year of my birth, working in Romania for a Soviet–Romanian oil company with the
imaginative name SOVROMPETROL. He returned when
I was several months old. His presence was immediately felt.
Before he came near me he spent a long time washing his
hands, like a surgeon before an operation. Then he said, 'So
let's see,' and I was finally shown to him. Like everyone else in
the small household and the extended family he was immediately besotted with the tiny person, the first grandchild. Later
that evening, when he realised that my sleeping pattern was not
very satisfactory, he declared that 'the baby needs discipline',
and insisted that they let me cry instead of immediately picking me up. Family rumour has it the treatment was successful:
I quickly got the idea and henceforth slept – well, like a baby.

He became very involved in planning my routine and my
earliest education, just as he had done when my mother was
little. There was a seriousness of purpose in his handling of
children and babies. He did not see them as doll-like miniatures
but as fully formed human beings who deserved utter respect
from the earliest age.

In 1956, when I was almost two years old, he made a list in pencil, on a thin sheet of company stationery he had brought back from his Romanian job, of all the words I knew at the time. Russian words. Under the heading 'Lenotchka is 1 year 10 months old, October 1956' he wrote down the words as I pronounced them, in his handsome, very clear handwriting. Next to my version, after a dash, he added the real meaning of each word. Thanks to my grandfather's loving attention to my early language acquisition, I know with complete certainty that I was able to say twenty words or phrases at that age:

Say
Bublik
Walk
Pencil
Candy
Stop
I don't want
Money
Scissors
Shoes
Take
Get up
Give
Play
Glasses
Box
Chocolate
Apples
Mushroom
Blood

Some of the words were phonetically very close to their intended pronunciation, others a little fanciful. I can imagine my whole toddler life from these words, with a large group of adults at my beck and call: my parents, my grandparents, other relatives, a live-in nanny. The latter was not a luxury; many Moscow families had them, very young girls from the provinces who held the fabric of a home together by taking care of babies, cooking, cleaning while the parents worked. Our nanny (or nannies: there was a succession of them) slept on a mattress in the kitchen. I was at the centre of everyone's attention, spoiled by my grandparents, my mother's sole focus and project. This never happened again in my childhood – six years later, when my brother was born she went straight back to work and there was no grandparental indulging going on, except when they visited us, which was rare. But my early years were a warm cocoon of sheer pleasure, not yet disturbed or even foreshadowed by the imminent move to Prague. My childhood in Moscow had a sweet taste for me, and those tastes I do remember: beige-coloured chocolate butter and milky vanilla ice cream.

The words I knew at the age of almost two tell a story. My verbs were just about all the simple actions I would ever need to master in order to communicate with and manage my world, then and now: say, walk, stop, take, get up, give, play. There was the crucial 'I don't want'. But what I did want, I remember, was to brush my grandmother's frizzy hair, or play a game, any game, with my grandfather, or – my absolute favourite – sit at my little desk and pretend to be really busy talking on my toy telephone and scribbling, preferably inside my books. I still have some of them, including the doodles; it's a very odd feeling to witness, from a distance of more than fifty years, evidence of my infant self's playing at being a busy adult, in exactly the same style as I do now. I still love nothing more than to sit at

my desk, talk on the phone, read, write and doodle. My grandfather's list attests to the fact that I knew the word for pencil as
early as I could pronounce it, or something like it.

The food I could name at that age is a clear giveaway of how
my grandparents indulged my sweet tooth, and perhaps their
own: sweets, chocolate and, for only slightly more solid nutri-
tion, *bublik* (a Russian kind of bagel). It seems obvious that I
liked apples too, and I can suddenly remember – in fact see –
my grandfather's large hands as he peels an apple, very smoothly
and skilfully, in one curved line. Then he would slice it neatly
and feed those small pieces to me like to a baby bird.

Shoes were a challenge – I couldn't put them on myself, but
really wanted to. Especially my winter boots, the *valenki* – they
made me roll forward through snow rather than walk. I was
wrapped in so many layers, the top one real fur, that in my
winter outdoor clothes I must have been much heavier than
my actual weight. In photos I look like a smiling winter doll,
pulled on a wooden sleigh by my young mother, also dressed
in fur.

A box was a different kind of attraction. I was mesmerised by
the little boxes my grandfather kept on and inside his desk, in a
special drawer. Many of them contained tiny toys and games –
for his own pleasure. My greatest, and rare, delight was when
he relented and agreed to sit down with me and slowly begin
opening the boxes, demonstrating, with pride, the toys he had
collected. My grandfather took the fun contained in inanimate
objects as seriously as I did.

The two words on the vocabulary list I can least account
for are 'mushroom' and 'blood'. For many years, and almost
to this day, a mushroom was the only thing I could actually
draw. Russian children's books frequently feature mushrooms
in a magical woodland setting. And blood: that's a great word
for a not-yet-two-year-old to own. A scraped knee, small

injuries, maybe a nosebleed? Was my over-protective parental and grandparental cocoon excessively attentive to my minor childhood injuries?

Like many other documents that could easily have been lost as I moved from house to house, city to city, country to country, continent to continent, this precious small piece of paper, just two years younger than I am myself, has always been with me, perfectly preserved. I said those words and my grandfather heard them; like a scientist collecting a body of data, he systematically and lovingly wrote them down on one particular day. My grandfather gave me the gift of preserving my first language, Russian, when it was just beginning to grow into my mother tongue.

And yet, it didn't.

No Goodbyes

There were many farewells over the years, beginning with the first one, in 1958, when my mother took me to live in Prague. The separation was hard on my grandparents, and the change drastic. Their apartment was suddenly emptied of what had filled their days with so much life: their beloved only daughter, and their three-year-old granddaughter. But they never asked my mother not to leave. On the contrary: they knew that living in Czechoslovakia instead of the Soviet Union could only make her life easier, and so they were happy for her. And they loved the man she would marry.

They would visit us in Prague (never together, as far as I remember), but not all that often – such travel was difficult to arrange, with special visas required, which had to be applied for, involving long waiting periods and uncertain outcomes. The same was true of my mother's trips back to Moscow from Prague. There was a finality in our departure, which I sensed and somehow understood. At the end of my first few years in Moscow there was a very long train journey to another country. And waiting at the end of that train journey was the man I would immediately accept as my father.

But Russia remained present in my life as my first literary home. I still have many of my early children's books, read to me by my grandparents in Moscow. In one of them there was a popular poem called 'Moydodyr' ('Wash 'em clean' or, literally, 'Clean 'til Holes') by Korney Chukovsky, written in 1924. It is about a dirty boy who is confronted by an anthropomorphised sink, a kind of general of cleanliness with an army of cleansing means at his command – soaps, brushes, toothbrushes, toothpaste ... The boy is so filthy that everything he comes in contact with flees in terror – his bedding, his clothes, shoes, the samovar he wants to use to get a cup of tea. As the boy tries to escape the scary sink in absolute terror, running down the streets of Petrograd (or Leningrad, depending on the decade of the poem's publication), he runs into Crocodile, another famous character from the same author's imagination, who defends him against the aggressive brushes but insists that the boy wash himself thoroughly, after which all is well again.

This petrifying ode to cleanliness is written in wonderful verse, animating every object, from lowly toothbrush to mythic sink, in a completely captivating manner. I was obsessed with it and had to have it read to me several times a day by every willing adult in the family. I knew it by heart, but the reading was an essential ritual which not only gave the right voice to the idiosyncratic cadences of Chukovsky's writing, but also helped me be less afraid of some of the more gruesome details of the story.

Another narrative children's poem by the same author was also a favourite of mine. In 'Mucha Tsokotucha' ('The Buzzing Fly'), the story was even more worrying. The heroine of the tale, a fly with a golden stomach, invites a multitude of insects to celebrate her birthday. They arrive, bringing gifts and cakes and sweets, and are pleasant in an obsequious manner. But when a vicious spider attacks the fly, threatening to kill her, not one of her guests is willing to help her. They are all afraid and hiding. At the last minute a tiny but courageous mosquito saves the fly by cutting off the spider's head in one quick move. At which point the guests crawl out of their hiding places and proceed to celebrate the fly's birthday. As a bonus, the heroic mosquito and the fly get married. I wonder if Chukovsky wrote these stories as clever allegories of life in the totalitarian Soviet Union, where cowardice and hypocrisy were a means of saving one's own skin.

Listening to my grandfather's melodic, expressive voice filled me with a feeling of deep comfort and security. Children crave, and deserve, a loving adult's undivided, absolute attention, and a sense that the outside world can be made to disappear into their own imaginary version of it.

As I only lived with my grandparents until the age of three, and they visited us in Prague no more than a handful of times, my grandfather could not have read to me very often. Yet when I immerse myself in Russian books my grandfather's voice is always with me. My grandmother rarely read to me, nor did she read to my mother when she was a child; my grandfather was the one who loved 'to work' with children – he called it *zanimatsa*, which means to engage in serious work and learning. Even our games were educational, teaching us skills he thought were important: clear thought, concentration, a deeper understanding of the world. He also taught me (and later my brother) how to play chess and draughts and backgammon, and how to enjoy caviar for breakfast, spread thickly on fresh, white buttered bread.

My most vivid memory of my grandfather dates back to the winter of 1963–4, when I visited Moscow for the last time. My grandmother, aged only sixty-three, was seriously ill; she was, in fact, dying from complications following a gall-bladder operation. But this was somehow kept in the background by my mother, who believed that children should be spared traumatic encounters with reality. I was never taken to my grandmother's funeral, and never really understood, or took in, the fact that she was no longer there. I never saw my mother cry over her mother's death. She must have done it when I wasn't watching, and she made sure I wasn't watching. She wanted me to remember my grandmother as she was when she was alive, and not to dwell on her death. I was nine when my grandmother passed away; by not being allowed to grieve with the adults, with my family, I was protected from understanding their sadness and from sharing mine. Perhaps it was due to this emotional mollycoddling that I simply don't know how to think of death and what it means. A few years ago, when I visited a close friend who was dying, she asked me, 'How can you console me?' All I could say was 'We'll all meet again.' I meant: death is not final, because I don't understand what that would mean. This friend's funeral was the first one I ever attended.

During the time of my grandmother's final illness I was kept amused and entertained, rather than included in what everyone was going through. My mother's intention worked out perfectly: my happy childhood was not affected. As a result of that trip I still remember Moscow as a real winter wonderland, made especially for children. The Russian version of Santa, Dyedushka Moroz (Grandfather Frost), is a more secular and less mysterious figure, and that winter he somehow merged in my mind and memory with my tall, elegant, always kind, affectionate, cheerful and playful grandfather. A well-placed relative had arranged tickets for the biggest *yolka*, a Christmas tree celebration for children at the Kremlin. This was a huge variety show with songs and performances and presents and sweets for each child. The audience seemed enormous to me – several hundred children with their parents. I was probably the only non-Soviet child in the crowd. When the presenter asked if anyone would like to perform a song my hand shot up without a moment's hesitation.

My grandfather looked on in amazement as I fearlessly walked up to the stage and announced that I would be singing a song in Czech, of my own composition (I should add here that I am a terrible, if enthusiastic singer, but at the time I was not aware of it). I had written it not long before, and still remember the simple, upbeat tune and lyrics: 'We will board the rocket ship and fly to the moon'. I began to sing, accompanied by a smiling accordion player. He hadn't counted on my song having about twenty verses, each picking up where the previous one left off, narrating the rhymed adventures and activities on the moon once our rocket ship had got us there. (I was under the profound influence of the Soviet side of the space race; clearly I favoured cosmonauts at the time.) The accordion player tried to end my song many times, with an appropriately bombastic finale, but I ignored him and just went on, and on, and on, until I was all done and there were no more verses left to sing. I received some applause from the audience but this was mainly an attempt to encourage me to finish my performance, as people had already started to leave. When I finally came off stage and rejoined my grandfather he said, with an astonished smile, 'I wouldn't have believed you'd have the courage to do this.' He was both proud and surprised. And to his own very musical ear, perhaps I was a disappointment. It was important for me to sing to this Russian audience in Czech, in my own language, to set myself apart from them. Growing up in Prague in the 1950s and 1960s, Russian was the language of the enemy. I was ashamed and embarrassed to claim it as my own, and outside my home I always tried to hide that I spoke it. This dichotomy became more pronounced as I grew older, and began to feel anti-Russian. My grandfather would not have understood.

This was the reason why, sadly, I never said goodbye to him. In 1969, not long before we emigrated to Hamburg, my mother travelled to Moscow to visit her father and tell him about the secret plans. Obviously this was not explained to us; it was simply a trip to Moscow, and she offered to take both my brother and me. I absolutely refused to go: so soon after the 1968 Soviet invasion of Czechoslovakia, I saw it as a betrayal of my moral principles and my loyalty to my homeland to visit the occupier. Not going to Moscow was my personal protest. But Maxim (who was nine at the time) did go, and how I envy him today. I wish I had seen Moscow one more time while my grandfather was still alive, and with my own, more grown-up eyes. He made several attempts to visit us in Hamburg in the early 1970s, and waited a very long time for his visa. Finally, it seemed as if he was about to receive it. Overjoyed, he immediately began out-lining his journey and wrote us a detailed letter about how he was going to travel, having consulted all the necessary timetables for trains between Moscow and Hamburg. With his characteris-tic meticulousness, he thought of every detail, every eventuality. He was bringing us gifts, thoughtfully selected for each of us. This letter is unbearably difficult to read today, because shortly after he posted it his visa request was denied. My grandfather died not long after. We were told by family members that the rejection completely broke him. Always an optimistic man, his last months were heartbreakingly sad.

I adored my grandmother Zelda. Even though I don't have as many and as detailed memories of her as I do of my grand-father, my sense of her as a kind of older version of myself was always very clear. She was a strong personality, but also very giggly, and loved setting up practical jokes. My favourite letter of hers is one she wrote from a river cruise she undertook on her own, down the Volga. Perhaps for the first time in her life, she was completely relaxed. Everything seemed to be in its place, she was retired and now had some time to herself – a real luxury. She describes with such joy the towns she visited during the cruise, and the wooden jewellery she bought for herself as souvenirs. I treasure these pieces as much as the simple gold bracelet that had belonged to my Jewish great-grandmother Rachel.

When my grandmother and my mother were evacuated to Bashkiria during the war, my grandmother worked in a factory seven kilometres away from where they lived. In winter, as she walked home every evening along an empty road in complete darkness, she saw wolves' eyes following her from very close by. The wolves were hungry. My grandmother was petrified. But she had no choice, and just kept walking. This is how her generation faced everything in life: by doing what they had to do, despite the ever-present fear.

In 1944 my grandmother was sent to work in a factory near Stalingrad. She and my mother, who was almost thirteen years old at the time, arrived in the city very early on a summer morning, when it was still dark. The sun was barely beginning to rise. A bent old man offered to guide them to the train that would take them to their destination. They followed him on foot as he carried their suitcase on his back. (Their main cargo, a beautiful shiny black upright piano and boxes of books, had been sent and stored separately; the piano – originally made in 1903 – survived the war and the following years, and ultimately made it to Prague, where I would have lessons on it until we left for Germany in 1970).

What my mother saw as a child walking through war-ravaged Stalingrad has remained etched in her mind with the veracity of a high-definition camera lens. She writes in her memoir, *The Watermelon Rind*, in the third person:

There were no more sidewalks. They walked in the middle of the streets, but these were no longer streets: they walked down a road on each side of which there were mountains of ruins, covering the remaining bits of sidewalk. The ruins were of various heights – depending on the size of building they used to be, big or small. And in this peaceful silence it was somehow hard to believe that under the city's debris there lay a multitude of corpses. Who were they? Were they the people who used to live in those houses and didn't manage to get away in time? Or were they soldiers – ours or the enemy's? No one could tell them who was under those fallen bricks, and how many there were. Their guide had no idea. And yet it looked as if these buildings had collapsed only yesterday, the ruins looked untouched. Only from time to time something rustled and moved in them. The old man said calmly that the city was overrun with rats. And fell silent again.

There was complete stillness. A very unusual kind of stillness for this morning hour. Birds were silent and dogs did not bark. And there were no inhabitants. What kind of a city was it, without inhabitants? It seemed as if the only survivor was this night guide. One couldn't even say that the city was asleep – the city simply did not exist.

In the dim light of the rising sun, against the pinkish-red sky, they could now see the dark silhouettes of multi-storey buildings, which seemed to have remained intact. By the time they came closer to them, it was completely light, and the sun's first rays fell on these houses. And only then did they realise that these were merely walls which remained standing, some with incomprehensibly connected floors, from which there were suspended, as if falling from one level to the next, metal beds, tables, wardrobes. Blankets, pillows and mattresses appeared to be strangely attached to the beds. On some of these walls there were pictures, mirrors; the window frames were ripped out but torn curtains were still hanging on them. And you could see exactly where there used to be a bedroom, a kitchen, a child's room. One chair lay on a fragment of a floor, another was suspended in the air; the slightest wind would blow it to the lower floor, or all the way down to the ground. And in one corner, something white: an overturned toilet, ripped out of the floor. Occasionally, when they walked near such a ruined house, you could even see mops and buckets; a doll in a red dress was miraculously hanging from a child's cot. It was as if people had just walked out of these rooms and would be back shortly to tidy them up again. But there were no more staircases for them to climb up to their homes. This part of the building was completely gone. The ruins were both alive and dead. The girl saw for the first time what war really meant and what it caused – not from radio or newspapers, nor from what people were saying when they talked about war and about the front. And although these walls had already stood there almost half a year, it seemed as if the war had happened here only yesterday, and that these buildings were destroyed only a moment ago. They looked untouched.

In this way, they crossed the entire city, which had ceased to exist.

My mother never told me about this frozen memory of the destruction of Stalingrad. There was so much she never talked about. Not because she wouldn't or didn't want to, but because there was so much to tell, and so little of it seemed even remotely translatable into my own experience. She didn't think I wanted to hear those stories, and she didn't feel she knew how to explain them. She could only write them. Mostly to herself – her book was almost an afterthought. And in her writing, spontaneous yet carefully burnished, she managed to keep alive and share what she had witnessed. Great movie scenes are made from a fraction of her visual precision.

As I lovingly translated my mother's memories from Russian into English I thought about how, in our family, we seem to be destined to live at great physical distances from one another, but our love is stronger than our separations.

The evening before my grandmother Zelda became ill, in late December 1963, my grandparents were out celebrating her brother's birthday. The following morning, still in high spirits, they were eating breakfast and listening to the radio when a quick Charleston tune came on. The music made her jump up and dance; she felt young again, joyful memories came flooding back. In mid-motion she suddenly clasped her stomach and cried out in pain. She went from intense happiness to fatal illness in a matter of seconds, almost dancing her way to the end.

Green Light

Although my father had moved to Prague as a teenager after the war, he returned to Russia to study history at Moscow University. This did not go according to plan; a former classmate from his high school in Prague denounced him for saying, privately, that Stalin's regime was anti-Semitic, and for telling an anti-Stalin joke. The friend's motive for doing so has always remained a mystery, but it had serious repercussions. My father was thrown out of the university and the Communist Party (which he had joined with youthful zeal – 'for five minutes', he always told me). He had to go back to Prague with a dangerously sullied political profile, was very lucky not to have been arrested, and was now allowed to hold down only factory jobs. Not for the last time in his life, my father had to start from scratch and reinvent himself professionally. He began translating from Czech into Russian, initially using various friends' names as his alias. In the early days he translated anything he was offered – technical texts, dry descriptions of items, newspaper articles ... Many years later he would translate film subtitles and works of literature. His best-known translation was a special edition of the Czech classic *The Good Soldier Švejk* by Jaroslav Hašek, under the pseudonym Maxim Rellib – my brother's first name and his own last name in reverse.

After the incident that ended his university studies, my father was officially no longer permitted to travel to the Soviet Union. Yet he found a way of doing so, visiting his parents on several occasions by joining organised tours with Czech youth groups. He met my mother a number of times, several years apart. They were first introduced at a party in 1949, by his brother Misha, who was a close friend of my mother's cousin. Later that same year, when my mother was at a geography field camp in deep countryside about 100 kilometres from Moscow, the two brothers suddenly arrived by motorcycle, on a surprise visit. My mother was barely twenty; they all had fun, as friends, talking and laughing late into the night, so late that the boys had to stay over, sleeping in the nurse's tent. The first spark of mutual attraction was there, but nothing more happened. (If it had, I once said to my mother, if they had fallen in love at first sight, she would never have become involved with Joseph – and I would never have been born. I expected her to express something like potential regret at this eventuality, but she only said, 'Oh well. Then it would have been someone else.')

In 1956, during one of his visits to Moscow, around the time when he was just starting out as a freelance translator, my father really caught my mother's attention at a party. He seemed much more worldly than any other young man she had ever met. And she attracted him by, without being drunk, dancing on a table and singing loudly (completely off-key), and laughing even louder. Walking back to the tram along with some others, they became separated from the group and he simply asked her, 'Would you consider moving to Prague?' And she answered, without hesitation, 'Of course!' They had one or two dates after that and, having done no more than kiss, they changed the course of each other's lives. Practically overnight, my mother found herself committed to a man who was asking her to live in Prague with him. The fact that she already had a child did not stop either of them. Immediately after they parted and he returned to Prague, each wrote a long love letter to the other, confirming their mutual love in almost identical words. My mother was relieved to receive hers – it meant that she had not been wrong about this unusual young man with a real sparkle in his dark eyes when he told hilarious jokes and stories. Semjon (or Sjoma, as everyone called him) was as seductive and warm on paper as he had seemed in real life. Their correspondence continued for almost a year, their plans to marry growing stronger from letter to letter.

One mild spring day my mother and Sjoma were strolling down a central Moscow avenue after their first real date. It had been a lunch at a fancy hotel restaurant. He was dressed with understated but impeccable Western European elegance, a look he knew how to produce without spending much money. My mother was not wearing a bra. The only bras she owned were home-sewn by my grandmother Zelda, made of coarse, sheet-like material; a real one would be a luxury. Her knickers, of the same provenance, were equally embarrassing – large chafing bloomers held up with elastic bands. Almost the entire population of a world superpower was dressed in extremely uncomfortable undergarments during the Cold War era.

On this occasion (as on many others, given that she didn't have much to choose from in her wardrobe: one dress, one skirt, one blouse), my mother was wearing a close-fitting blue and white chequered skirt and a tight white blouse. The young man, always an aesthete, was put off by the unsexy red scarf around her neck. He thought she looked like a Young Pioneer, not mature enough for her age (twenty-six). But she was extremely pretty and vivacious, and he was smitten in a way that felt much deeper than his many flings in Prague.

They were well-matched – both were short, dark-haired, good-looking, and both had a quick, natural way with words, though his was a great deal quicker. She preferred to listen, and he liked her attentiveness. He also liked her laugh, loud and open, and especially her blue-grey eyes. Together they looked like shining Hollywood stars playing dressed-down parts in a drab post-war movie.

Life writes scripts novelists often try to imitate. The couple accidentally bumped into another young man – Joseph, my biological father, who at the time was still an occasional if rare presence in my life. He was dressed in outlandish – for 1950s Moscow – trousers with a zip (everyone else wore them buttoned), a hand-me-down he had received from relatives in America. Over his arm he carried an oversized camel coat from the same source. Both young men were introduced to one another by my mother; she told each the other's name, and who they were. They were not of a dissimilar type: both were dark, very Jewish-looking, attractive, bespectacled. But Joseph was much taller, had bright blue eyes, and a shy voice with a slight stutter. This encounter on a sunny spring afternoon was brief, casual and quickly forgotten by all; yet my entire life was already in the hands of this young trio.

There is a scene in my mother's memoir that always makes me cry. She writes about our first night in Prague, in the one room we were all now sharing. I was finally asleep in my new cot, my long braids flung in opposite directions across the pillow. Though we had just arrived from Moscow, my new father had a deadline the following morning and had to finish editing a translation. My mother describes, in warm, vivid strokes, how she looked over his shoulder, saw his work for the first time and offered to help. They sat there together, reading and editing the Russian text he had translated from Czech, until late into the night, in a room filled with green light. The light was created by a cloth they had put around the bright ceiling bulb so it wouldn't disturb my sleep. My mother remembers their shared concentration, how close their lips were, almost touching ... When the editing was finished her new husband had tears in his eyes. 'I can't believe I am finally not alone. We are now together. Will you always be here with me and for me?'

He was probably overwhelmed by the enormity of what they had accomplished, against so many odds. And he didn't even fully understand how lucky he was – not yet. My mother's love for him was of the unconditional kind, absolute. Still, she wasn't his first big love. Eva, a beautiful Jewish girl from his home town, was my father's first serious passion, also adored by his family. She left him and broke his heart. When her marriage failed and she wanted to return to him, he refused to take her back. Instead, he found my mother – who has always felt some- what inferior to Eva. My father was suddenly keenly aware of the emotional security he had gained by marrying my mother. He had been fiercely independent as a teenager, living with his older brothers but without parental authority. He relied on himself for everything. His sense of responsibility for their new family unit must have suddenly kicked in that night after our arrival from Moscow. But there was more: the understanding that he now had his own slice of Russia, and of real, authentic Russian, by his side. His Russian would always remain excel- lent, but having a Russian-speaking wife, especially one who was also able to help him edit his work, was a priceless source of support in his profession. She would continue to help him edit his translations, especially the literary ones, and he in turn would be her first reader, typist and editor when she began publishing her own writing. My first night as a brand-new, not-yet-four-year-old émigré was spent in the sign of things to come: translation, one language into another, old commingling with new, under a roof of love my parents had created without any concern whatsoever for its chances of survival. They were very instinctive decision-makers: what felt right could be done; *had* to be done.

On neither side of my family, no matter how far down one goes, is there a trace of real, bona fide Russianness. And now here they both were, inside a cocoon of very pure Russian, in Prague. It was the Russian language that defined my parents' cultural identity, and still does – even when they now watch endless hours of very bad Russian TV (via satellite) in Hamburg or Prague.

So much has survived in our family archives, despite all these moves: photographs, books, notebooks, letters, personal knick-knacks ... But the first two love letters my parents had written to one another simultaneously, which crossed en route – those did not survive. Worried that they may contain compromising information, my mother destroyed them in the early 1960s, during a time when the family was under heightened sur-veillance due to an uncle's failed attempt to emigrate, and his subsequent arrest.

My mother took these letters to a friend's apartment not far from ours, and burned them in his coal oven. Their Russian words of passion are lost, but their bond has endured. It contin-ues to feed on their tempestuous love, and on the impassioned arguments they have on a daily basis, in a timeless Russian kept in pristine condition. They were both émigrés, each in their own way, and their inner island of very literate and literary Russian was an oasis they inhabited together, and with their children. We were all émigrés, in staggered stages. Russian was the first casualty of all our wanderings.

Blurred Vision

'Don't rely on your emotional memory,' my mother once told me. I liked the poetic mystery of her phrasing, so I never probed behind those words, for fear they might dissolve into something mundane along the lines of 'check your facts'. But I have no memories whatsoever of my first year in Prague, between the ages of three and a half and almost five. I have to ask myself: did my emotional memory erase itself, did it block a period of transition during which I appeared to be a cheerfully happy little girl to my parents but was, in fact, finding my way in a new family, new language, new environment – perhaps not without some pain?

Years later, when I was about ten, my mother inadvertently closed the car door on my finger. I remember having two simultaneous reactions: agonising, mind-shattering pain and, seeing the horror on her face, an instant decision not to show it, to spare her feelings of guilt for my injury. Before she could even ask, I said, 'It's OK, it doesn't hurt.' She looked at me with both shock and relief. She couldn't believe me, and yet she wanted to. This was our modus vivendi from the start: everything was kind of true between us, except when it wasn't allowed to be. It was a grey area between truth and almost-truth, as dictated by circumstances.

If I can't rely on my own memory of my first year in Prague (emotional or otherwise), I have my mother's reported view of things – and many of her photographs. She was an avid, artistic photographer.

Her story begins with our train ride from Moscow. My mother, not yet thirty, leaving her old life behind, advancing towards her new one at the speed of a train's rickety progress on Soviet rail tracks, then, much faster and softer on Czechoslovak ones, to marry a man she hardly knew, but knew she loved. It is essential to add the 1950s Iron Curtain dimension to this picture: in 1958 a move from Moscow to Prague was equivalent to a personal liberation. Czechoslovakia may have seemed like a grim Central European outpost of the Soviet empire to both Western visitors and its own citizens, but to a Soviet arrival Prague was a dream of civilised beauty, full of seductive promise and unheard-of freedoms. It wouldn't take my young mother long to morph into a Czech patriot – with a Russian accent. She fell in love with Prague as quickly as she had fallen for her new husband.

There was only one moment she must have dreaded, a little (or possibly a lot, depending on the kind of truth she was telling herself). My new father was to join us at the small Slovak border town of Čierna nad Tisou. How would I react to him? Everything depended on that first encounter.

I know I must have been well prepared for the meeting. My mother would have told me fun things to make me excited with anticipation. It worked. When this father joined us in our train compartment, bringing me sweets and a doll, apparently I greeted him with a cheerful 'Papa!' and a hug. And that, as far as my parents were concerned, was that. We were a family.

In one instant Sjoma changed from being a single young man living in close quarters with his older brother Misha to a family man with a wife and daughter (but still sharing the same ground-floor lodgings). His responsibility grew immensely from one day to the next, but he had wanted it that way. The initiative had been all his. He was a dynamic, gregarious, hard-working young man, but without a personal anchor. My beautiful mother materialised like a sudden answer to his dreams. They simplified and complicated one another's existence. Their life together was a tango danced by an amateur couple learning the moves as they went along. 'I didn't really think I would stay with him for ever,' my mother declared one day, at the age of eighty-two. She said she never thought about her life that far ahead.

It was my mother's love – adventurous and fearless – that brought me from Moscow to Prague. I was about to be transformed from a Russian child into a Czech child. This process of linguistic and cultural layering is a familiar one to all immigrant children. One language is spoken at home, another in the world outside, with children mastering the new language while their parents, with their accents and imperfect grammar, remain forever foreign. Even a small child begins to feel superior to his or her parents, sensing their language inferiority in the domain outside their home.

After a brief stint at a Russian nursery close to where we first lived, I began attending a regular Czech kindergarten when we moved to another apartment. I wish I could make my memory light up and illuminate those moments, but in this first virginal encounter with being foreign I can now only recall the pleasure of suddenly knowing Czech.

My mother says that for the first two months after joining my Czech kindergarten I didn't speak at all – not a word. I was absolutely silent there, like a mute child. After two months

I started speaking in complete, perfect Czech sentences, as if I always had. This sounds accurate, even scientifically so: a four-year-old child needs about two months to internalise the vocabulary and syntax of a new language, mastering it in its entirety rather than in tentative stages, the way adults do.

But my first perfect Czech sentence was spoken at home – not to my parents, obviously, with whom I continued to speak Russian, but to our Czech neighbour. I was sitting on my potty in the hallway of the apartment we now shared with a very nice Czech family, a policeman and his wife and young son. As the policeman walked in through the front door I greeted him from my little throne: '*Ahoj, vojáčku!*' ('Hello, little soldier!') I do have a vague memory of his uniform and my vantage point, possibly reinforced by the multiple retellings of this apocryphal story of my initiation into Czech.

I love it, mainly because it encapsulates, in two words, the extent to which I had already absorbed the grammatical and even satirical intricacies of my new language. I used the correct declension for the noun *vojáček*, inflecting it in the vocative case. I also immediately found a diminutive for soldier – *vojáček* rather than *voják* – and in just two words managed to convey a tender yet ironic greeting. Blurring the difference between a soldier's and a policeman's uniform was not a mistake but rather a cheeky provocation: my first joke in Czech! Or, to be precise, my first Czech words were a joke I made myself. It was, as I quickly understood, a great language to joke in, to be funny in, to tease in. Provoking a uniformed man into laughter while sitting on a potty was a very Czech moment.

I am laughing – not just smiling, really laughing – in most of the photos my mother took of me in my early days and years in Prague: playing in various parks and beautiful, very old gardens; lending my shoulder to my father, who is fast asleep on a park bench; amusing a crowd of participators in one of the obligatory parades celebrating the victory of the proletariat; dipping my feet in a country brook on a hot summer day. The adults around me are laughing too. My parents' Prague of the late 1950s seems to have been a cheerful place. I know that this enjoyment came with a heavy price, and wasn't what it seemed. But privately, at least, away from the unbearable political demands the regime imposed on every single citizen, life was good for our young family.

My fully developed memories of Prague begin with my first day of school. But from my kindergarten days I retain two key moments.

I arrived in Prague with very long hair, two thick braids tied with silky, rustling ribbons. My mother said she couldn't take me anywhere without hearing from strangers '*To je hezká holčička!*' ('That's a pretty little girl!'), mainly on account of those very Russian braids. One day she decided she wanted to use my hair for a hair extension, which was the greatest fashion accessory of the day. I remember very clearly sitting in a hairdresser's chair about to have my long hair cut off, without my approval or interest. My mother rationalised the deed by telling me that it would be good for me to have a haircut, and that my hair would grow back even thicker. But in the meantime I had to present myself to my kindergarten teacher and friends with a very short, rough haircut. As I entered my kindergarten I immediately announced I was a new girl, with a made-up name. No one really believed me, but they did at least pretend they did, for a while. Reinventing my identity was becoming quite easy.

The other very clear memory from my pre-school days in Prague also involves my mother, albeit indirectly. I was playing in the kindergarten playground when she came to pick me up. Seeing her from a distance, I was so happy I began running towards her as fast as I could, not noticing I was heading straight for a barbed-wire fence. I hit the wire at eye level, eyes wide open. There was a sharp sting. My vision went blurry for a while, but I was lucky: I had missed the most sensitive part of the eye, and there were no serious consequences. The sensation of freely running towards my mother in an open space, then suddenly not seeing her, exhilaration followed by momentary blindness, followed by the relief of a lucky escape has stayed with me. My early childhood was full of such contrasts: fun and games on the periphery of danger.

My original point of entry into Czechoslovakia, the sleepy Čierna nad Tisou, would ten years later become a place of ominous significance. In the summer of 1968 the Czechoslovak leader Alexander Dubček, hero of the Prague Spring, was forced into a meeting there with the Soviet leader Leonid Brezhnev, to justify the Czechoslovak experiment of 'socialism with a human face' and to prevent the inevitable: a military invasion of his country by the Soviet Union and four other armies of the Warsaw Pact. He failed, and on 21 August 1968 my new country was brutally invaded by my old one. This would cause our emigration to yet another new country, and whatever trajectory I and my family had been on until then would undergo a complete change.

But not yet.

Marbles

Like all émigrés, I have recurrent exile dreams about walking down the streets of my childhood and realising I am utterly lost. It's not unlike that other dream everyone has occasionally, of not being able to unlock a door despite holding the key in your hand. There is a mysterious incompatibility between the real and the remembered or imagined context: the dream is about withholding, about being kept on the outside of a world to which I cannot return. By removing myself from it I have been sentenced – or have sentenced myself – to never again finding a way back. The betrayal of the émigré is both a self-inflicted wound and a grave sin. The dream cityscape of my childhood is a map I can clearly see but no longer follow.

Yet in my undreamt memories my childhood geography is vividly real, and I can navigate the map of where I lived with timeless ease and without any heavy burden of loss. In fact, they feel so light and airy that whenever a breeze reminds me of the freshness of my Prague springs and summers and winters and autumns I am very easily transported into after-school playtime, running around the park with my friends and being utterly free.

I grew up in Vinohrady, one of the central quarters of Prague, just west of Václavák (Wenceslas Square). My neighbourhood consisted of elegant tree-lined streets in genteel disrepair, much like the rest of the thousand-year-old city. Peeling stuccoed walls, unpainted heavy entrance doors and loose black and white cobblestones; beauty everywhere, not only where tourists (not many then, masses of them now) would notice or be told to look. Prague seems to have been dreamt up rather than built, like a perfectly imagined sculpture slowly chiselled into ageing stone by a succession of artists who shared the same vision but were given free rein to follow their own whimsy.

Vinohrady means 'vineyards'; I never knew, while I lived there, that very close to my home there was indeed a small vineyard, and that the area had once been covered in them. I learned local patriotism and urban snobbery from a young age, well aware that neighbouring Žižkov (just a few streets away) was considered a far more run-down part of town; Žižkov had the postal code Praha 3, whereas Vinohrady was Praha 2, and I knew that between those two codes there was simply no contest: Praha 2, my Praha 2, was the desirable one.

In 1965 we moved to a bigger apartment, within walking distance of the old one. They had some basic features in common: each was located on the first floor of a handsome, tall art deco building, in a quiet street leading directly onto a park. The first, in a street called Laubova, was a remodelled half of a previously shared flat (remodelling apartments, or rather supervising others doing so, is one of my father's great talents). We had two bedrooms and a living room; the kitchen was a former pantry, tiny but fully equipped for my mother's culinary adventures, mostly based on recipes from the Soviet cookery book she had brought with her from Moscow (and which now has (unused) pride of place in my own kitchen). The second apartment, in Krkonošská, was quite substantial: four large rooms with high ceilings, and our very own gas boiler shimmering in metallic grey in a black-tiled bathroom. I used to volunteer for the job of cleaning it; I loved making the tiles shine darkly while the boiler hummed and its blue pilot light hissed and flickered.

The parks these two streets bordered on couldn't have been more different: Jiřák, a flat, not very large open space with rows of benches and some grass next to Laubova, and Riegrák, one of Prague's largest hilly green spaces next to Krkonošská. Those were nicknames, of course. They were really called the Square of Jiří of Poděbrady and Riegrovy sady (Rieger Gardens), respectively. The former was basically the front yard of a large church, the latter a cultivated urban wilderness you could really get lost in, or pretend to.

When I was in primary school I loved playing marbles alongside the massive side wall of the church. Built only thirty years earlier, in the 1930s, it looked to me like an enormous rectangular ship in dark grey and white. The tower was over forty metres high, with a massive clock I would look up at when it was almost time to go home. Long before I became aware of Prague's singular beauty I was immersed in this corner of it, with its futuristic kind of magic. Seeing it daily, I absorbed the imposing, spectacular architecture as if it were an ordinary sight. Only the wall mattered. We formed a long line parallel to it, along a loose chain of shallow holes in the ground. We had to dig fresh ones only in spring; after that they lasted, for daily games, rain, mud or shine. Our marbles had a hierarchy, progressing from plain blue ones to large multicoloured glass balls we called *duhovka* ('like a rainbow'). It gave me very deep satisfaction to win the biggest possible marble, smooth and heavy and so dense with colours it looked almost black. And it gave me even greater satisfaction to trade my baby brother for the best marbles his grinning little face could buy me.

By the time Maxim was born in 1960 I couldn't remember

having any other home except our apartment in Laubova. I was six years old, in first year of primary school, with a wide circle of local friends, some of whom I had known since nursery. My Moscow roots were already a distant memory, present only in the Russian spoken at home with my parents. The boundaries were clear: Czech was my language, Russian was theirs. Sometimes I would play one language off against the other. One day I was driving my impatient father crazy by lacing up my shoes at a snail's pace when he was late taking me to kindergarten. 'You are drinking my blood!' he screamed in Russian, using a common idiom for one's patience being tested to the absolute limit. I looked up at him from my still-untied shoes and replied, semi-innocently, in Czech, 'How am I drinking it? From a glass or from a cup?' My father burst out laughing. This may have been another reason – aside from linguistic purism – that my parents never let me mix my languages: in Czech I had the upper hand.

I never noticed, or was not aware of, my mother's pregnancy. It was not discussed, at least not with me – until, towards the end of that summer, I was told I had a baby brother. My grandmother had arrived for an extended visit, to help, and I was sent to my first residential summer camp at around the same time, for about a week. When I came back there he was: my very own sibling, from then on and for ever my closest friend and ally. I immediately informed my parents that bringing him up would be entirely my responsibility. They laughed and pretended to agree; or maybe they actually did agree. Maxim, or Maximek as I called him in a tender Czech diminutive ('little Maxim'), was indeed all mine as soon as he grew out of infancy.

I announced his birth with great pride to everyone at school – my fellow classmates, my teacher – but also to the general public in the park, consisting mainly of older ladies who came out daily to sit on benches and watch us play. I loved chatting to them. I would hop off my scooter and stand in front of them, hand on hip, talking a blue streak about anything that came into my head. For many months my favourite subject was my brand-new brother. I was not at all shy to declare that he was the most beautiful baby boy in the world. The old ladies nodded and told me they couldn't wait to see him. By the time he was old enough to sit up I was allowed to take him to the park by myself and parade my dark-eyed, dark-haired baby Maxim between the benches like a young prince.

I was immensely proud of him simply because he existed. His arrival marked the end of a period of my life in which I felt outnumbered by my parents as a unit. Suddenly I was no longer alone; I had my own unit – of two! – and it made a huge difference. My new role of older sister excited me very much, awakening my maternal (and didactic) instincts. At first it was like having a live doll, but very soon my little brother became the one with whom I shared my world, real and imaginary. When he was old enough to understand I would tell him a new story every single day, stories I invented just for him. My parents and grandparents had read to me, of course, but those were finished, burnished narratives, tested by and on millions of children. When I started reading myself it instantly ignited my imagination: every story I read made me think of another, untold and unread. Maxim was the first recipient of those ideas, my first listener. Having a listener is a very serious commitment: it taught me to bring each idea to a proper conclusion while keeping his interest from beginning to end. The stories I used to tell him when he was little had to be very visual; I had to make him feel as if the story were happening and developing right before his eyes. There is no better way of tasting the essence of what a writer has to do. In this way, we both did. (Maybe this story-telling had something to do with my brother becoming a writer; he sometimes says so.)

He was especially fond of funny recurring characters, such as a talking parrot with anarchist tendencies. That, too, was an obsession I had passed on to him. I can trace my fascination with the idea of animals having a human face and character to my early years in Prague, when I discovered there were people, all of them men, called Fox (Liška) or Birdie (Ptáček) or Hedgehog (Ježek) or Goose (Husa) or Fish (Ryba). These are common last names in Czech. As a four- or five-year-old I was in awe of my parents receiving phone calls and visits from foxes and other animals. In Russian, the man's last name would usually have a suffix, concealing or distracting from the morphological derivation. So it seemed to me that in Prague animals occupied the same level as humans, commingling in daily life and speaking the same human language – Czech. Many of the stories I made up for my brother began with sentences like this: 'Once upon a time, there was a parrot who wanted to go to school ... '

While Maxim was still a baby I discovered that showing him off to my friends in the park was a lucrative business. They would beg me to let them push his pram, to borrow my special prize for a while, and they were willing to pay for it in the highest currency we had: marbles. In the manner of Tom Sawyer, who convinced his friends that the chore of painting his fence was such an honour that they were keen to pay him for the privilege of being allowed to apply a few brushstrokes, I would grant permission to my friends to wheel my baby brother around, receiving a few marbles in return and a bit of free time to play with them. There was a small hill in the little park, which I used strategically to showcase Maxim's laughing face as I briefly let go of the handles and let him roll down 'by himself'. This was what my friends wanted to do too: to push the pram around the park and up that hill, and then let go, catching up with him at the bottom. Miraculously they (and

I) never failed; it was a small hill, really only an elevated bit of concrete, but the pram could easily have overturned. It was certainly moving fast enough for my brother's eyes to widen in excitement – or so I thought. Now I believe he must have been terrified.

When he was older we walked to the park together. We would leave home with a small cotton bag of about five marbles each, and return with a bounty, rather unevenly distributed between the two of us; obviously I had won the biggest ones and was (very happily) carrying the heavier load. But he kept getting better at it, fast, and I soon forgot to make allowances for him as my baby brother when we played: he could win with ease. One day a boy my own age or a bit older threatened me. Tiny Maxim suddenly appeared out of nowhere, like my own little Superman. Stepping between us he said, 'Leave her alone or I'll beat you up.' Everyone around us laughed, the bully retreated and I realised Maxim's 'little baby brother' days were over.

I could see the distant, fairy-tale Prague castle from many spots in my neighbourhood, but my very own Kafka's castle was the church, a powerful magnet whose visual reach was omnipresent. One Sunday I was playing close to the church entrance while my grandmother was wheeling Maxim around the park. I saw a big crowd streaming through the massive front doors. I had never been inside, and wanted to see what went on there. I joined the crowd and a service in full swing. I heard majestic organ music and a heavy, hushed silence. I looked around and saw people kneeling, so I did the same. But I wasn't in a pew, I was standing in the centre of the church, near enough to see up close the enormous gilded figure of Jesus Christ. I didn't know who he was but I thought he had to be important, like the main character in a children's theatre production I had seen not long ago. I must have been the focal point from any direction, a little girl kneeling all by herself.

Suddenly the doors opened with a loud and powerful groan, and then I heard heavy steps behind me, echoing loudly as they approached. People turned around and stared, and I did too. I saw my father, marching in a determined, furious manner to my spot, where he scooped me up like a little puppy and carried me outside, from the sombre darkness and silence of the vast church into the broad daylight and street noise just outside its massive doors. My grandmother stood there, waiting. She tried to calm my father down in Russian, but he would have none of it. I received a slap, and this: 'Don't you EVER go in there again, and don't you ever kneel to pray. We're Jews.' I didn't really understand, but the message was clear: as far as I was concerned, this amazing church wasn't mine. My grandmother was appalled at my father's explosion of anger, but she reinforced his message in her own way when she soothed me, saying, 'He shouts too much, but he's right.' It was the first time I understood, under rather dramatic circumstances, that there was another side to my identity. Now I knew that I wasn't allowed to kneel, like so many other people did, and that this church was only a backdrop to my childhood. It was just a wall; a place to play marbles.

When I was nine years old a lady stopped me in a street near my home and asked, 'Would you like to play a part in a film?'

'I'm not allowed to talk to you,' I replied, very suspicious of her motives. But she laughed: she was actually a well-known film director and had spotted a child she would like to audition for her new film. She later spoke to my parents and I was invited to a screen test, competing with dozens of others. We had been told to dress lightly, but my mother insisted on wrapping my head in a scarf, and made me perspire under several layers of sweaters and two cardigans, plus a padded winter coat. The other girls were wearing light summer dresses and spring jackets, and were immediately ready for the summer scene we were filming. I had to borrow someone else's clothes for the audition. I was mortified.

The scene required that I whistle, loudly, to attract the attention of a group of older boys, who had to come running, in awe of the little girl's authority. I didn't pass the audition: I made the boys laugh rather than tremble with fear, and my parents were later told that 'it was decided to give the part to a blonde child, who looked more like a Czech village girl'. Rather unjustly, I blamed my mother for the tragic loss of my acting career, when, in hindsight, it was clear that, in terms of my looks, I was perceived as a foreign child.

I started reading and writing in Russian at the same time as I was learning to read Czech at school, aged about six. I remember teaching myself the Cyrillic shapes while I was being taught the very curved Czech handwriting. The teacher stamped my diary with three beautiful stars for reading the first full page in our reader out loud. I have a very clear mental snapshot of her warm smile as she said to the class, 'This is how I want you all to read.'

But now I wonder: was her praise meant for a child who had quickly mastered fluent reading, or was it also – or even primarily – for the foreign child who had surprised her by learning to read Czech very quickly? I felt as Czech as all my classmates. Yet in the eyes of a teacher who must have met my parents and known my personal history, I was a Russian child.

Where Books Come From

Our next apartment may have been bigger, more grand, and my adolescent life there more exciting, but while we still lived in Laubova I had everything I wanted and needed to feel very, very happy.

I was not especially aware of what my parents were going through at the time. Politically, they had to contend with an extremely repressive regime in the 1950s, a grey prelude to the more liberal, more colourful 1960s. It was an era when political and personal spheres merged into one, regardless of who you were or where your sympathies lay. Like any new couple, they were in the process of establishing themselves as a young family, as young professionals. By the time my father's earlier political 'transgressions' receded into a relatively distant past, a much greater disaster loomed: his brother was arrested for attempting to emigrate to the West (this was illegal in communist Czechoslovakia) and, shortly afterwards, their father was arrested in Russia for 'economic crimes', along with a number of others in a well-known Soviet show case. It is not clear whether he was executed or died in prison or a labour camp, though the family assumed the former. My father never really recovered from this tragedy, which was all the more difficult to deal with due to the complete impossibility of communicating or obtaining reliable information. My parents continued to function as if nothing had happened. They dealt with grief by not giving in to it.

But I did not know any of this. I was raised in an atmosphere of complete, cultivated insouciance, encouraged by my parents to see life as my very own playground. My birthday parties were socially lavish, in my parents' spirit of generosity. When I was seven I informed them I had invited all my girl friends. My parents were outraged: what about the boys? I was instructed to immediately go out and invite all the boys I knew. This included not only my classmates, but also the boys I knew from the park. 'Come to my birthday party on Sunday,' I told them, one after another, or in groups. They all came. Our apartment was completely filled with children. There was no party enter-tainment – an unheard-of concept in those days. My friends were simply allowed to play with all my toys, in any room, any way they chose. The freedom to just run around my house and play (I'm sure there were about fifty children present) was intoxicating to all of us. And then my parents served lots of food and a huge cake, and the more noise we made the happier they seemed. I'm not sure about our neighbours; our family partied Russian-style.

By my tenth birthday the gift-giving became a more con-scientious affair, and my parties a little bit (though not much more) selective. From then on, most of my presents were books. I still have many of them, with neat inscriptions in my classmates' tidy handwriting. We all loved a small but well-stocked bookstore in our neighbourhood. In the communist Czechoslovakia of my childhood, books were a standardised fare, in the sense that we all read the same ones. But that doesn't mean they were inadequate – quite the contrary: the Czech authors and many translated ones were really excellent. With the exception of some obligatory so-called socialist literature produced by editors at state-run publishing houses under ideological duress, my early childhood library has withstood the test of time. I still cherish it.

It is our family tradition to leave gifts by the birthday child's bed late at night, so that they wake up surrounded by presents. On my tenth birthday I pretended to be fast asleep while my mother placed a mountain of new books on a chair by my bed and tiptoed out of the room. As soon as she had closed the door I started reading them by the light of the street lamp just outside my first-floor window. My birthday is in December, so that night didn't turn into day for many hours. By the time the yellow electric light gave way to the milky greyish-white of morning I had read all of my birthday books cover to cover. I was in heaven: I had completely lost myself in each one, and loved them all. Most of them were in Czech, but a few were in Russian, sent by my grandparents from Moscow. I absorbed all the stories, characters, illustrations: it was like a night full of vivid dreams.

All my friends had lots of books, but when I realised I had a few more than the others I decided to play librarian. I spent an entire day numbering each book, creating library cards and a full list of my stock. Then I invited friends over to borrow them. I wrote their names on the cards and the date they took them home; they were allowed to keep them for one week. Some were never returned. When I see a circled number inside one of my old children's books it connects me immediately with that game, and that day in my life.

We lived under the leaky umbrella of totalitarianism, but the freedom we had as children was intoxicating: running around without adult supervision, doing whatever we liked with our days, choosing who to spend time with and where. And Czech children's books, television programmes and theatre played a big role in this feeling of living in a magical land. Czech literature for children is built on subtle irony, on characters who are gently subversive and very funny. Despite our six-year age difference, Maxim and I were glued to the same animated series. And to this day, our nicknames for one another are based on two Czech cartoon characters, little woodland dwarves who lived together in a hut in loving disharmony.

Living a free childhood in an unfree society sounds like a paradox. It isn't. Childhood is a world of its own, a dream within the reality one was born into. The reality dictated that some dues were to be paid to the totalitarian entity that ruled not only my country but the entire Eastern Bloc. I had to be a Young Pioneer, which meant that on festive occasions such as parades and special assemblies I wore a red scarf, pleated blue skirt and a white shirt my mother never quite managed to iron perfectly. Before I was a pioneer I had to be its infant version, *jiskřička* ('sparkle'). At a very young age all this was fun rather than a chore I felt forced into. From my point of view as an adult, it's almost embarrassing to realise just how irrelevant the crippling ideology behind these activities was to me as a child. But only as a very young child: by the time I was in my teens that complacency had turned into something very different. Its opposite, in fact.

I was allowed to go to shows at a children's puppet theatre by myself. Not just any theatre, but the greatest: Špejbl and Hurvínek, two idiosyncratic comic puppets created in the 1920s by a famous Czech puppeteer. They were father and son, speaking in odd, high-pitched voices: Špejbl, a retired teacher completely out of touch with the real world and always exasperated with his son's ideas; and Hurvínek, a streetwise, articulate, hilariously naughty little boy. I loved them so much I was practically living in their world. It was very sophisticated comedy that worked on many levels, but was mainly carried by extremely sharp dialogue. Czech culture never condescended to children. There was no Disney cuteness or prettiness. Writing for children was one of the few areas where even adults could escape into a semblance of freedom.

The adults in my life were actually still very young at this stage. Only a few years earlier, in the 1950s, my father had served in the Czech Army. This is a period of his life he actually does love to remember and talk about. Now in his eighties, he sings dirty songs and tells the crudely funny jokes from his days as a young soldier, his face comes alive, he laughs at his own memories of his younger self. It is as if the army had been his playground, where, in spite of the regimented routine and the political pressures of the times, he could forget about his actual responsibilities. When I asked him, 'What did you actually do in the army?' he replied, in Russian, with a mischievous smile: 'We knocked pears off trees with our dicks.'

I have a T-shirt with an amusing photograph of my young father printed on it, wearing his soldier's uniform but also a bow-tie, and saluting, with a big cheeky smile on his face. Behind him is a small bookcase, containing both Russian and Czech books. It was partly hidden by our dining table, and this was intentional: some of the books on those shelves were forbidden. Among them was a fat historical tome about T. G. Masaryk, Czechoslovakia's first president and the most enlightened philosopher–politician of his time. My beloved first teacher, Paní Plhová, once told our class about him in an unforgettable, soft-spoken manner: 'Children, I am not allowed to tell you this, but a long time ago we had a wonderful president, Tomáš Garrigue Masaryk. I just want you to remember his name.'

She was taking a serious risk – if any of us had blabbered about it at home or told the wrong person there would have been political consequences for her. Communist Czechoslovakia was supposed to forget its capitalist bourgeois beginnings, when it became an independent state in 1918 after the break-up of the Austro-Hungarian Empire and blossomed in the 1920s before falling to Hitler's Germany in 1938. Of course I asked my parents who he was, and why the book about him was hidden behind the table. My father repeated what my teacher had said – that Masaryk was a great man, and that I shouldn't talk about him. My parents exchanged a glance and my father said to my mother, 'Very brave of her.' I knew he meant my teacher.

Parents could not trust their own children. We were never told the whole story; secrets and lies and evasive answers and meaningful glances and concealed real opinions were a normal part of our daily discourse. Irony and double entendre were essential ingredients of our language. I may have wanted the honour of being a Young Pioneer, but even then I knew that under that layer of officially orchestrated certainty there was doubt, disbelief and, somewhere deep down, the real truth about how things were. This truth could not be discussed, it had to be guessed, worked out on the basis of clues and suggestions like a reverse treasure hunt: the farther away you moved from the core treasure – the truth – the safer you were. The safer you were, the easier your life was.

My father's work brought him into close contact with many Czech writers, film-makers and other artists. I heard frequent references to a place he loved to spend time in – *filmák*, short for Filmový Klub. This film club was where many creative and personal connections were made, and my parents' social life and their friendships with Prague intellectuals began to flourish. They had noisy get-togethers in our house almost every night, with animated discussions and much laughter. Their lives were transformed: suddenly they were right in the middle of something very exciting.

I will never forget my own first encounter with a real author. The Czech Jewish writer and journalist Ludvík Aškenázy lived across the street from us in Laubova. His wife was Heinrich Mann's daughter, as I found out years later. My father translated some of his books into Russian, and I read them in both languages as a child. They were unlike anything I have ever read – before, or since. Minimalist, witty, deeply moving gems based on poetic dialogues between characters who were clearly fictional creations but felt like people you knew very well.

I saw him sitting on a park bench, alone. He was a very rotund man, not large but somehow imposing. I sat down next to him and started chatting. 'So is this where you think up all your books?' He smiled, and said 'Sometimes.'

Later that evening, when I mentioned this to my parents they told me off for being rude and bothering an important, serious man. But I was very happy. I felt I had just come a little closer to understanding where books came from: From the heads of great writers sitting on ordinary park benches. In my own town, Prague.

Prague Journals, and Trees

A large black, ruled notebook. The front cover is filled with blue-framed labels, each with a red title in my mother's massive, clear handwriting, in Russian:

THE HOUSE DIARY [added in my hand: of Billers]
Rada (mama)
Sjomka (papa) also known as 'bad daddy'
Lenochka (daughter, also Lenka, also sister)
Maximka (son, also Maximorus, also brother)

1 January 1963 (possibly from 24 December 1962)

EVERYONE WELCOME

Inside the notebook there is a loose sheet of paper. Again, in my mother's ten-inch letters, in red:

I PROPOSE!
   A DIARY OF OUR HOME. WRITE WRITE WRITE WRITE!!!!

EVERYONE!!!
BIG AND SMALL. AND THOSE GROWING UP.
VOLUNTARY PARTICIPATION!
ONLY FOR THOSE WHO ARE INTERESTED.
OPEN TO GUESTS.
(Those who suffer from the absence of publishing houses
and publishers.)

The language of this family diary was Russian. My
mother's own idea received an exuberant introduction (by
herself); the beginnings looked promising. Today, I am
struck by her allusion to publishers and publishing houses –
as if this family joke were actually half-serious: we're real
writers here.

After her enthusiastic opening lines, and a short paragraph
from each of my parents, I became the only one writing reg-
ularly, updating the diary almost in Facebook-status style,
documenting occasional events and situations. In 1963 I was
nine years old, and could only print in capitals in Russian. (Of
course, I could write in joined-up handwriting in Czech, but
this diary was a Russian-only zone):

25 December 1962
    PAPA WENT FROM ROOM TO ROOM AND DID
NOT CLOSE THE DOORS.
    MAXIM IS SITTING AT THE TABLE AND
DRAWING A CAT.
    MAMA IS LYING ON THE COUCH.

26 December 1962
    I AM WRITING FIRST INSTEAD OF MAMA.
    PAPA IS SHOUTING AT MAXIM.

MAMA IS SITTING ON THE COUCH AND LAUGHING: HA-HA-HA.

MAXIM IS GETTING ON EVERYONE'S NERVES.

27 December

MAXIM IS DRINKING WATER.

PAPA IS STANDING BY THE CUPBOARD.

MAMA IS COOKING.

PAPA IS TALKING TO MISHA.

28 December

LENA GOT AN 'A' IN MUSIC.

THEY TOOK A SWIPE FROM OUR BUMS AND PAPA WAS EMBARRASSED TO SHOW THE DOCTOR HIS BUM.

MAMA IS WALKING FROM ROOM TO ROOM AND NEVER CLOSES THE DOORS AND DOESN'T TURN OFF THE LIGHT JUST LIKE PAPA SOMETIMES.

MAMA IS SINGING AND ROCKING HERSELF LIKE A TINY MAXIM.

21 March

LENA TRANSLATED THIS: A CIRCUS WITHOUT HORSES SHOULD BE ASHAMED.

24 April

WE ARE SITTING AND LISTENING TO THE RECORD 'OLIVER TWIST'.

So much for 1963. The last entry was the hit song in Miloš Forman's film *Konkurs* (*Audition*), sung by a seamlessly edited succession of extremely earnest, plain-looking, very real teenage girls: 'I should not have read that novel / A hero was hidden in it / I love him / His name is Twist / Oliver Twist ... ' It is one thing to suddenly remember an old song, but to find evidence in a diary that it had once had a (completely forgotten) presence in one's life is a surreal step back into the past.

No one used this diary to record that it was the year my grandmother Zelda passed away in Moscow, almost exactly a year after my mother started this attempt at a family chronicle. Nothing was written in 1964 either. Then, in 1965, I suddenly resume my role as the family historian, but now I am writing in cursive Russian and occasionally insert a few Czech phrases for witty effect. I make some pretty funny Russian puns – I would have no idea how to translate them into English today. I state that we have now (in October 1965) moved, the house is a mess, my father agitated 'about everything except his loving daughter'. My grandfather, on a visit from Moscow, is 'learning Czech'.

The following year receives only one brief update, about a family 'idyll': Maxim is ill and singing, I am writing, my father is typing on his typewriter and my mother is cuddling Maxim. Moving right along to 1967, I begin (and end) that year by drawing stick-figure 'portraits of each family member and their thoughts this year'. For myself I draw hearts and a boy kneeling, declaring his love. The heart contains my initials but not his: we have a secret, a mystery. I was thirteen, and I can confirm that there was a boy I was hoping might fall in love with me. (He did, but not that year.)

Maxim's thought bubble contains a copy of the drawing of himself, but dressed as a cowboy. He has a gun, which is pointing upwards, and is going off: *pimpimpim* (that's Czech for *bangbangbang*).

My mother, in her own bubble, is thinking about London, Italy and Paris, plus strings of pearls and a fancy watch. She did travel to London around that time, by herself, for a conference. During that trip she met the Queen; she also walked into a Soho strip club ('I was curious') and bought Paul Anka and Beatles records. She was in love with Paul Anka.

Finally, my father is depicted as holding an envelope and a letter (clearly an angry one, from Maxim's teacher). In his bubble there is a belt in his hand, directed at Maxim, and I am in that bubble too. It looks like a threat of corporal punishment; all three of us are crying long chains of tears, which look exactly like my mother's pearls. Maxim's tears and his father's meet and intermingle, forming a circle.

The final entry, still in 1967, mentions only that I won second prize in a poetry-reciting competition. Then nothing.

Despite its meagre content, this family chronicle has, in fact, served exactly the purpose originally intended by my mother, as a time capsule of our life as a family at a time when we were all still at home in Prague, our roles clearly assigned. My father was the temperamental presence, demanding that doors be closed and lights turned off, yet frequently not abiding by his own rules. He was the figure of irascible authority and unpredictable yet regular bursts of tenderness. My mother was a permanent source of tenderness, with frequent outbursts of song, dance, loud laughter and occasional fury. She lived in her own *inner* bubble, using her complex moods and her physical exhaustion as a shield against the outside world (which included all of us). Maxim, a very small boy, was already causing trouble and courting disciplinary disaster while secretly craving peace and quiet; my parents' noisy ways were hard for him to take. For me, he was at the very centre of my family universe.

My own part in the family quartet is also quite obvious. I was hiding behind my persona of a neutral observer, somewhere between my parents and my much younger brother, understanding and loving them all, watching and registering everything, yet not insisting on being understood myself. I saved my deep talks for my close friends, never for my family. My exuberant chattiness had them fooled; they always mistook it for openness. 'You always told me everything,' my mother once said, years later. By this she meant that I would give a breathless daily account of my day in school and other easily relatable matters. But I did not reveal to either of my parents my feelings about – anything, really. I felt like the family interpreter, connecting them all, skilfully leaving myself out of that equation without anyone noticing, fiercely guarding my own domain against theirs, and without their language. My Czech against their Russian.

The move referred to in the diary for October 1965 was from Laubova to Krkonošská Street. Just a few blocks away, but a completely different neighbourhood, dominated by a vast, hilly park full of old trees and large green spaces. No church here, and an end to my fixation with playing marbles. Instead, I became a proper tomboy, and spent my free time running around the park with boys, climbing those trees. I decided that girls were a fake species, backstabbing, gossipy and full of envy and petty jealousies. Some were my best friends, but their complicated machinations bored and annoyed me. By contrast, boys were direct, simple and not too wordy. My parents never supervised my homework, and they didn't control how I spent my time outdoors. My brother was perfectly happy playing football with much bigger boys in the street right in front of our building (the occasional cars were dodged, without many incidents). This left me completely free to roam the park with the boys. They would come knocking on my door, or I on theirs. I loved the excitement contained in the simple question: '*Ahoj, můžeš jít do parku?*' (Hi, do you want to go to the park?'), anticipating our adventures.

Oddly, most of the neighbourhood boys I was friends with at the time shared their last names with types of bird. There was Bažant (Pheasant), Špaček (Starling), Vrabec (Sparrow). One was even called, generically, Ptáček – 'Little Bird'. I don't remember their first names because we addressed one another by our last names, an unwritten rule applied to social inter-actions between boys and girls. To them, I was Billerová. My parents loved it when, say, Starling came calling for me, but I was already out with another boy, so they could say 'She's up in a tree with Sparrow.'

We would wander around the busy park, disappearing into the thick foliage, our secret refuge. Then it was a question of finding the first good, solid tree branch we could easily reach; once we were on it we would grasp the next one, higher up, and keep climbing until we were on the highest branch, where we could just sit and stare at the people below. This was freedom: close to the real world but inside our own. We didn't talk much. The pleasure was in climbing a tree, for no particular reason.

Trees are the real survivors of history. Ever since my tree-climbing days in Prague I have loved getting lost in forests, in their silence, tranquillity and concealed drama once lived by others. And now when I visit this Prague park I look for trees that could be the ones I climbed as a child. Unlike me, they stayed here; while I wandered, rootless and uprooted, they never moved. Their roots grew deeper into their own bit of earth.

But ultimately, it wasn't this romantic vision of a childhood wonderland that I took with me when I left Prague. The indel-ible picture in my mind was of Soviet soldiers and their tanks stationed in our park for many months after the invasion. Their outdoor latrines made it stink. As I passed them every day on my way to and from school that year, their presence and the accompanying stench seemed like a cruel joke. My friends and I teased the soldiers by putting tiny pencil drawings of stick figures inside a matchbox and pretending we were taking photos of them, until they confiscated our 'cameras'. I never once revealed to them that I was a native Russian-speaker.

The real diaries of those last years in Prague were the ones I secretly wrote myself. The invasion triggered a new earnestness in me, a feeling that I was an intended rather than accidental witness of this period of history. The two volumes of my first Czech diaries refer to political and personal events as part of the same continuum. On the day of the invasion itself I only managed a full-page headline framed in black like a death notice:

21 AUGUST 1968 – a black day in the history of Czechoslovakia and mankind

A few days later, I added a full account of how I had experienced it:

On that day I was in a summer camp in Chřibská near Děčín. It happened while I was working on my badge of silence. I came back from the bathroom to our room – and all the girls were crying. I didn't know what was going on and J.Z. told me. I forgot all about my badge and started crying – terribly. Everyone was thinking just one thing: how is it going to end, and that Russkies are bastards. Yes, exactly that. Then we watched TV and listened to the radio, almost all day long. By the afternoon we calmed down quite a bit. And what actually happened? Soviet, Polish, Hungarian, German and Bulgarian armies invaded our territory – Prague is occupied. When I read this years from now, I will probably cry again and again.

I remember so much more than I chose to reveal in my diary. The sense of helplessness, of an entire country being violated. The strange, dreamlike sensation of watching myself as if in a movie, and of life going on in spite of the national trauma. The strong sense of solidarity. The funeral in January 1969 of Jan Palach, the young student who burned himself to death in Wenceslas Square, so close to my home, in protest against how quickly the recent Prague Spring was being forgotten, and the country forced to return to 'normal'.

On the next page, only about two weeks later:

Of all my teachers, I hate Smolíková (geography) and Pivoňka (physics) the most. But Smolíková more so – she is a disgusting, evil bitch!

And another week later I write about the pain of losing my best friend Katja, who emigrated soon after the occupation – as did many others. The first wave of exiles from Czechoslovakia occurred instantly. The question we had all immediately asked ourselves – How is this going to end? – was being answered, in stark colours, every single day. Our country had been violently attacked; we were hurting, and felt helpless. Life went on.

For me, exile was not even remotely on the horizon. I immersed myself in an exciting, bittersweet mix of adolescent emotions and the sense of living at the very heart of history. No other place in the world, I thought, could match Prague's soulful beauty and tragedy. I was where I was meant to be, and I was beginning to write about it. In May 1969 I published my first poem in a real magazine. The poem was entitled 'People' and the magazine was called *Větmík* (*Pinwheel*, formerly *Pionýr* – *Pioneer*). It was an unrhymed, somewhat rhythmic prose segment in poem form, about discovering what's inside a person and finding the key to connect with them, for love or for friendship. Both were becoming my main obsession, and have remained so. I was fascinated by ways of gauging the difference between love and friendship: how blurry were the boundaries? My first love grew out of a deep friendship with a classmate – but maybe it was the other way around?

Seeing my little poem in print was exhilarating; but getting paid for it was even more so. (I still have that pay slip, as well as the acceptance note, addressed to me as 'Reader, Jelena Billerová, Krkonošská 3, Praha 2'.) It meant professional respect and recognition, nothing less. It cannot be underestimated how crucial it is for writers to be paid, even at a very young age. For me, it was a sign: now I really was, or was becoming, a writer. I was on my way. It felt good. It felt right. It was meant to happen. I was sure I would publish my first novel by the age of eighteen.

I wrote much more prose than poetry, and published some too (mainly satirical stories in a humour magazine), but poetry was my way of playing with language in complete freedom, jazzing up random words or snippets of sentences into a coherent whole that began and ended at just the right moment, preferably unexpectedly.

Immediately after the invasion, while still at summer camp, I decided it was essential to write a letter to my grandfather in Moscow, to make sure he understood how evil it was that his powerful, barbaric country had invaded my helpless, small, enlightened one. 'We don't need those soldiers ... They should go home. We have our own socialism, we don't need anybody's interference in our affairs ...') I was really worried that my Russian (or rather Armenian) grandfather, a Soviet patriot, would not grasp the nature and extent of the monstrous injustice my country had just suffered, and what it meant for me personally. I also added a postscript, addressed to the censor: 'For the comrade who will be reading this letter at the border. Uncle, you are a human being, too! I assure you that this letter will not cause a revolution in the USSR – and your people will not rebel. You can let this letter through – it tells the truth.'

Apparently I was convincing, or lucky, because my grandfather did receive it. He later told my parents he had found it astonishing. I have the original: my mother brought it back from one of her visits to Moscow years later.

The invasion was a direct stab to the country's heart, but the wound bled slowly, almost invisibly. Despite the presence of Soviet soldiers in most cities, the press did not immediately lose its freedom, and it took a while before the government shut the borders to the West. In March 1969, almost eight months after the occupation, Czechoslovakia's national ice-hockey team beat the USSR in the World Championships in Stockholm, twice: 2–0 and, a week later, 4–3.

These numbers are etched in my memory as the last euphoric moment of pseudo-freedom in Prague. As soon as the second match had finished, late at night (I think it was past midnight), everyone started moving in the direction of Wenceslas Square: normally a ten-minute walk from our apartment, this victory march took many hours. My father said, 'Take it in. You won't see this ever again.' We merged with joyous masses of people as soon as we left our building, and the entire throng rolled like lava down the wide main street. The sense of pride and excitement, and of having the moral upper hand was written on people's faces. I heard, and joined in, shouts of the victory scores – 'Two–nil! Four–three!' – and saw witty slogans playing on the idea of beating the Russkies – at hockey, if nothing else. At that very moment more than half a million people marched and celebrated in almost seventy cities all over the country.

I sometimes watch grainy documentary footage of this demonstration and hope to spot myself and my father in it. History was now a drama I had a small part in. Suddenly my life felt at least as interesting as the books I was reading.

My Prague Spring

Shortly after our move to Krkonošská I also moved schools. This had been my parents' idea. There were a few elite schools in Prague where foreign languages – real foreign languages, in addition to the obligatory Russian – were taught on a daily basis. For some reason my parents had decided long ago that the language I should study and know was French, and to that effect they hired a private tutor for me, an elderly Russian lady called Madame Olga Nikolayevna Prokopenko. She belonged to the much earlier generation of White Russian émigrés, from an aristocratic family. She used to tell me stories whose historical context I did not really understand at the time, for example about her brother who angered and endangered their father by participating in 'an uprising against the Tsar' in 1905. Like all Russian aristocrats she spoke perfect French. Olga Nikolayevna not only taught me French grammar and vocabulary, both of which I found fascinating, but also introduced me to the magical world of reading in French. There is a saying in Czech that roughly translates as 'You have as many lives as the number of languages you speak'. It wasn't until I began to understand French that the true meaning of enriching one's life via a foreign language really became clear to me.

Olga Nikolayevna gave me a special gift: a French children's classic she had been raised on herself, *Les petites filles modèles* by La Comtesse de Ségur, originally published in 1909. Bound in red leather with gold-embossed lettering, it had quaint, witty illustrations depicting nicely dressed children and elegant adults. It surprised me very much that I was able to follow the children's mischievous adventures without understanding every word. My teacher said to me, 'When you read in a foreign language, never look up every word in the dictionary, but only those words you notice coming up often.' It was the best advice I have ever received – a brilliant, very natural method of speeding up one's acquisition of a language, without a major effort. I have since shared it with many.

When I read Vladimir Nabokov's memoir *Speak, Memory*, I found out to my great amusement that, growing up in an aristocratic Russian family, he too was raised on *Les petites filles modèles*. And I learned from his book that La Comtesse de Ségur was herself a Russian aristocrat (her real name was Sofia Feyodorovna Rostopchina), and that the French country-house setting is actually modelled on a Russian aristocrat's home. It is ironic that thanks to my first French teacher I was temporarily immersed in the kind of pre-revolutionary Russian aristocratic culture my communist environment required me to detest.

Olga Nikolayevna prepared me very well for the French entrance exam to my new school. That is to say, I passed, but the teacher who tested me seemed rather amused by my accent. She assumed it was due to my Russian background, but it was simply my perfect imitation of Olga Nikolayevna's speech. The ink of her dedication on the inside leaf of the book she gave me has faded over the years, but her old-fashioned Russian handwriting is still perfectly legible: *Dorogoy Lenotchke – O.N.* ('To dear Lenotchka – O.N.')

I switched schools in the middle of an academic year, joining an already fully established class who had been together for several years. I walked straight into the second half of an art lesson. Art and physical education were my worst subjects. The art teacher, an imposing bearded man who looked quite a bit like Hemingway, asked me what mark I had received for art at my old school. He was pleased when I said it was an A. I wasn't lying: although I couldn't draw or paint, my previous art teacher was a very progressive, very young and pretty woman who encouraged us to make collages – no drawing required. I was good at collages; all it took was a good eye for spotting interesting photos in magazines, then cutting them out and pasting them into imaginative compositions. The more playful we were, the more she admired them. But in my new art class they were making potato stamps. I was handed a potato and a special knife, and told to carve out a certain shape. My failure to do this was abysmal. A few years later the same teacher would add citizenship to his repertoire of subjects, and there I managed to shock him again. He was trying to impress the school principal and a visiting dignitary with his dutiful teaching of the meaning of 'comrade'. I raised my hand. 'Yes, Billerová?' 'I just wanted to say that the word "comrade" was already important in Ancient Greece, because there is this line in Homer's *Illiad*: "And every comrade was carried by three goats."'

Everyone laughed, but my art-cum-citizenship teacher turned a dark, furious red.

Another who was often red in the face, though for a very different reason, was our lovable physics teacher, who kept a bottle of wine under his desk and took frequent sips while demonstrating experiments that never, ever worked.

Some of our educators were formidable characters, with many eccentricities. Our maths teacher was extremely strict, but if you were a supporter of his football team you could do rather well. Before tests he would tease the class by asking one of us to predict the outcome of an upcoming match; if you dared predict his team's loss you were invariably called to the blackboard to solve a difficult equation. I was bad at maths and had no real interest in football; my fate in his class was doubly sealed.

My favourite subject was Czech, both literature and grammar, but I had a secret: I found the Czech classics we were supposed to read and write compositions about so boring that I never read them. To this day I have not read *Babička* (*Grandmother*) by Božena Němcová, one of Czech literature's most celebrated classic novels. But I wrote several essays and exams about it, all of which earned me As and my teacher's praise. I picked up everything I needed to know about the book's contents from what was said in class; the rest was convincing filler based on my imagination. I never felt guilty about this. I was reading the books I really wanted to read, working my way through my parents' library and a public library, as well as borrowing from my friends. I was not the only one; many of us were reading secretly under the desk while pretending to listen to the teacher. I remember one of my closest friends reading Hemingway during our physics class; we were thirteen at the time.

My new school was in Ostrovní, just behind the imposing National Theatre building, in one of the most elegant central quarters, only steps away from the Vltava (a scenic but temperamental river, with dark mood swings). It took me about twenty minutes to get there by tram or by bus; in winter I preferred to walk all the way, the pristine morning snow crunching under my feet all through Wenceslas Square and beyond. I loved that commuting interval between home and school, and often did my homework while standing on a crowded tram. I learned to control my handwriting while in motion and keep it neat by pausing when the tram lurched forward.

Unusually for a Prague school building (formerly a convent school), ours had its own swimming pool. Some of my classmates' parents were well-known academics, artists and intellectuals. One girl's father was a 'big beast' at the Ministry of the Interior. Another classmate's mother was an important school inspector, which made some teachers a little bit afraid of her. She also had the biggest breasts in our class and was extremely pretty, with one long braid slung over one shoulder like a stunning accessory. The school itself had had some famous pupils, for example Hana Mašková, the Olympic figure skater who would die tragically at a young age. In a parallel class, one of the pupils was Norodom Sihamoni, the present King of Cambodia and son of King Norodom Sihanouk. The prince arrived each morning in a chauffeur-driven limousine, carrying the simple slippers we were all required to change into. When he didn't do well he was teased: 'His Excellency has failed again.'

I was a very late bloomer, and looked like a twelve-year-old until I was fifteen. I was famous for my regular tardiness – my daily late entrance had an almost theatrical quality, and was usually greeted with collective laughter – and my constant talking during lessons. I couldn't help it: behind me were the two smartest and funniest boys in the class, so my back was turned to the teacher as often as I could get away with it. We had so much fun chatting and laughing we hardly noticed that the friendship between one of them and myself was slowly metamorphosing into first, deep love.

Our country was metamorphosing too. The Prague Spring, which officially began in January 1968, was a sudden explosion of freedom and reform from within the core of the Czechoslovak Communist Party itself. There was an instant, radical change of tone; the borders with the West opened up; censorship was abolished. Newspapers, radio and television could now say whatever they pleased. This was 'socialism with a human face', a phrase coined by Alexander Dubček. The world was watching Czechoslovakia with amazement and admiration, and that felt good. Unfortunately, the Soviet leadership was watching as well; the heady days of the new, democratic Czechoslovakia were numbered, and would be over by August. But we did not know this, or didn't want to know. The entire country felt like a cancer patient who had suddenly been cured. The sense of euphoria was all-pervasive and exciting. My mother's Czech made a big leap forward in 1968. For the first time since her arrival in the country she began to really read newspapers and books; like everyone else, she was addicted to the galvanising 'events', as we all referred to the Prague Spring and its aftermath. Despite her Soviet background she became a Czechoslovak patriot – her thick Russian accent notwithstanding.

As teenagers, we felt this intoxication with special intensity. Our parents were suddenly no longer grey, tired people, but excited, hyperactive, news-hungry, ever-partying adults. There was an erotic charge in the atmosphere, affecting everything: a blast of fresh air, of optimism, of new energy. We were all so happy to be in Prague in 1968. It felt like a magic number, a magical year – and a magical place.

I can easily conjure up the sounds and images of 1960s Prague, the songs we listened to and films we watched back then. The lyrics, stored somewhere deep inside my brain, come floating back and I can sing along, word-perfect, to songs I last heard four or five decades ago. The soundtrack cuts like a razor through the other cultures I have since added, revealing my much younger brain, not yet burdened with languages that were not, and would never be, mine. It is a little spooky when I hear myself sing a song I was obsessed with as a thirteen-year-old, suddenly understanding and appreciating its lyrics, discovering nuances I had missed. We connect with music on such a profound, subconscious level; we unpeel the layers of who we became, who we once were. Deeply hidden identities can go even further back than childhood, or actively remembered lifetime: rather mysteriously, I have discovered a connection to the old Russian songs and music played and loved by my grandparents.

Music, art, literature, theatre, film: for me and my close friends the Prague Spring became synonymous with being part of a new wave of creativity, obliterating boundaries between adults and young teens. Almost overnight we had access to the same experiences. We went to plays, concerts, exhibitions, films, without any age or time restrictions. We were treated as equals by our parents and teachers, all of us part of the same liberating experiment. We dared hope that life would be this free, this wonderful, this true for ever.

Less than two weeks after the Soviet invasion, in September 1968, our teachers gathered us all in the gym for a special assembly. There were tears as they talked to us about what we had witnessed only days ago – the rape of our country. Soviet tanks were a daily sight in the streets of Prague; the Soviet military and political presence, of so-called brotherly advisers, would continue for many years to come. The occupation had been swift and overwhelming because the armies of the 'friendly' Warsaw Pact had not only penetrated all of Czechoslovakia's borders, but had also landed military aircraft in Prague, carrying tanks and other materiel. This, we were told by our teachers, would become our new reality. There would be changes, they said, 'normalisation'. They warned us to be careful.

Our heroic, unforgettable, brilliant history teacher (a very elegant, beautiful woman) welcomed us to the first post-invasion class by saying, 'I don't know how long I'll be able to continue, but while I'm here there will be no textbooks. Write down everything I tell you and study only from those notes and the sources I give you. Go the library. Read historical novels, read literature, read everything you can find translated from other languages. Literature can teach you more about the world than any history lesson. I don't care what the curriculum says. This year, I will teach you everything about modern world history. You need to understand it in order to comprehend the meaning of what is happening right here. It's all connected. Don't just listen to me; think about everything. Think, argue, ask questions. I want you to feel free as long as we still can.'

She managed to maintain this illusion of freedom until I finished middle school, in the summer of 1970. Gradually, though not very slowly, most of our teaching staff were replaced. Our school was too liberal for the new regime, and some of our teachers too outspoken. Perhaps there were pupils whose parents sympathised with the old – now new – political regime. Mistrust was returning, becoming the norm again.

Our class, like others, was missing some pupils: every once in a while, another one or two emigrated. My turn came in the summer after we had all graduated. In the autumn, we would have gone our separate ways, to various high schools of our choice.

1969 was a bittersweet year for me, filled with the pain of political disillusionment and the joy of first love. I roamed the night streets of Prague with an unusual, soulful boy – we were classmates by day, barely touching lovers by night. We would go to concerts of beautiful baroque music in ancient churches, and he would walk me home, before walking back to his house at the other end of town. We were fourteen, fifteen years old, and already knew the importance of silence in love. When we found ourselves – much too soon – in front of my building we would stand there, extending the moment. Neither of us wanted to go back to our routines, to our respective homes. And yet the very next morning we would be talking in class again, as if nothing had happened. Our very special love-friendship continued for many years after my emigration, in letters. In his witty, crystalline Czech prose he kept me connected to what I had left, and what I needed to forget so that I could remember it again, without pain. When I was seventeen and living in Germany, convinced that becoming a writer was a plan and a dream I now had to abandon as I had lost my language, he surprised me with a letter saying that I should write, 'even if my first efforts turned out like misshaped sweets in a candy factory'. I still have, and treasure, all of his letters. He lost all of mine in a move from one Prague apartment to another.

During my last year in Prague I fell in love with the city as if it belonged only to me, my own private treasure. From school I could quickly reach a bridge to cross over into Malá Strana, an historic quarter full of mysterious old streets, hidden gardens, churches and parks. I often did, all by myself, sometimes even during school hours, or after school, instead of going home. I walked and walked, and inhaled Prague's beauty at every step, almost as if I had a premonition that my days of having a home there would soon come to an end. Prague's beauty is like that: it touches your heart deeply, like music, and also like a drug.

Many years later the postman delivered a book-sized envelope to my house in London. It came from my brother in Berlin, following a recent trip to Prague. 'I'm sending you a surprise,' he had told me on the phone a few days earlier, so it wasn't a surprise. Inside was a book, a Czech novel I'd read as a teenager: *At' žije republika: Já, Julina a konec velké války* (*Long Live the Republic: Me, Julina, and the End of the Big War*) by Jan Procházka. It is the story of a boy's experience of the end of the Second World War, in a small Bohemian village. Julina is his horse, whom he rescued from cruel treatment by the retreating but still arrogantly defiant German Army, at great risk to himself and his family. Published in 1966, the novel was unusual in its frankness.

The end of the Second World War was normally an ideological opportunity to declare the Czechoslovak nation's gratitude to its Soviet brothers for liberating it from Nazi occupation in 1945. The official end of the war, 9 May, was celebrated with military parades and endless speeches reconfirming the Czechoslovak–Soviet brotherhood. No mention was ever made of the fact that parts of the country had actually been liberated by the Americans, and that the liberation soon, or in fact a priori, created the basis for the annexation of Czechoslovakia to the Soviet sphere of influence. The 1939 Stalin–Hitler pact may have been short-lived as a strategically useful lie between dictators, but it had fateful implications for the post-war map of Europe. What Hitler attempted to conquer and lost, Stalin liberated and kept. When the war was over and Nazi Germany defeated, Stalin's Russia continued to reap long-term political benefits from its military successes and those of its tactical allies, but ideological enemies, Britain and the United States. From a proud if small Central European country with one of the most robust democracies in the West (and a top army it never used), Czechoslovakia morphed into a powerless Soviet satellite state, and is even now, more than two decades after the Velvet Revolution, still coming to grips with its past. A country's trauma is not an abstract blemish; it is the inner story of every man, woman and child, passed from generation to generation. Its healing is its history.

Long Live the Republic was the first novel, and certainly the only one for a non-adult readership, to depict the perceptions of one little boy – the author's alter ego – at a crucial historical crossroads. It was a brief moment when past and future overlapped: German soldiers, Russian soldiers; the boy's neighbours and friends suddenly showing the gamut of human characteristics, from heroic altruism to greed, betrayal and cruelty. It was the first contemporary novel I had ever read about the political situation that was not black and white in its analysis; in fact, it had no ideology at all. It made me understand that the truth about history is in the eye and heart of the boy fighting for his beloved horse. On the back cover the author added a personal afterword: 'I had to write the end of my war because reading about those days was only full of the sweet smell of lilac, the waving of flags, the singing of *chastushkas* [Russian folk songs]. Yes, there was that. But not only that. I believe that truth is the biggest and most basic responsibility of literature.'

His book, a slim paperback with a shiny red, blue and white cover (the Czech national colours), was still a familiar sight after all these years when it slipped out of the envelope Maxim had sent me. A small yellow Post-it note was attached to the front, with a black-penned note in Czech:

Look what I found in a second-hand bookshop, the
Bolshevik that stole our apartment probably sold it. – M.

I opened the book. On the title page was a dedication from him to me, in blue ink and a child's handwriting in curved Czech letters:

To Jelenka on her 16th birthday from her little brother Maxim.
Praha, 16th December 1970

I was speechless. Both Maxim and I love to browse in second-hand bookshops and flea markets, looking for old treasures with some sort of significance. Having lost our homes, we are jealous of the steadfastness of the homes of others. We need to latch on to their roots and connect with stories that will never be ours.

But here was the reverse: my brother had found something in a junk shop that had once actually belonged to us, at a crucial time in our family's history. It had meaning for us, but had to be meaningless to those who inherited it along with the apartment we had to abandon when we fled Czechoslovakia. Our lives froze in time; we moved across the border to Hamburg, and while the objects we left in Prague were full of our memories, to strangers they were worth either money or nothing. This book, which had meant a lot to me, was clearly just another item on someone's pile of junk.

I called Maxim right away, feeling very moved and excited. 'Wow,' I said. 'Incredible. Where did you find this? Was it that little junk shop on Vinohradská?' I figured it was likely that the book had ended up not too far from our old home.

He started laughing hysterically. Something was wrong. Then it hit me: he had made it all up. Well, not all: he did find the book in a second-hand bookshop, and bought it because he recognised and remembered its significance for me. Then he wrote the dedication, trying to imitate his handwriting as it would have looked in 1970, when he was ten years old. And then he added the faux-émigré narrative – the abandoned possessions tossed away by those soulless apparatchik thieves of our memories . . .

It was funny, it was sad. It was a bittersweet reminder that after leaving Prague, émigré narratives were all we had.

Eau Sauvage

My Prague school recommended that we write to a French children's magazine to find pen pals, in order to practise our French. It was called *Vaillant*, and was a communist youth publication with a long history but not much of a future (its last issue came out in 1969). I was quite clueless about its political orientation, though it did surprise me that all the French teenagers who replied to my published offer to 'correspond with a fourteen-year-old girl in Prague' happened to be from communist families. This led to a period of intense daily letter-writing in French. Coming home from school, I couldn't wait to open my post: at least five letters every day, windows into the lives of girls (and a few boys) from many different cities in France (and a few in Romania). The most exciting envelopes were the ones that felt a little bulky, a little uneven: a tangible promise of something inserted in addition to the letter. These were usually photographs – of my pen pals and their families – but often they would also send little gifts, and I would reciprocate. Somewhere in France, in an old box or drawer, there could be these old letters from me, with photos ... I managed to keep mine – or rather theirs – for many years. I learned new French words and expressions from my pen pals. One of them wrote that I looked *ravissante* in my photo; when I looked it up in my pocket French–Czech dictionary (which I also still have!) I felt very flattered.

But within a year most of them stopped writing, and I was left with only two loyal correspondents: Catherine from Marseilles and Maria-José, a Spanish girl living in Paris. Both loved spending summers in socialist summer camps, and were proud of their working-class roots. Catherine seemed quite poor; when we finally made plans for her to visit me she explained that, actually, her family couldn't pay for her to travel anywhere. Eventually I had only one steady correspondent: Maria-José. We took our pen pal friendship to the next level when we exchanged visits in the summer of 1969.

My parents delivered me to her house on their way to their own holiday. They used to spend their summers driving around Western Europe in a car packed full of tinned food, in the manner of all East European tourists who had to travel on a minimal foreign currency allowance. Perhaps it was during these poor man's vacations that they first played with the idea of leaving Prague for good. My memory is oddly selective when it comes to travel. I remember my arrivals very well – in Paris and earlier in Prague, or in Moscow on a visit, all the way back to my earliest memory of suddenly being in the garden with cherries in Kuntsevo. But I have no recollection whatsoever of getting to any of these places. I don't remember the long train journey from Moscow to Prague at age three and a half, nor the flight from Prague to Moscow when I was nine. And I don't have any memory of our drive from Prague to Paris. It is as if the journeys occurred without any travel: the only thing my mind retained was the change of locale.

I do remember that when we first arrived in Paris my parents met up with a Czech family of older émigrés, who spoke fluent

French and took us to my pen pal's home. We discovered that Maria-José's address, which I knew by heart after our long correspondence and pictured to be a working-class area, was actually in the very wealthy northern suburb of Enghien-les-Bains. Jéjé (her nickname) lived with her mother, grandfather and two cats in a beautifully furnished apartment. There was thick olive-green wall-to-wall carpeting throughout. This impressed me very much; our Prague rugs (some antique, some modern) on top of polished parquet floors seemed old-fashioned in comparison.

My French began to improve from the moment I met Jéjé face to face. She looked striking, with long dark hair, a distinctive, curved nose and a very athletic build. Her expensive clothes and shoes were preppy rather than sexy, and she was always enveloped in lashings of Eau Sauvage, a distinctive male fragrance. She was combative and uncompromising, a very strong character. She seemed to be in a permanent state of fiery anger with her mother, shouting and arguing about small things like the state of her shoes or the length of her skirt, as if they were a matter of life and death. I had never encountered such impassioned disrespect towards one's parent; she fascinated me. Before I was left alone with my host family for a month, my mother took me aside and said, 'If you don't get along, don't worry about it. It will be an interesting experience for you no matter what.' She turned out to be right. And as my French improved, I began to understand that the arguments between my hosts were a matter of passionate temperament rather than animosity.

Jéjé's parents, both Spanish expats who had fled Franco's regime, were separated, but closely connected with each another. It was a very unorthodox arrangement. Her mother, still of the communist-socialist persuasion, held a lucrative job as a translator at UNESCO. With her substantial salary, she supported not only her daughter and elderly father but also her ex-husband's expensive lifestyle. Jéjé's father was an anarchist, a dandy, and the owner of a famous political bookshop in Paris. He wore very elegant suits and designer shoes that cost astronomical amounts of money (as his wife often told me). He looked charming and theatrical. When I first met him, he said, 'You are Jewish? That's OK, but I don't like Israel.' I didn't really know what he meant; not at the time.

I felt threatened by Jéjé's almost permanent, very personal criticism of me, until I realised (after retreating into my elegant guest bedroom and crying into my fluffy pillow, with one or both of their cats for company) that she meant absolutely no harm. Her mother explained this to me one day, saying softly in what I now identified as Spanish-inflected French, 'It's her character to shout. She is like her father. She doesn't mean it. We spoil her, I know. She is our only child.'

In fact, it turned out that Jéjé was kind of proud of me, as her Czech pen pal. None of her friends had one. She showed me off to them and even took me to her high school. After a week of sitting in on most of her classes, I was in love with French school stationery, French school fashions and a number of her male classmates. It was a very posh suburban school, and Jéjé was quite a star. I had a small slice of short-lived, exotic fame in her shadow. When one of her friends told me '*Tu parles français vachement bien*' I was truly excited – about the compliment, but especially about the fact that I now knew enough French to decipher and completely understand a bit of their teenage slang. This was the transition I had been hoping to experience: from learning a language via its grammar and school exercises to really living it.

My best time in Paris was when Jéjé left for her own holiday, in England. She was not looking forward to it, and told me horror stories about the English, and their unpalatable food, bad hygiene and eccentric habits. She regarded her visit as a necessary evil, 'Just to learn their terrible language.' Before she went away she gave me several pairs of colourful tights to wear with my miniskirts, 'to look more Parisian'.

Once she had gone I became her de facto replacement in the house. For two weeks her mother showered me with the kind of attention and affection she was used to bestowing on her daughter. I loved it. I was constantly asked what I would like to eat, where I would like to go. I learned all sorts of new habits I would have to forget for many years to come, such as starting each family meal with a freshly boiled artichoke dipped in vinaigrette. I had never seen an artichoke before in my life, and had to be taught the slow process of tearing one's way to its prickly heart.

Jéjé's mother worked full time, and took me to work with her every day. This was my first-ever experience of a suburban commute: everything I did in Prague was within walking distance or just a few stops by bus or tram. I was used to living in the centre of my city; here I saw people travelling by train and underground to their places of work. During these long journeys I watched the transformation of plain-looking women into stunning beauties as they applied their make-up on the train in minute, meticulous steps, utterly absorbed by their own reflections in their little mirrors. I watched them pursing their lips, lowering their eyelids, opening their eyes wide like dolls, colouring their faces with fingers, brushes, little sponges and other tiny utensils. Some were even able to paint their nails. I learned a great deal about adult womanhood on those suburban trains. It seemed to boil down to an ability to transcend the ordinariness of everyday life by a conscious act of external metamorphosis. I longed to be all grown up and able to look the part of the woman I wanted to be, just like them. I admired their sophistication. The only woman I knew in Prague who

seemed equally capable of floating above her own life was my
best friend's mother, a theatre actress. I had seen her perform
in plays; I had watched her be herself, then someone else, then
herself again when we visited her backstage. I wanted to learn
to be like that too. There was a brief period in my life when
I secretly dreamt of becoming a film star. My father had been
an interpreter at the international film festival in Karlovy Vary,
and in the 1960s he boasted about a playful flirtation with Gina
Lollobrigida. In fact, she looked a bit like my young mother,
even without make-up.

The daily commute to Jéjé's mother's place of work was
meant to teach me how to get there on my own, so that I could
sleep in and join her in the afternoons. It seemed easy enough. I
managed the train without a problem, but got lost in the Métro.
I would get off at the right stop but go to the wrong exit, or I
would miss my stop and have absolutely no idea where I was.
There was no underground in Prague at the time, and the Paris
system was very confusing to me. When I realised I was lost I
would go to the nearest person in Métro uniform and inform
them that 'Madame R. is waiting for me, but I cannot find her'.
They would ring her office number, someone would relay the
message to her, she would come to the phone and, exasperated,
tell me to wait for friends of hers who lived near that Métro station. On one unforgettable occasion, as I had no money on me, a
Métro driver was told to look after me in his cabin while driving
the underground train, to make sure I got off at the right stop.
The friends – complete strangers to me – met me and I was fed
and invited to spend the night at their home. When I awakened
in the morning, I had a strange feeling of being at home; even
sitting down to their family breakfast felt incredibly familiar.
The world, I remember feeling rather than thinking, is the same
everywhere: families sleeping and eating under one roof, speaking in different languages but about more or less the same things.

Jéjé had pointed out that I wore my skirts much shorter than was the fashion in Paris. And indeed, when walking around the city on my own – at the age of fifteen, still looking rather prepubescent (I had spent many years waiting for my breasts to grow) – I attracted a lot of attention from French men. It was both unpleasant and a novelty to be noticed as a young woman when I still felt like a child. One of my miniskirts (a West German import) was made of bright blue imitation patent leather; that one earned me the frequent question: 'Américaine?' One man was even kind enough to explain that I dressed like an American girl, and seemed completely taken aback when I told him I was from Prague.

When my parents came to take me back home, Jéjé's mother was visibly relieved. She told them that if I stayed any longer she would probably have a heart attack. We made plans for Jéjé to visit me in Prague, soon.

She arrived on her own, like a grown-up, by plane. Now it was my turn to show her off to my friends (all my school friends spoke French and could communicate with her very well), and to show her my city. After a week of observing our life there she suddenly said, with disdain, 'People here don't dress well. I don't understand this: I thought you were more advanced than us, because you have socialism.'

We debated this and other points, never really agreeing. The socialist ideal she had been raised on while living a capitalist lifestyle had nothing to do with the socialism – once oppressive, then reformed, then violated and becoming oppressive again – that was my own reality. But by now we had an understanding, and something like a real friendship.

Hamburg: A Port of No Return

In the summer of 1970 my parents said they had a fun plan. My father had been offered temporary work in Hamburg, in the north of West Germany, and we would all join him there for a year to learn German. But first, I was given the opportunity to improve my French even more: a young Belgian family my parents had met on their travels and had hosted in Prague invited me to spend the summer with them. Any trip to a Western country sounded like a dream come true, so I did not question it. Once again I was dropped off in a foreign country and city (it was Gent; the family were in fact Flemish, but spoke French at home for my benefit that summer), and once again I don't remember the journey. I had a very relaxed time playing with their new baby, accompanying them on their beach holiday, sightseeing, being a part of their family for a couple of months. Then I was taken to Hamburg to join my mother, my ten-year-old brother and my father for that 'fun' year. I was almost sixteen.

Ours was a far cry from the typical Czech story of emigration. Usually, Czechoslovak citizens either stayed in the West if they happened to be there at the time, instantly severing their ties with their closest family and friends at home, or they loaded their cars with their belongings and drove across the border, usually via Austria or Germany and an unpleasant sojourn in a refugee camp. Czech and Slovak refugees were very fashionable after the 1968 Soviet invasion, and most were received with open arms by many countries and on several continents. For us, this situation did not arise. My parents created a transition that camouflaged the finality of the move.

My father's job was in a sleepy suburb called Farmsen. Through a personal connection, he had been given the position of a clerk for the big mail-order firm Otto-Versand. This meant a guaranteed, if extremely modest, income for him. It also meant a complete transformation of our lives.

Initially, my father rented a room in a nice suburban house with a garden. His landlady was a middle-aged widow with a teenage son. When we arrived we were all – all four of us – sharing this room for a short while. I don't really remember this boy but I do have a clear mental picture of his habit of eating cornflakes with a sliced banana for breakfast every morning. This seemed very Western to me; my brother and I copied him. The tiger on the cereal box was, in our eyes, the cartoon-ish embodiment of Western freedom – all fun and games. I thought I would have so much to tell my friends when I went home later that year. I thought I would begin by introducing them to cornflakes.

During this 'temporary' year in Hamburg we moved four times. First to a very small cube of a house on a noisy main road, which had been provided by my father's employer. This was a novel experience. We had only lived in apartments before. It was odd to suddenly have a tiny yard of our own, and to come home to a very plain, modern, Lego-like two-storey house made of red brick.

My parents' love of antiques was by now a distant memory.

In Hamburg we quickly filled our new home with furniture collected, literally, on the streets. Once a month, on so-called *Sperrmüll* (bulky waste) days, Hamburgers disposed of their slightly used living-room sets and various tables and chairs. My parents, nearly penniless during our first months in Germany, found almost everything we needed. It felt a bit like furnishing a doll's house.

My father's job was no less makeshift. It consisted mainly of ticking off warehouse inventory. Years later I asked him how he felt about that – having gone from translating books and films to being the equivalent of a barely literate (in a foreign language) office clerk. He laughed, and remembered how ridiculous he, the foreigner who spoke little German, must have looked, arriving every morning with a copy of *Der Spiegel* under his arm while his colleagues carried the *Bild-Zeitung*, a crass tabloid. He claimed he found it amusing. I didn't believe him. In 1970 my parents were only forty, much younger than I am today. They had been at the peak of their professional careers, they had been happy and fulfilled; now they were nowhere.

That's exactly how it felt to me. Hamburg seemed grey, cold, angular and sterile. In its cool, remote way it was a pleasantly efficient city, but one with which I had absolutely no connection. I missed Prague's mystery, its moody, neurotic beauty. I even missed its sense of resignation and collapse.

Within days of arriving, at the end of August 1970, Maxim and I began attending the local school – middle school for him, the *Gymnasium* for me. It was a large, modern, sprawling suburban school, nothing like our old urban buildings in Prague. I was introduced as the new girl from Prague who could only speak French. I did my homework in French and communicated with my new classmates in French (they studied both French and English), while trying to learn German as I went along.

During my first few months there an Israeli academic visited the school. His aim was to meet with German children and teenagers, to talk to them about their views on their country's past and their own lives.

He asked them simple questions, such as: Who was Hitler? What do you think of him? What do your parents tell you about him? It seemed crystal clear to me what the answers to those questions were, or were likely to be. So it shocked me very deeply to hear some of my classmates say things like 'Hitler was a Nazi, but he was good because he built the *Autobahn*.' Or 'Hitler wanted to save Germany.' But also 'Hitler was a swine like all Nazis.'

The Israeli academic smiled, and patiently engaged with the very young students in an open discussion. I was silent. Afterwards I went up to him and in my simple German told him that I was from Prague and that I was Jewish. He shook my hand and said 'This is not your home.' I said, 'Of course not. I am going back to Prague.'

Maximantel

I was sitting on a garden swing in our landlady's suburban garden, repeating '*Eins, zwei, drei*' out loud each time I propelled myself high above the ground, with *drei* marking the highest point of my arc. I was practising making my German sound native. The previous year, while we were still living in Prague, my brother and I had been sent to a private German tutor, obviously in preparation for this 'adventure'. I really enjoyed learning new grammar, and German was no exception. To fill a brand-new notebook with homework exercises was an interesting way to pass the time. But it was an abstract language to me; I had never actually heard it spoken by native speakers. Until I arrived in Germany that summer I'd had no idea that the 'r' in German sounds similar to the French 'r', yet different. I could pronounce the French 'r' very well after my time in Paris. Now I decided to drop any hint of a rolled Czech 'r' and any semblance of the exaggerated French 'r'. To achieve this, I had to keep repeating '*drei*' until I managed to move my 'r' from the back of my throat to the front, soften it and make it vibrate a little. Suddenly, I had it. I stopped the swing and listened to the sound of my own voice in a new language.

This was more than an exercise in phonetics; it was my moment of understanding that I was on the verge of yet another linguistic migration. It did not, at that time, seem final. Just possible. I realised that, if I had to, I could wear this new culture like a costume. I could play linguistic dress-up.

It did feel like a game. Some of my Prague classmates used to spend time abroad, returning with new clothes, stationery and records, and an improved knowledge of French or other languages. I thought this was my turn: I was simply adding German to my arsenal, and I was quite determined to rejoin them in a year's time. Some of us would be attending the same high school. While I was gone my Prague friends kept me informed about the contents of 'our' new lessons; a neighbour who was a year older even sent me her school notebooks for that year, so that I could follow all the subjects. I expected to have to pass exams on the material I had missed.

Most of my new classmates lived near by, some in elegant suburban houses with large gardens, others in modest flats. We were friends and neighbours, often visiting one another after school. I never felt excluded – quite the opposite. I listened to their conversations in German and gradually tried to join in. I had to make an instant transition from adolescent philosophical thoughts about the meaning of life (in Czech) to simply naming things, like a baby learning to speak. Every object, every action had a name that had to be learned. I was particularly fond of compound nouns, like *Plastiktüte* (plastic bag), *Staubsauger* (vacuum cleaner – literally 'dust sucker'), *Damentoilette* (women's toilet). I was even quite attracted to *Bundesrepublik*. The most magical double word of all was *Maximantel*, but not because of its sound.

The *Maximantel*, a very long, heavy winter coat reaching down to your ankles, was the trendiest fashion item that season, my first winter in Germany. There was something

nineteenth-century about them, slightly puritan yet very provocative at the same time. The point was to wear a really short
miniskirt underneath, with tights and high boots. But among
teenagers in Hamburg this fashion was more subdued. To fit in
I quickly learned to dress down rather than up. Our 'uniform'
consisted of denim or corduroy jeans and flat-heeled, high-top
suede shoes with laces.

I had the jeans and the shoes, but the *Maximantel* – the ubi-
quitous, essential *Maximantel* – was an unattainable dream. All
of my friends had them, but my parents couldn't afford to buy
one for me. Our emigration – even if I still didn't believe it was
'for real' – had tangible, unpleasant consequences. One of them
was the fact that, ironically, we were now significantly poorer
than we had been in Prague. My father's salary at Otto-Versand
was a thousand Deutschmark per month, and it was at the time
our only income.

In Prague I'd had a modest wardrobe, with only a few
choice fashionable items – my orange paisley dress, for example, sewn for me by a private dressmaker who made most of
my mother's very beautiful clothes from imported fabrics. But
in Hamburg it became more important to blend in. I spent
all of my free time with my new friends; I even had a new
boyfriend of sorts.

Deafeningly loud disco parties were held on weekends in
the *Aula*, the school's assembly hall. Long-haired boys and
girls shook their bodies ecstatically more or less opposite one
another, or sat on the floor in a long row along the wall, their
heads bobbing up and down to show their appreciation of the
electrifying guitar licks slicing through the smoke-filled air. I
was offered both cigarettes and puffs on the joints circulating
in full view of any teachers present (I refused both). A sweet-
faced blond boy called Volker told me he smoked *Haschisch* and
asked if we had any in Prague. I said defensively that we did,

of course – but the truth was I had never come anywhere near it. During slow dancing I watched bodies rubbing against one another without embracing, touching intimately yet actually not engaging at all, looking away from one another, not holding hands, barely talking. The soundtrack to this adolescent trance was mostly the rich, rocky complexity of Cream and Deep Purple. I wondered what my Prague friends were listening to. Before I left we had been fans of a Czech rock band called Blue Effect. Their decision to sing in English, including their own material, and to embrace current Western music and style trends did not save them from absolute anonymity on the international stage, no matter how good they may have been. I was beginning to understand that the country I had come from was not the centre of the world: it was very small, very distant indeed, despite being less than a day's drive from my new home.

At school on Monday, there was no trace of this night-time mix of excitement and awkwardness. Everyone was friendly, laid-back, easy-going. Someone came up with the idea of a group of us going to a Pink Floyd concert. I was invited to join them. I had to wear a *Maximantel* for that, like everyone else. It became an emergency. The cheapest one I could get cost ninety-eight Deutschmark from C&A, the cut-price fashion store.

My desire had a secret subplot. I fantasised about returning to Prague that same winter, wearing a maxi-coat. My Czech friends would be so impressed, I thought! And showing up in Prague in my *Maximantel* would also prove that our stay in Hamburg was, indeed, only temporary, a mere shopping trip.

I was rescued by my little brother Maxim. He was such a photogenic child that when my father suggested he could try earning some money as a model for his employer's catalogues he was immediately accepted (I auditioned too, but failed). When

Maxim was ten he had long wavy hair, a prematurely adult, understated, slightly sarcastic smile and a surprising ability to pose in front of the camera with professional ease. In those catalogue photographs, he looks like a dark, debonair, very foreign body among the mostly blond, awkwardly wooden German child models. He also looks older than them: a miniature adult.

Maxim was paid very nicely for looking like a wax doll in ridiculous outfits: a checked suit, a *Knautschlack* (lacquered faux leather) jacket described as *im Rennfahr-Look* ('racing-driver look'). And with his fee from Otto-Versand, my baby brother paid for my very first, utterly unforgettable *Maximantel*. It was the one from C&A, for ninety-eight Deutschmark, and a dream come true. Very dark navy blue, with a stiff straight collar and large metallic buttons all the way down. I slipped into it as naturally as if it had always been mine. Wearing it to school the next day I finally felt I had what *they* had, I wore exactly what *they* wore. I could pass for cool in Hamburg. I belonged, kind of. I remember all of us wearing our maxi-coats to the Pink Floyd concert and never taking them off. Somehow they went with the music and the frenetic lighting.

My brother – who would grow up to become a German writer – refers to this period as a very unhappy one for him as a child. But at the time it seemed to me that he had seamlessly transposed himself onto a German childhood. He played football with friends as he had done in Prague, was glued to the television (mostly *Tarzan*), and read a lot of books – mainly adventure stories about the American Wild West.

His modelling career didn't last very long. One day, when he was summoned to pose for some new photographs, he was more interested in playing football – and was never asked again. The money he earned as a model was never used for his own dreams. My parents needed it to buy a *Brotmaschine*, a bread-slicing machine we had never possessed, or needed, in

Prague. What Maxim really wanted (and for some reason never received) was a plastic race track with little cars, called a *Carrera Bahn*. I expect he still dreams of it today. But he gave me one of my dreams – my long coat and a way to fit in.

'Paper is patient'

I was so involved in dealing with my new life and language that it never really occurred to me to observe what was happening to my parents, how the move had affected them. Their relatively young age – early forties – might explain their fearlessness, and why they never stopped to think about the consequences of the choice they had made. As a prominent Russian translator, my father was afraid he would be forced to do official work for Soviet authorities. The decision to emigrate from Soviet-occupied Czechoslovakia had been a rational one, and probably a necessary one too; choosing to make our new home in Germany, of all places, was quite the opposite.

In actual fact, my father's courage was not unlimited, and his choice of Hamburg was not a random one. He followed an old family friend, the writer and journalist Gabriel Laub (known in family circles as Grisha), who had emigrated in 1968 and by the time we arrived was already a well-established author there. A linguistic genius and speaker of many languages, he not only learned German within months but almost immediately began writing in it, making a name for himself on the German media scene as a sharp literary wit and lovable *bon vivant*. Everything about him was rotund: his plump figure with a large balloon-like belly, his perfectly round face and his head of small curls.

My first encounters with Czechs living abroad took place at Grisha's home. It was a spacious, high-ceilinged apartment on a leafy street in the central quarter of Eppendorf, where he entertained a constant stream of gregarious, merrily drunk visitors. Grisha loved to cook. I was in awe of his abundantly stocked kitchen, his book-lined study and his cosy living room. The kitchen and the study were a kind of sanctuary; he reigned in both, happily chatting to any guests but remaining firmly in charge. His study was the first real writer's office I had ever seen. I admired it. Against a backdrop of hundreds of books he sat behind an enormous desk and a small black typewriter. Opposite his desk was a comfortable armchair I loved. He was easy to talk to.

There was a story he repeated almost every time I saw him, especially when there were others present: 'I used to carry a photo of you in my wallet. You were about four years old, but you looked like a beautiful young woman, with very long hair. I used to tell people, "That's my girlfriend," and they believed me!'

I was flattered but also a bit uncomfortable when he said this. There was a voraciousness about Grisha that extended to all his appetites – for food, for women, for company, for popularity. He was never out of sorts, always a calm, cheerful, amusing centre of attention. He and my father competed for that spot, taking turns telling Jewish jokes, singing dirty or maudlin folk songs in Russian, Czech, Polish, Slovak, Hungarian. Their paths had first crossed in Prague as young expat Jewish men with Russian connections but very much at home in Czechoslovakia. Grisha had been born in Poland but spent the war years in evacuation in Asiatic Russia, like both my parents. He had been a prolific journalist in Prague, writing with ease in a language he acquired as a young adult, and spoke without an accent. When they were alone, they always spoke Russian, and appeared to be connected almost like brothers. Yet their dispositions were polar opposites: Grisha was soft-spoken, calm and slow-moving, whereas my father was quick, loud-voiced and temperamental. They were linked by a long friendship steeped in secrets.

I felt a distinct difference between my parents' approach to life and Grisha's. His was, or appeared to be, devoid of all the taboos that hung so heavily in the air in our family. He followed a simple, direct path to his aims, the easiest, most convenient route. He was cuddly, but hard: I sometimes saw a layer of cold steel under his smiley, benevolent exterior. He pleased only himself, and with the innocent narcissism of a man without insecurities he never doubted his actions and decisions.

A Czech émigré woman I met in his apartment one Sunday afternoon asked me, 'So when did your family emigrate here?'

'We didn't,' I replied, 'we're only here for a year. We're going back to Prague in June.' She burst out laughing. 'Sure you are. Listen, darling, you're émigrés, just like the rest of us.' I wanted to argue, but I suddenly realised that she was right. My parents had lied to us: this was no fun year abroad – it was final. There would be no going back to Prague. I caught Grisha's smile from across the room: he clearly knew about my parents' real plans.

My parents' inability to tell the truth about such things upset me. They always had their reasons for not presenting things exactly as they were. I began to resent being excluded from their decision making.

Grisha's guest had been right – our stay was to become permanent. In 1970, if you crossed the border between Czechoslovakia and West Germany, there was no way back. You cancelled your old life and lived with the consequences.

After a few months we had moved out of the suburban cube and into quite a nice apartment in Eimsbüttel, a central quarter not far from Grisha's Eppendorf. For reasons I could not really account for or justify, I found the building and the area deeply depressing. I hated living there. Maxim and I continued to commute to our suburban school for a while. But within months everything changed again.

Three things happened, more or less simultaneously. Both my parents found jobs that tapped into their real abilities, including, in my father's case, his skills as a translator. We moved again, this time to a beautiful, very spacious apartment in a quiet, leafy street. It would be our family home for many years to come; my parents continued living there long after my brother and I moved out. (In fact, they have lived there far longer than in any of their previous homes, separately or together.) And Maxim and I switched to excellent schools that were very close to our new address. We would stay at those schools until our respective high school graduations. Emigration was forcing us all to grow new roots.

There are two toilets in my parents' Hamburg apartment – 'his' and 'hers'. My father's toilet is bare-walled, large, white-tiled, minimalistic, neat. When he needs something to read there he'll take it in with him and bring it right out when he's done. My mother's, in contrast, is a smaller space, cluttered with all manner of stuff to look at. One of the items is a large calendar permanently open at a page with a quote by Gabriel Laub: 'Paper is patient. It can take everything, even the truth.' My mother sees that sentence every day, more than once; my father must have seen it too.

Gabriel Laub was an important extra in our family tableau. His life was intertwined with that of my parents in ways that became more obvious as time went on and our émigré experience became the norm. Grisha was certainly aware of my real roots. He knew my father before my mother and I became a part of his life; he was there to welcome us when we came to live in Prague. In a photograph from my earliest days there I am standing – with only a hint of a smile – between my father and Grisha, who are both crouching down to match my height, and laughing. My father could have remained as carefree as Grisha clearly still was at that young age (they were in their late twenties), yet he chose to take on the responsibilities of a parent.

Grisha never alluded to anything from their past, but in Hamburg, his presence was an essential reminder of the life they had left behind. Year after year their joint (and jointly competitive) moments of jovial singing and anecdote-telling became more a showcase for the entertainment of their new German friends than a natural way to spend their time together. Grisha and my parents had begun the slow process of ossification that befalls all émigrés: a kind of freezing-up of their real identity into something that makes sense in their new context, but is a semi-conscious denial of who they really are – or would have been, had emigration not cut their lives in two (or in three, in my mother's case). And, watching them, I knew it was happening to me too.

I never had a conversation with Grisha about such matters. But much later, after his death, I read in an article he had given me, and I had kept among my papers for years without really looking at it, his real thoughts on being a writer in a foreign language:

One of my aphorisms is: 'The most important thing for a writer is language, provided he has something to say.' Of course an author needs to feel at home in the language in which he writes, but it does not always need to be his mother's home. As an adult, one often feels happier and more secure with the woman one loves. The list of authors who have written major works in languages other than the first one they learn would be endless, beginning with the Ancients of many nations, who wrote Greek and Latin, and later French, and including the Poles Joseph Conrad and Jerzy Kosiński in English, the Romanian Eugène Ionesco and the Czech Milan Kundera in French, and the Hungarian Arthur Koestler in German and English ... I speak and write four languages with more or less equal ease. I have had more practice in German by now. People often ask me what language I dream in. As far as I know, it is a mixture of all my languages, with a few added ingredients from those I am not so good at. I have a four-language home. So what?

Would Grisha understand why I couldn't stay in Germany and write in German? Or would he have said 'So what?' I once told him, rather arrogantly, that the reason he wrote aphorisms and elegantly construed texts, but not much live, natural prose and dialogue, was because German never did become his real language as a writer. He agreed.

I have a video made in the 1990s in which my parents and Grisha stand together and, as a joke, sing the Soviet national anthem in mock-festive voices (the men very well, my mother off-key) until my mother's Dalmatian Adon jumps on them and they burst out laughing.

Kafka in Hamburg

The move to B—strasse, my parents' address to this day, was the real beginning of our – now permanent – life in Hamburg. I loved this apartment, and still do. It was on the first floor of one of two identical white art nouveau buildings facing a row of low, very pretty older houses. Some time later these houses were demolished, and while their demolition was in progress I saw them ripped open, with some of the interior details still intact. I imagined that this was how European cities had looked when they were bombed during the Second World War. The older buildings were replaced by a concrete wall belonging to the adjacent post office. It was ugly at first, but was gradually overgrown by green vines, a kind of creeping urban jungle.

I knew this would be a permanent home for us when I saw that it was on the first floor. All our previous apartments – the ones that counted – were on the first floor, and had small balconies, large windows and high ceilings. Our new Hamburg street had been built at around the same time as our old apartment building in Prague, at the end of the nineteenth century or the very beginning of the twentieth (very new for Prague, rather old for Hamburg), at a time when one could move from one city to the other as if they were part of the same geographic and political continuum, despite being in different countries. There was a linguistic connection too: being a part of the Austro-Hungarian Empire made Prague a multilingual city, with German very prominent among the languages spoken there. Now there was an impenetrable border between Hamburg and Prague, between West Germany and Czechoslovakia. It was a complex border, built of layers of dark history on both sides. History, I was beginning to understand, was not a lofty subject analysed in heavy tomes of descriptive writing. It was simply – or not so simply – the story of what happened to people as they lived their lives according to, or against, rules created by others. My own place in my corner of history crystallised faster in Germany than it would have done in Czechoslovakia. Partly because living in Germany made me be more aware of my Jewish roots in addition to my Czech and Russian ones, but also because emigration is like a sculptor's chisel: it helps carve a shape out of a mass of raw ideas.

The move to the new apartment was smooth and almost festive. One flight up a white marble staircase, through a tall, glass-filled wooden door, and here it was: our new home. Two large rooms on the left – the living room and, behind white-lacquered sliding doors, my father's study – then a slightly smaller one just in front of the entrance door (my parents' bedroom) and, at the other end of a very long corridor, two other, big adjoining rooms: one mine, the other Maxim's. It was as if this apartment had been waiting for us, made exactly to fit our internal family structure: our parents on one side, my brother and me far away on the other.

My room was a little bit nicer than Maxim's. It had a large double window and more space and light. It also bordered only his room, whereas behind his wall you could hear the neighbours' children. On the other hand, he had a better view of the small theatre that backed onto the courtyard we faced. Every evening during the interval we could see and hear the audience pouring out onto the balcony, drinks in hand. Watching them from the privacy of our rooms felt a little like theatre too.

I immediately asked around about local high schools (there were several very good ones, all within walking distance), chose one mainly because of its interesting name – Helene-Lange-Gymnasium – and went there by myself to register. It was so simple. I arrived without any appointment, walked into the secretary's office and said I'd like to switch to this school from my suburban high school, there was a brief discussion with the headmistress and I was immediately accepted and invited to join the second half of their Year 10.

The very next day I became a pupil at the first all-girls school I had ever attended. It was a novel experience. Boys had always been my closest friends at school; I couldn't imagine a daily life without them. But this class was a very pleasant surprise. The absence of a male contingent made for an intimate atmosphere. What struck me immediately was how bright and communicative my new classmates were, and emotionally open. I found them interesting; fascinating, in fact. I became friends with many of them, and we spent a lot of our free time together.

The first year at this school was so smooth and pleasantly uneventful I didn't notice that I was now speaking German without really thinking about it. It felt natural. After two years of teaching me German literature, my favourite teacher suddenly exclaimed in class, 'You do have an accent! That's the first time I noticed it.' One of my umlauts did not sound quite German enough when she saw me perform in a school play (I played a Mother Superior!). It was said in a very friendly manner and was, in fact, a compliment.

Our school theatre was a big part of my life. My favourite

role was the minor but energetic part of Mabel Chiltern in Oscar Wilde's *An Ideal Husband* (in German: *Ein idealer Gatte*). The performance was very favourably reviewed (by one of our friends) in the magazine I created with my close friend Thomas, who also played the part of my love interest. This was a little later, when my girls' high school merged with two neighbouring boys' ones, creating a very unusual, almost university-like structure. We could choose classes and teachers in any of the three schools, and all of those classes were mixed. This brought boys back into my daily life, and a greater variety of challenging teachers.

The magazine was called *Kacktus*, an intentional misspelling of *Kaktus* to imply the word 'shit'. It was basically a more mature version of a magazine I had started in my Prague school, which I had called *Bác*, meaning 'boom'. I was dedicated to both and wrote and commissioned most of the pieces, though in Hamburg I had a passionate co-editor in Thomas, and many other friends contributed articles. They were sharp and satirical, outside any mainstream that existed beyond the school walls. We had our own life, feeding on the books we were reading and talking about, on music, and very much on one another. A small core group of friends evolved during my Hamburg school years, with whom I became very close. During breaks between classes (and sometimes instead of classes) we spent many hours drinking tea and analysing each other. We had a favourite café near the school, but an equally frequent destination was my room. I had a small coffee table and two armchairs, and really enjoyed hosting my friends there. I didn't talk to them about my past; I had buried the yearning for my lost roots deep inside myself.

Very early on, a few months after I became a student at Helene-Lange-Gymnasium, I wrote my first big essay in German. My teacher suggested that I write about Franz Kafka, because he was also from Prague. I immersed myself in his books and stories, and especially his diaries. And suddenly I realised that I was now able to read and appreciate Kafka's pristine, lucid prose in German, his native language, and not in a Czech translation. My emigration brought me closer to possibly the greatest writer in the world, who came from my city, Prague, yet wrote in German, my new language. The link between all these facts was Kafka's Jewishness – and mine. It was in Germany that I was to become fully aware of how being Jewish was an intrinsic part of my identity, something I have continued to reflect on for the rest of my life. I was looking at Kafka's life and writing as if it were a window into my own. My teacher gave me my first A in German.

However, it was becoming clear to me that I wouldn't stay in Germany, despite the overall pleasantness of my experience there. It was a good country, but it was not for me and never could be, because the longer I stayed the more aware I became of the absolute impossibility of my becoming a writer in German. 'Using their language' is how every émigré writer feels. There is something illegitimate about it. But for a Jewish writer in Germany this is compounded by the constant unwritten and unsaid requirement to justify oneself, to explain how one deals with the Jewish dimension of one's identity in a country that once tried to destroy it. For me, this situation flattens and removes several layers from my writing by forcing it to conform to such expectations. I did not want to write in such a context, where I felt reduced.

Many years later I edited an anthology of writings by young German Jewish writers, called *Jewish Voices, German Words*. I suggested the idea to an American publisher because I saw a literature emerging in a Germany of which I was not a part, but which I understood and was fascinated by. In the introduction, I wrote:

From the moment I realized that the sense of history of the Germans – including those of my generation – did not exactly match my own, I no longer saw Germany as a country like any other ... Once, I dozed off on an express train from Hamburg to Munich; when I opened my eyes, we were passing Dachau. The station's signs – Dachau-Dachau-Dachau – triggered an emotional turmoil I can describe only as a flash of collective memory. To the German friends traveling with me, Dachau was just another town.

The same extremely knowledgeable and inspirational German teacher, Dr Ilse Köser, who had suggested my Kafka essay was also the reason I immersed myself in German language and literature. I studied, both critically and reverentially, German classics, German contemporary authors, German translations of world literature. Dr Köser was very surprised, and sorry, when I later informed her that I felt myself to be emotionally incompatible with the German language. I told her I would move away, in search of another adopted home and language.

She said she understood. She was the only person of her generation I have ever met who was honest about what she witnessed during the war: 'Of course we saw what was going on. We saw Jews being rounded up and we knew where they were going. Anyone who tells you they were not aware is lying.'

After we had been living there for a while we discovered that our new Hamburg address was actually in the former Jewish quarter. There was a former (soon to be restored) Jewish school around the corner. And when a memorial art installation began to spread through the streets, consisting of copper tiles set into the pavements, engraved with the names of Jews who had lived at that address and had been murdered by the Nazis, our street needed more than one tile per building to list all the names.

Maxim: Our Shipwrecked Club

Maxim was ten years old when we moved to Germany; I was almost sixteen. This new life in Hamburg was the first emigration we shared. It sliced through my adolescence and his childhood; now we were both severed from our roots. Each of us knew how the other felt about this permanent wound, though we never talked about it. We just lived it, together, under our parents' roof. We continued to speak Czech to each other, and Russian only to our parents. Eventually the loss became our new roots, connecting but also separating us as we went our different ways in life.

Because of his young age the transition from Czech to German seemed smooth for Maxim. And because of the ease with which he quickly absorbed the new language I never noticed how unhappy he was. Yet while I was received with friendship and a certain amount of curiosity about my foreign background, but never any kind of hostility, by my new classmates, Maxim's experience was radically different. Many years later he would repeatedly describe his early Hamburg years as 'a horror'. When we first arrived he had expected the children in his new school to be like those he knew in Prague. Instead they teased him, made fun of him as a dark-haired foreigner, attacked him, punctured his bicycle tyres. His response was what he called 'an intelligent defence': he soon realised that a couple of sharp, smart sentences was enough to stop the bullies in their tracks. The self-assured outspokenness that has become his trademark as writer and journalist has its roots in his Hamburg schooldays: his verbal power was a weapon against his German classmates' physical and psychological one. He probably would have confronted any other bullies in exactly the same way. But there is no denying his sense of isolation in an environment where he was the only Jewish child. That he was also a Czech child who spoke Russian at home rendered his ethnic make-up almost incomprehensible to others. Just like me, Maxim truly discovered his Jewishness in Germany, and found that it defined him. Under the layers of the languages we spoke and the cultures we borrowed was a much deeper link to where we had originally come from, via our unknown or forgotten or remembered ancestors. Our Jewishness became increasingly vital for holding the rest of our identity together.

The anti-Semitism I experienced in 1970s Germany was a trickle rather than an assault. During my last two years of high school I had a Saturday job working in a ladies' 'boutique' in Hamburg's main shopping area, the Mönckebergstrasse. It wasn't really a boutique at all but a very standard clothes shop, with ordinary, not especially fashionable styles for mostly middle-aged women. I was paid fifty Deutschmark for a day's work. To earn a small commission we were told to flatter the customers when they tried things on, to encourage them to buy them even when their midriffs bulged under too-tight dresses and skirts. The full-time sales staff were very good at this, and I copied them. But one day, when I had been a little too successful and earnt a nice bonus at the end of a long Saturday, one of the saleswomen commented, 'Herr Kohn won't be pleased to have to pay you this much extra. *Sie kennen ja Ihre Rasse.* [Well, you know your race.]' I was completely taken aback. My race? Not only had I never thought of my Jewishness as belonging to a race – rather than a religion, a people with a shared history – but it had never occurred to me that these women I worked with every weekend classified me in that way. We had never talked about my religion or background. But now it was plain: they had seen me as being of the same race as their hated boss and owner of the shop, the diminutive, fussy and always friendly Herr Kohn. I felt a sudden whiff of the Weimar Republic, of that Germany where Herr Kohn and I would indeed have been very much of the same *Rasse*. And not for the first time in Germany, I wondered what role these ladies and their parents would have played, perhaps did play, a few decades earlier. One of our neighbours, a very friendly man in his forties (whose gregarious wife knocked on our door almost every evening with a bottle of wine), told me during a New Year's Eve party that 'the Jews' fate is their own fault'. He said this while drunkenly trying to dance with me.

Our school was a very liberal environment, with freedom extended even to the way many of our classes were taught. We could sit, stand or walk around, the teacher in a sort of free-flowing conversation with us based on mutual respect. We were treated as adults. Smoking was allowed, though only in one especially designated room, *das Raucherzimmer.* I didn't smoke myself, but liked spending time there with my friends. We could barely see one another's faces in the thick grey air: the smoke from so many cigarettes hung like a heavy, malodorous curtain.

Even in this atmosphere of almost absolute personal freedom, my brother managed to be the misbehaving rebel. Teachers complained that he insisted on sitting on top of his desk rather than behind it; that he was rude and argumentative, and too opinionated; that he didn't want to do anything he was asked. All good things, I thought.

The transformation from his quiet, introverted years into this new, in-your-face teenage Maxim seemed sudden. He used to spend his time reading *Asterix* comics, watched a lot of TV and was very interested in ancient history. His room had a piano in it. We both took lessons, picking up from where we had left off in Prague. I played under duress, whereas he seemed to genuinely enjoy learning music – despite our morbid teacher Frau V, who taught in her somewhat rancid apartment which was around the corner from ours. We disliked those lessons so much that sometimes we rang her doorbell when we passed by, just to annoy her. Hearing her prim voice through the intercom – '*Ja, bitte?*' – made us dissolve in giggles before we ran away. We took turns at her piano during the lessons. Maxim progressed, I stagnated. I enjoyed the lessons in Prague, but not in Hamburg, even though the language of music, at least, was not a new one: notes have the same names (though pronounced differently) in Czech and in German – c, d, e, f, g . . .

Piano-playing turned out to be my Proustian madeleine. Compositions I played as a child in Prague, and can still play at more or less the same basic level, instantly conjure up a sense of a much younger me, and of my piano teacher Paní K. It had been my father's conviction that a child's education is incomplete without piano lessons, possibly because he himself had never had any. I enjoyed the regularity of my lessons, and the serene one-to-one with the teacher. Yet I played badly, and hated practising. The daily hour at the piano at home, going through my assigned pieces and études, was the worst part of my day. I tried to avoid it, and whenever possible secretly did so. Sometimes I would prop up a book instead of my sheet music and read while pretending to be practising the same étude. One time, when my father came to pick me up from my lesson, my teacher mentioned I hadn't been practising. He exploded with anger. Paní K was shocked and so was I. This too comes floating up as a sharp memory whenever I play the piano.

Each December when Paní K went away on holiday her husband, a professional musician, took over her classes. There was a very different feel about them. He listened to my playing with a serious expression, not paying attention to my mistakes but to the tone of the music. When I finished he jumped up from his seat and exclaimed: 'So the young lady has talent! Why don't you use it?' I promised and resolved that I would. But never did.

My brother, however, played not only what we were taught but often his own compositions as well. He would sit at the piano and improvise. It sounded good. He could sing and write songs too, and maybe that was the reason why I was so certain he would become a pop star, with music as his métier. It actually surprised me when he became a writer.

Maxim's growing teenage rebellion coincided with my leaving the school – and, a year later, Germany. When I finished high school I had a very good grade average thanks to having been able to graduate only in the subjects of my choice: three languages (or rather, literatures) – German, English and Latin – and biology, as the one compulsory science. But I had absolutely no idea what to do next, no preference for one field over another. So I thought, I love languages and am good at them: why not study the science that explains how language works?

So began the most uninteresting year of my life, as a student of linguistics at Hamburg University. What made it especially boring was the fact that the university was even closer to my home than my high school had been – literally a one-minute walk, just around the corner. There were very few lectures and seminars, and all were easier than anything I had done in high school. I made a few friends, but there was no real student or campus atmosphere. I felt that my life had come to a standstill. Hamburg had become suffocating for me.

The only amusing (and lucrative) highlight of that period was my newly discovered ability to teach Russian. My father had been asked to tutor a group of postgraduate students of Slavonic studies, but had no time or inclination so he passed them on to me. They were four very tall young men in their late twenties who arrived twice a week, sat in the low armchairs around the coffee table in my room and became little boys, listening to my every word. I made them strong Czech coffee and proceeded to teach them Russian conversation. I would choose a topic and make them talk. I also gave them homework, which they did religiously. We laughed a lot but I was also strict, and the method I used worked: they really did learn Russian, and told me so. It was the first time I had become aware that a language that was native to me could be formalised into clear rules for others to follow. I had one other pupil, a middle-aged gynaecologist, who wanted solo lessons several times a week as he was preparing for a trip to Russia. It was these lessons rather than the theoretical lectures in linguistics that confirmed I was probably on the right academic track: I did enjoy learning how language worked.

Around this time, my little brother began morphing into a hirsute young man, with a head of curly hair and a beard. He wore oversized fur coats, had many girlfriends, stayed out very late and on one occasion had a wild party that attracted a destructive bunch of drunken gatecrashers. (My mother captured this incident in one of her short stories, as a fleeting but very sad moment of estrangement between a mother and her teenage son.)

After only two years of living in Hamburg, our family's internal linguistic lines had been redrawn. Maxim and I spoke fluent German, a language our parents were still struggling with, despite working full time and using it to the best of their abilities to support us. Maxim's new language was to become his instrument of lovehate with Germany; it made him a quintessentially Jewish writer, on a large Russian canvas, with Czech wit, in beautiful, almost old-school German prose. Despite his strong sense of isolation and not-belonging, he stayed in Germany.

Our ways began to diverge; I was actively looking for a way to leave Germany. After a couple of short trips to Israel I was beginning to see it as a potential new home – just for me. Maxim happened to be in England, on a summer language programme, when I upped and moved to Tel Aviv in 1975. He told me many years later that he had never known about my plans to leave, or at least not that they were final. He said he returned from England and found me gone. Suddenly he was all alone with our parents. He had a difficult time dealing with our father's temper. There was a hardness in their mutual chemistry that could no longer be alleviated by my presence. And then, during this time, Maxim fell seriously ill and spent several months in hospital.

We began a new, long-distance phase of our close relationship. Letters, postcards, phone calls, visits. By phone, our contact would become almost daily. We now had another loss in common: each other.

After high school, Maxim decided to move to Munich, where he lived for many years; then, much later, to Berlin. By staying in Germany, and with the German language, my brother beat me to a more direct route to becoming a writer. Along with his serious literary presence he also became a sharp polemicist, starting with a provocative column in the very trendy *Tempo* magazine in the 1980s. This was the only time when he actually felt good in Germany; at twenty-something, he was writing for fashionable magazines and looking the part of a cool young writer. He was a literary celebrity.

His column was entitled *'100 Zeilen Hass'* – '100 Lines of Hatred'. By hatred, he actually meant anger, and by anger he meant the righteous kind: in each short column he zeroed in on someone or something in German society who he felt needed exposing as doing something wrong or immoral. The column was widely read and quoted, yet self-destructive: even before he had published his first collection of stories he had accumulated so many enemies among Germany's cultural and political elite that his literary writing would, for a long time, be regarded as springing from the same uncompromising source. As his own voice developed and matured, he realised that his controversial opinions and cutting tone had led to his increasing isolation, and some bitterness, as a writer. This perception wasn't wrong: Maxim's fiction is as fearlessly truthful as his most provocative journalism. Yet his stories and novels also give him the tenderness of a storyteller who sees and tries to understand everything human and wants his readers to do the same.

He was given a typewriter at the age of thirteen, an Olivetti Praxis 48. He wrote his first story on it, about a man sitting on a bench in a park. At eighteen, he spent a couple of sleepless nights writing a story per night; they were so terrible, he thought, that he never did it again and resolved – unlike Kafka – to never write at night. As a mature writer he rarely digressed from his routine of writing in the morning and editing after lunch, then going for a walk and watching TV to relax. I don't know why I have always felt the need to call him exactly when I know he's writing, and why he always picks up. He says, 'Quick. You know I'm working.' Then we proceed to talk, regardless, and these conversations, no matter how light-hearted and silly, truly sustain me.

I once wrote a profile of my brother for the German weekly *Die Zeit*. I felt a need to explain his mix of soft centre and hard edge to German readers. I thought I was the only one who could really do this. The editors gave my piece the title *'Mein Bruder, der Biller'*. 'My Brother, the Biller'. He had become *the Biller*, known by his last name alone. When I asked him questions for the profile, he said: 'I'm a Jew for them but one that doesn't play the role they expect from me. If I could have chosen another country to emigrate to, I would have chosen one where others don't always force me to answer questions about Jewishness. Walser writes about Germans, Barnes about the English, Oz about Israelis – Biller about Jews. I shouldn't be asked why I do that, it's self-evident. German critics can't forgive me for creating my own world using their language.'

This is why I did not stay in Germany, but my brother was right to stay; as his publisher Helge Malchow once told me, Germany needs him. He described my brother as 'an irreplaceable, unique author in Germany. He writes in German but he is not German. Our literature needs his outsider's point of view and his kamikaze-like precision and sharpness.'

I once saved a text message from Maxim, written in Czech: 'I'm on a train from Turin to Milan. It's gorgeous here. Berlin teaches me to love the rest of the world.' It captures so much that is characteristic of him: his inability to write a plain, uninteresting sentence; his so often frustrated longing for a (new) place to love; and his affection for Czech, the native language we share.

During our last winter in Prague it snowed heavily. Together with a friend, Maxim and I had founded the Shipwrecked Club. We called ourselves Jim, John and Jane; we drew maps leading to hidden treasures and felt blissfully lost on an imaginary forgotten island. Meanwhile, unbeknownst to us, our parents were plotting a life where we would be both saved and shipwrecked, never to return.

Israel: Prelude to a Home

I first discovered Hebrew in Prague, when I was about thirteen. It happened through music. I found an odd record in my parents' collection and played it on our Grundig record player. It didn't sound like anything I had ever heard before, and it was love at first sound. A male voice and a female voice took turns and combined to sing a very beautiful, strange melody. I tried to sing along by following the lyrics printed on the back of the cover. The Hebrew letters were as mysterious and striking as the music. I could not read them, of course, but I was able to guess some, matching the song's printed lyrics to the sounds. I kept replaying the small '45 record, over and over, until the sounds came to me naturally and somehow connected with the exotic words on the page. I had absolutely no idea what I was singing; there was no translation, and my parents had no clue either. The language sounded completely foreign yet also oddly familiar. There was something about it that made me long for it to be mine.

My initial encounter with real Hebrew occurred much later, when I visited Israel as a tourist in 1974, a year before I moved there. The hot, humid air and steaming tarmac at Tel Aviv's Ben Gurion airport were my wake-up call. This was Israel, a real country in the very real Middle East, with its own climate and character, far removed from Europe: the tall palm trees; the dusty roads and sandy houses that seemed neither old nor new but some-how unfinished, in perfect harmony with their raw surroundings; and the people (most of them very young) confidently showing off suntanned flesh, looking upbeat, very beautiful and sexy.

Before that first visit Israel was not a country I could really imagine, neither physically nor emotionally. It was, to me, more a distant concept than a real place. My point of reference was my (one-dimensional, as I would soon learn) knowledge of Jewish culture, which was mostly rooted in European history. I was discovering that to be Jewish was to have a personal link to a collective memory of a people who had remained an exiled community against all odds, surviving organised persecution and genocide. I knew Diaspora Jewishness, knew it well, and was very familiar with how it defined itself as a vast sea of sadness and mourning. My father, anti-religious and a staunch believer in materialism (my question to him, at age twelve: 'What happens after we die?' His decisive answer: 'Nothing.') would always tear up when he heard Jewish prayers.

My parents had travelled to Israel several times before my trip, visiting friends and family they had reconnected with since our emigration to Germany. These were people they had known in Prague, and who had left for Israel in 1948. The immediate post-war period, during which it was possible to imagine Czechoslovakia going the way of other Western democracies, like Italy or France, was irreversibly over; the Iron Curtain was about to be drawn. A few Jewish relatives on my father's side had survived the Holocaust and had been starting new lives in Prague, but after the regime change to a communist dictatorship they chose to immigrate to Palestine, or the just-established state of Israel. Several Jewish friends and acquaintances went there in 1968, after the Soviet invasion of

Czechoslovakia. But this was an immigration rather than emigration; a kind of homecoming.

Oddly, the possibility that Israel – a remote ideal they identified with – could actually become a home for our family had never occurred to my parents, not even when they were contemplating leaving Czechoslovakia. It wasn't until they began visiting from Germany that my father realised he loved this tiny country like a lost home. His sudden passion for Israel surprised me; it seemed to be an emotional replacement for the home he had given up when we left Prague for good. And yet he wouldn't uproot himself and his family and actually go and live there.

In the 1970s Soviet Jews began to arrive in Israel, in ever-increasing numbers. In due course they would include close relatives of both my parents. And still my family stayed in Hamburg, ever the visitors, never the *olim*. Perhaps my father hated the idea of being mistaken for a Soviet Jew.

There is a town south of Tel Aviv called Rishon Le Zion, meaning 'the first of Zion'. My brother joked that our father was Acharon Le Zion – the last of Zion. He would criticise Russian relatives who chose to emigrate to Canada or Germany instead of Israel, yet he never made the move himself. I think I was sent to Israel as a kind of emissary; my father was directing me towards a place where he hoped I would want to live as an alternative to Germany. My mother, I knew, had no such wish.

I was met at the airport by my father's Czech-speaking relatives, and their Hebrew- and English-speaking daughter. The relatives were about ten years older than my parents; the daughter about my age. Although the actual family link was remote (my 'aunt' Klari was related to us by her sister's marriage to my father's great-uncle), the connection was real and already very deep. I found myself in the Middle East and yet also in close contact with people who had come from a Central Europe that long predated my own memory of it.

I was instantly drawn to the older generation: the survivors who had lived the history I had only read about in books. They had come from my corner of the world, but were now part of something completely new and young. Klari had survived Auschwitz with her sister; her husband Zoli had spent the war fighting as a partisan in Slovakia. They were heroes in the most real sense of the word, but these experiences were not something they chose to talk about, unless asked. Klari and Zoli were gentle, warm, easily accessible people who made everyone feel at ease. As soon as I entered their ground-floor apartment, where the front door was never locked, I felt completely at home. Klari worked in a knitting shop in central Tel Aviv owned by another Czech friend; Zoli was a bus driver. In post-war Prague they had run a small shop and told me, with much laughter, how my father, then a teenager with militant communist convictions, accused them of being capitalists.

Their home in Holon, a suburb south of Tel Aviv, would become my base whenever I visited Israel. I tried, but completely failed, to connect with their daughter's local circle of friends. This was my first exposure to the social power of the Israeli *shechuna* (neighbourhood): people who grew up together and never lost touch, living at home with their parents after a tough three-year military service. The young men looked manly, there was much partying and having fun, but the trajectory of their lives seemed very simple, by my European standards: after the army they all were determined to marry as soon as possible and settle down not too far from their parents – often in the very same neighbourhood. I became the object of one young man's marriage plans: without much of a preamble, after going out for ice cream a couple of times he appeared to be asking me to marry him. We communicated in less than perfect English, but his intentions became very clear.

I did not particularly mind his attentions on a subsequent visit to Israel, when I decided to spend a few months on a kibbutz. Yuval was a paratrooper and looked handsome in his uniform, sporting a red beret. He travelled to see me occasionally, on Fridays, presumably pursuing the idea that marriage could still be an option. Being 'attached' to a *tsanchan* (paratrooper) was a sign of prestige; it provided me with a cloak of protection against unwanted attention from the kibbutz population of temperamentally laid back but sexually febrile young men who were spoiled by the constantly moving and changing feast of volunteer workers from all over the world – Jewish or otherwise. To be a city boy's girlfriend meant they couldn't show too much active interest in me. This was both useful and annoying; I was not in the least interested in being considered out of bounds. On the contrary: the kibbutz environment was pleasantly conducive to a sliding scale of loving relations, from casual to deep friendship, from tentative flirtation to, not infrequently, real love. Fortunately, after a few futile visits Yuval got the message and stopped wasting his precious leave on coming to see me.

I came to this particular kibbutz, which lay prettily in the green-hilled heart of the Jezreel Valley near Mount Gilboa, because friends of my relatives knew a family of Russian old-timers, the Gorens, who had kindly agreed to be my kibbutz family. This did not mean that I stayed in their house – not even their own children did, from a young age. But I could drop by any time.

The kibbutz arrangements had a natural simplicity: identical small houses; all the meals served in a central dining hall; one shop for all, where things were handed out for free in restricted quantities. All this was based on the original socialist ideals of the kibbutz movement, put into practice in its self-contained collective communities. My personal experience of state socialism had taught me that it brings out the worst in people: greed, envy, cowardice, aggression. The kibbutznik, however, was supposed to be someone who felt comfortable with living under all sorts of restrictions. So I found it very funny when the shop gave me a simple T-shirt and sun hat and a lady witnessing the exchange complained bitterly that it wasn't fair: 'I've been waiting for this T-shirt for months and these volunteers arrive and are handed freebies on day one?' In her eyes, I was a privileged visitor to her world; moderately useful to the kibbutz, but nevertheless an interloper.

As volunteers we did not really mix with the kibbutz population, except at the weekly disco that took place in a bunker on Friday nights. Work was assigned on a rotation basis; we were expected to experience everything from kitchen duty (highlight: peeling hundreds of potatoes) to field and farm jobs, as well as helping out in children's houses (they lived separately from their parents). Eventually I was assigned to the chickens. Or, to be precise, their eggs: my task was to stand by a conveyor belt and place the eggs collected from the battery hens in the appropriate containers, at the right speed and without breaking too many. I did not, at the time, give any thought to the cruelty of this procedure. We were a fun group at this conveyor belt, and there was a great deal of joking and laughter in a mix of languages: English, Hebrew, German, Dutch, Spanish ... It was a much sought-after job, because even though we started at five in the morning we were finished by eight. After a delicious breakfast consisting of a huge and colourful variety of cheeses, salads, fruit and, yes, egg dishes, I was free to lounge by the pool, sleep, read, socialise and generally enjoy a blissfully carefree existence for the rest of the day.

In the early morning the pool was generally empty and the water still cool. I decided to use this time to teach myself how to swim. I was a borderline non-swimmer at the time, but having this pool all to myself, morning after fresh, blue-skied morning, I just kept swimming back and forth, cautiously, until my fear was gone. After two weeks of this regime my skin turned a new, much darker colour and I was told I looked like a *sabra* – a native-born Israeli. Sometimes it felt as if life in Israel was mainly about having a nice tan: Zionism as sun worship.

There were quite a few volunteers among us who had been on the kibbutz for a very long time, and showed no sign of ever leaving. One or two simply had no money for a ticket back home or on to their next destination; staying indefinitely was their way of coping with a financial or personal crisis. A Dutch volunteer had spent two years on this kibbutz. One could forget about the existence of the outside, real world as all needs were taken care of. My stays were relatively short – about a month at a time, on several occasions. After that, I began to feel stifled by the greenhouse atmosphere of the kibbutz. It was safe, pleasant, fun, yet ultimately an artificial oasis of a life far removed from anything that was relevant to me.

But it was during these short trips to Israel – and it did not take too many – with some time spent on the kibbutz, some in cities, visiting family and friends, that I began to feel, for the first time since leaving Prague, that I could feel at home in a new country. I loved the old-timers whose Hebrew had so many different tinges of European, Middle Eastern and other accents. I loved the fact that Israel was not a country inhabited by any kind of Jewish-looking stereotype, but by people whose looks could not be categorised at all: everyone looked different, carrying their families' international gene pools in their own physical make-up. They were fantastic to look at. In this genuine melting pot, where everyone either came from somewhere else or had parents and grandparents who did, I could suddenly see myself blending in, having a home. Here, it turned out, I had a historical right to return to the birthplace of my ancestors. The Israeli passport, and various new immigrants' benefits that came with it, could easily be mine. The Zionist ideal, the dream of Theodor

Herzl in turn-of-the-century anti-Semitic Central Europe had by now been translated into a reality that had a direct impact on my life. I had the right to call Israel my country.

What did this actually mean? The political and historical complexity of Israel as a Jewish homeland was not lost on me, even in those early days of my acquaintance with the country. Once, as I was being shown around the campus of Tel Aviv University, my guide (an Israeli student) suddenly stopped and said, 'You do know a part of this campus is built on top of an Arab cemetery? We could be walking on some graves.'

Travelling to and from various cities, usually by bus, I became aware of a change in the landscape whenever we passed an Arab village. Their buildings seemed to emerge into view with an air of older permanence, dominated by pale green shutters. Even from a distance there were visible signs of the unfinished, or rather ongoing, construction of houses that looked as if they had found their place in a haphazard way, rather than as a result of a plan. The inhabitants of these villages were citizens of the same country I too could become a part of. If I did, I would be a brand-new addition to it, an *ola hadasha* – a new immigrant. Israeli Arabs, on the other hand, had been there long before me. Yet so too had many Jews: in spite of the dispersion after the destruction of the Second Temple by the Romans, there had always been a Jewish presence in Palestine. This surprised me. My knowledge of Jewish history was proving to be embarrassingly meagre. I was beginning to discover Israel's history by immersing myself in its present.

Chance encounters with strangers would have a profound effect on me. A woman whom I had asked for directions in Jerusalem suddenly said, after understanding that I was a tourist possibly thinking of staying, 'Well, this is how we live here, between wars.' The most recent had been the Yom Kippur War of 1973. I suddenly saw a seemingly peaceful, exuberant country superimposed on a bleeding layer of perennial conflict. I had never experienced war except as a history of my parents' generation. Here it seemed both remote and tangible.

One very hot day I was walking down a quiet street in northern Tel Aviv, looking, to all intents and purposes, like a native – very suntanned, wearing shorts and sandals. I was stopped by an old lady in an elegant white summer dress and white hat, carrying a white handbag. She took out a blue airmail envelope and immediately addressed me in German, without asking whether I spoke the language: '*Bitte, können Sie mir diesen Brief übersetzen?*' I recognised her Berlin accent, as strong as if she had left days, not decades, ago.

She wanted me to translate the letter in her hand, from English into German. I did so, as if such a request were not in the least peculiar or unexpected; as if a burning-hot summer afternoon in an Israeli city were the most natural place in the world for an old German émigré to address a young girl in German, and also to assume that she knew English. When I finished (it was a mundane letter, about someone's previous and planned visit – dates, arrangements, pleasantries), the old lady said '*Danke schön,*' and walked on.

For some reason this meeting didn't feel random to me. The elderly lady was like a living apparition from Germany's past, which she had miraculously survived. The Germany where I now lived did its best to erase and camouflage that past. I began to feel that I could actually belong in this country of contrasts, where one could arrive from anywhere and speak any language, or several, yet feel at home, and be connected by Hebrew.

When I returned home I told my parents I wanted to study in London or New York – or in Israel. My father vetoed the first two options by saying he could not (or rather would not) support me there. But in Israel he would, as it was more affordable, and it was a plan he liked.

Double Immersions

I wasn't thinking about the void my permanent absence would cause at home. But my mother was, and began to fill it with frantic preparations for my leaving. We spent that summer on a dedicated shopping spree, as if I were being sent to the other end of the world without access to basic necessities. I had never before been allowed to indulge in buying so many things, just for me, and on such a large scale. As a new immigrant to Israel I was given a certain allowance, a very small shipping container, to carry the beginnings of my life from the old country to my new one. I didn't really own or want anything at all, and so my parents decided to use that allowance to provide me with things I might need later, and over a long period of time: clothes, sheets, towels, dishes, some appliances ... It was a bit like a dowry – not for a bride, but for a young woman's newly independent life. I loved the novelty of being an actual owner of such items, and I adored the clothes. It was 1975: there were some colourful tiered maxiskirts, cropped tops, flared jeans and white trousers, platform shoes and sandals, short dresses. My mother bought one of the skirts, a turquoise one, for herself; in it she looked like my slightly older sister. She was so young then, only forty-five to my twenty. She looked about thirty.

She also organised a ten-day holiday just for the two of us – our last opportunity to be together, before my move. I did not really understand – not then – why it was so important, and why my departure marked the end of an era for her. It wouldn't occur to her to stop me going, or even to hint that I shouldn't; nor would she let me see her pain. My mother always translated sadness into positive action. Things need to be done, regardless of how one feels about them, and by focusing on the details and practicalities of mundane tasks one can manage to mask one's feelings, even to oneself. What she actually felt at that time was an echo of her own past separations: leaving her parents in Moscow and moving to Prague, in her mid-twenties; then, at forty, leaving Prague and emigrating to Hamburg. Each time the political barriers between the countries she moved to caused her to sever her links to her parents for a very long time, and ultimately for ever. This was not my situation. I might have been moving to the Middle East, but I was not crossing any political boundaries. Accessibility would not be an issue. Still, I *was* going away.

We didn't travel very far for our holiday; for some reason, my mother chose a town called Plön, about an hour's drive from Hamburg. We stayed in a small hotel, went for quiet walks, ate solid meals and had frequent tea and cakes among near-silent, stone-faced north-German tourists. It was the most German environment I had ever experienced, in odd contrast to my parents' lifestyle in Hamburg, which had always retained their own noisy, colourful Russian/Czech/Jewish style, very much enjoyed by their German guests. On the last day my father came to pick us up (he had also dropped us off) with Maxim, who had just returned from England. My mother filled the car with beautiful local flowers and plants she had been buying almost daily, in yet another attempt to distract herself from feeling sad. It was on the car ride home that Maxim finally understood I was only going home in order to leave Hamburg, this time for good.

I was excited. I couldn't wait to start my new life at the beautiful, sunny and green-lawned campus of Tel Aviv University, with its own luxury pool and cafeterias serving Middle Eastern delicacies. I had been accepted into the second year of a BA in (theoretical, as opposed to applied) linguistics, starting in September. But first I would spend my summer learning Hebrew at an *ulpan*, an intensive course for new immigrants. Mine was at the same university where I would be studying.

We were an international group, but most of my fellow students were from North America. After learning their personal stories I arrived at my own interpretation of Zionism. My new understanding was that ideology played almost no role in many of these young people's decisions to come and live in Israel. Most typically, they were trying to get away from their families, to resolve or escape issues with their parents (especially their mothers), to put a safe distance between the places where they grew up and their new home, and to have fun for a few years while discovering their Jewish identity. Not many of them ended up staying, though they all talked about it with real seriousness of purpose.

The Hebrew lessons we had were based on the immersion principle: only Hebrew was used in class, even – or especially – to explain what we didn't know, whether grammar or vocabulary. This very effective method helped erase all linguistic differences among us and created a *tabula rasa* we all shared, and could quite easily build on. Outside our classes we all communicated in English. For me, it was the beginning of a double immersion: Hebrew and English. Hebrew was the language of my new country, but it would take several long years before I would really absorb it and feel its texture from within. In the meantime, I was drawn into English in a new way.

This was not my first encounter with English. Only a couple of years earlier, when I had just arrived in Germany from Prague, I had been faced with a new-language double whammy: I had to become fluent in German, of course, but I also had to learn English almost as quickly in order to keep up with my classmates who, at sixteen, already had several years of English classes behind them. Remembering my earlier linguistic immersions – in Czech and, later, French – I knew that this was the most efficient method of acquiring a new language.

So during my first summer holiday in Germany, a year after our arrival there, I contacted a Welsh family recommended by the parents of a school friend. My letter to them went something like this:

Dear Mr and Mrs Matthews,

   I am from Prague, but I now live in Hamburg. I am sixteen years old. I need to learn English. I would be very happy if I could help you as an au pair this summer. I look forward to hearing from you. Thank you very much.

                                    Yours sincerely,

                                               . . .

I received a very kind reply by return post. The Matthews family would love to have me. They explained that they lived on a farm in South Wales, had two daughters aged ten and six, and that they would meet me at the train station in Bridgend, their nearest town. A travel agent in Hamburg quickly worked out my cheapest route: an overnight ship from Hamburg to Harwich, a train from Harwich to London's Liverpool Street station, then another train from Paddington to Bridgend. The ship was full of students, staying up all night, drinking and having fun. I don't really know how I managed to find all my trains and platforms, but I did. On the train to Wales I got into a conversation with a mother and daughter sitting opposite me, who were travelling to Cardiff. They were horrified that I was all by myself, going to stay with people I had never even spoken to. The mother said, 'Here is our number. If you have any problems, please call us, we'll come and help you.' Here were complete strangers trying to protect me from other strangers. I loved Wales already!

The Matthews family – all of them, including the grandparents – were waiting for me in Bridgend. As I stepped off the train they immediately surrounded me with hugs and smiles and a lot of melodic chatter I did not yet understand. They called me Ellen and treated me like a precious guest in their home. Although I tried to be as helpful as possible I was not in any sense an au pair. The Matthewses were kind and very lively people. The girls – dark-haired Mary and very blonde Jane – were my main source of English conversation; to be exact, they talked non-stop and I listened. They talked to each other, to me, to all the adults, to the family dogs and other animals, in sing-song voices I immediately fell in love with and started to imitate.

It rained every single day of my stay on the farm, and life followed a calm rhythm. We had freshly made chips and milky tea every evening while watching *Coronation Street* (the only time no one was allowed to speak). For three weeks I merged with this family as if I had known them all my life. And without paying any conscious attention to learning it, English was suddenly a language I understood and spoke and read as if I had been studying it for years. My teacher in Hamburg was very impressed with my progress, and very amused when he heard the Welsh accent I had acquired.

This immersion was so successful I wanted to do it again the following summer. I decided I had to be a real au pair this time, not a guest. An agency found a family for me, in Croydon. Once again I travelled by ship from Hamburg to Harwich, then by train to London. But this time I was picked up from the station by Mr Cunningham, dressed in a light summer suit and driving a fancy white car. He was elegant and soft-spoken. Mrs Cunningham, on the other hand, turned out to be neither. They had two very sweet children, a seven-year-old boy and a three-year-old girl. The evening of my arrival, they were hosting a dinner party. I wasn't invited to join them, though I was briefly introduced as 'our new au pair'. The following morning Mr Cunningham left – he worked somewhere in the Middle East and was rarely home – and Mrs Cunningham explained my daily routine. I was to get up before everyone else and make breakfast for the entire family: bacon, eggs, toast, tea, coffee, the whole English deal. Then it was my responsibility to clean the entire house from top to bottom, and help Mrs Cunningham with the cooking. In the evenings I was to play with the children and read them their bedtime story. While I was busy doing all this Mrs Cunningham, who did not work, spent much of her time sunbathing in the garden (weather permitting), looking after the tan she had recently acquired on their holiday in Spain.

At the end of my first day I called my parents and cried. My mother said, 'You can come home if you want to. But try to deal with it.' So I stayed. I burned their bacon almost every morning; I was terrible at my cleaning duties. I felt like a maid in a Victorian costume drama. One day I slipped and slid all the way down their carpeted staircase on my back, hitting a fragile antique table when I reached the bottom. Mrs Cunningham cried out 'Oh no, she broke it!' while Mr Cunningham, who was at home at the time, timidly asked, 'Darling, shouldn't we check if she's all right?' That fall was just another bad moment in a difficult summer. I did, however, connect with the children, and really loved reading to them and spending time in their strange, whimsical world. They were sweet and emotionally vulnerable, or so I felt. Perhaps I was projecting.

My parents had given me the phone number of a well-known Czech writer and translator who had emigrated to London. On one of my boring Sundays off, I decided to call him. Another Czech émigré writer, whose name I no longer remember, answered. He said the other writer was not there, but that he would be delighted to see me himself, because 'If I can't spontaneously meet a young girl, then my life is over.' I found him funny, and I loved hearing his very Czech voice. He said he would pick me up from Croydon and take me out to a pub near by. This made me feel very grown up, and even more so when he introduced me to my first gin and tonic. When he arrived he turned out to be a charming bald man who looked middle-aged to me, but may have been no more than forty. Mrs C was visibly charmed by him; I had never seen her so giggly. On the way to the pub he told me (in Czech) that my boss had very sexy *zákolení*: did I know what he meant? I wasn't sure, so he explained it was a beautiful Czech word derived from the word *koleno* (knee), describing the back of the knee. This, he said, was a very erotic spot on a woman's body, and he could always tell, just by looking at it, whether the lady in question was sexually hungry. This was a whole new take on Mrs Cunningham, and actually made the rest of my stay in Croydon a bit more bearable; whenever she treated me badly I just thought about her *zákolení*, and laughed to myself.

I never saw the writer again; he seemed like a character out of a Kundera novel. His injection of Czech humour and sarcasm had briefly interrupted my English immersion, and was a refreshing reminder of my pre-Hamburg roots. And the following summer I went back to the farm in South Wales. The girls were older now, and I knew the family and their routine so well it felt like coming home. One hot day a dog was breathing heavily in the doorway. A teenage boy who was helping out on the farm pointed at my miniskirt and said with a serious face, 'I'll soon be panting like this dog.' I loved this earthy compliment, and I was very happy that 'panting' was a word I knew and understood. My English immersion – this stage of it, at least – was almost complete.

Deep Structure

A few weeks before the start of my first semester at Tel Aviv University I stayed with a Czech friend, Dan, whose parents had known mine in Prague, and who had visited us in Hamburg. We were of more or less the same age and had fun speaking Czech. He knew several families who had come from Prague in 1968 and now lived in the same neighbourhood. Israel seemed like the place where everything came together full circle, where all the roots and personal trajectories reconnected.

Dan's parents were away that summer, and I had a standing invitation to live with him until I found my own room in a student apartment. On one of those evenings he hosted a dinner party for some of his Czech friends (several of whom were in serious relationships, though I couldn't quite figure out who was linked to whom), and a very tall young married couple who were more international: she was from Vienna and he from Toronto. I liked them both, but noticed him especially. I had a kind of instinctive feeling, as if we had met before. After dinner, when everyone had gone and Dan and I were cleaning up, he told me that Shalom – his Canadian friend – and his wife were splitting up: in fact, this was their last evening together before her departure for Vienna. They had an adorable baby daughter named Miriam, he said. It was a very sad situation, but he (and his parents) had always felt that they were mismatched.

Such mature relationships – marriage, serious dating, separation – were not even remotely on my own radar. I was twenty, and felt closer to my unbound teenage years than to plans of becoming a proper adult. I was not in the least interested in looking for a husband, or even a boyfriend. And yet, two years after this first meeting, Shalom and I were married.

The day after the dinner party I was surprised to see him stepping out of the bathroom at Dan's. I noticed his smiley blue eyes and blondish curly hair. His wife had left for Vienna, he explained, but he was staying. We talked. He was only twenty-four but already had a PhD in philosophy and a full-time job as a university lecturer. I had never met anyone so close to my age who seemed so focused and so brilliant. He had also studied and taught linguistics at Tel Aviv University, where I was about to enrol.

The Linguistics Department had been founded and was headed by the eminent American professor Robert Lees, who had come there from the University of Illinois and was a famous early fan and proponent of Noam Chomsky's linguistic theory. When I went to see him in his office soon after my arrival for my now-permanent stay in Israel, he gave me a gruff talk about my new life, with a special warning: 'Do not get married young. This country is a trap. Everybody is obsessed with weddings here. Don't fall for it.' I mentioned that I knew Shalom, his former graduate student. Professor Lees was astonished. 'You know him? How did you meet him? He's a genius.' Then, after a pause, 'You're going to marry him, right? Don't.' I laughed.

Lees's department was a replica of any similar institution

in the States. All the classes were taught in English – mostly American English – and so my double immersion continued, now in my academic life. In lively and informal lectures and seminars I was introduced to the hot topic of the day, transformational-generative grammar, as defined by Chomsky and his adherents. It was based on the premise that all languages shared a universal deep grammatical structure of basic semantic relations, mapped onto a variety of surface structures via so-called transformations. It fascinated me that language could be seen as an abstract concept, to be analysed scientifically and mined for data to support or refute a theory. My knowledge of several languages was now a source of ideas for seminar papers, and for finding examples and counter-examples for my professors' theories. It amazed me that most of them did not speak any languages except (American) English and some heavily accented Hebrew. To be a linguist, it was explained to me, was not synonymous with speaking a variety of languages; it was a scientific title, like mathematician or physicist. I wondered if I now had a split personality: was the linguist I was becoming receiving data from the multi-language speaker I had been for most of my life, somewhere deep inside my brain?

The best part of this stage of my life was my new freedom to live on my own – or, more exactly, in apartments shared with other students. There were usually three of us. Shalom had put me in touch with a friend of his called Zvia, a petite, beautiful girl who was a former linguistics student. She was now studying speech therapy but she knew all my teachers and the material I was learning, and so I found myself talking linguistics even outside university hours.

Zvia had been born in Cochin, in the state of Kerala, South India, where her father had been education minister in the local communist government. Her native language was Malayalam.

She had immigrated to Israel with her entire immediate family (she had nine or ten siblings) and other relatives. We became best friends instantly, and whenever we moved from one apartment to another it would be the two of us plus another roommate. My English immersion continued with our intense conversations in a variety of accents and inflections – American, Canadian, Indian, South African ...

At weekends I was often invited to stay with Zvia's family. Her father was a tall, very distinguished gentleman, gentle and soft-spoken but awe-inspiring. Their Rosh Hashana celebration was a real eye-opener for me. Instead of the customary apple dipped in honey for a sweet year, their festive table, or rather several long tables linked together under sparkling white tablecloths, was covered in every variety of fruit, in a stunning display of colours. Jewishness, I suddenly saw, came in as many varieties as all this fruit: adapting to each country's human climate, merging with each host yet retaining its own flavour, character and roots. I was as Czech or Russian as Zvia was Indian, or our friend Janet from Johannesburg was South African. All our different yet shared roots had been in this country, new to some of us, native to others. Time had a different flavour in this tiny slice of the Middle East: past and present merged in a slow yet intense flow.

In Israel I felt neither foreign nor exotic. My cultural trajectory was no more complicated than anyone else's.

My Guy

Shalom, whose divorce had been an amicable, though certainly not painless affair (his daughter Miriam was now living in Austria with her mother), became a part of my life soon after we met. We fell in love quickly and self-evidently. Being together felt very natural to us both. Thus began yet another foray into the English language, through the time I spent with him and, quite often, with his very lively and interesting family – he had three younger siblings, all living in Israel. They had emigrated from Toronto almost ten years before we met. His parents' library was my first real window into American and Canadian literature, especially the Jewish literary greats: Bernard Malamud, Saul Bellow, Philip Roth, Henry Roth. I began reading their books while taking in the family's background and dynamic, their conversations and arguments. His mother was originally from the Bronx and grew up speaking Yiddish to her Russian-born parents. Her father had been a Yiddish poet, and one was never allowed to forget the significance of this fact. Shalom's father, who was fifteen years older than his wife, had been born in Poland, and immigrated with his family to Canada as a child, in 1926. He also spoke Yiddish to his parents (who, I was told, never really learned good English).

Although the language at my future in-laws' home was English, I learned that there was a rivalry between them about the quality of each other's Yiddish. Russian Yiddish was considered superior to Polish Yiddish, by speakers of the former. Or, in any case, by Shalom's mother Adah. His father, Ben, didn't seem to care.

Adah was a fiery, striking dark-haired and blue-eyed woman with a husky voice, or, often, no voice at all due to her chain smoking. She nevertheless always managed to produce a very assertive whisper. In the family dynamic she was the irascible New Yorker while Ben was her gentle, soft-spoken Canadian counterpart. They were both passionate readers and loved talking and arguing about books and articles. It was in their home I discovered the *New York Review of Books* and *Encounter* magazine. Adah read constantly, usually curled up on the living-room couch; she absorbed the printed word like oxygen. Ben was more private; in fact, I rarely saw him with a book, though he obviously read almost everything his wife did, and often more. She was a talented editor and translator, whereas he had the quirky creative mind of a born writer. Ben was a distinguished professor of social work and wrote books on the subject, but always played with the idea – or longing – to be a novelist. Eventually he would dedicate his retirement to working on his long-planned novel. He wrote and revised it for many years. Its topic was a man's complex relationship with being a Holocaust survivor. I was most struck by his description of his character's powerful attraction to a difficult woman and her scatological language.

Shalom often joked that my parents and grandparents, as opposed to his, had missed the boat – meaning the immigrant boat from Eastern Europe to North America. He was right: going back a couple of generations, we were from exactly the same environment. Not that my grandparents and great-grandparents had actually ever actively tried to leave Eastern and Central Europe. And one day I would discover that missing the boat would acquire new connotations for my place in my family's hidden history. I would find that I too was a descendant of exactly the same pattern in my paternal grandparents' immigrant narrative: an escape from Eastern Europe to America, a new life in New York. But then, that narrative was reversed; my paternal grandfather did not exactly miss a boat – on the contrary, he took it back to his home country, in the service of his belief in its ideals.

Ben loved to pose the same question every time he saw me: 'Who is the greater Jewish writer, Bellow or Roth?' His mind was made up, but he enjoyed the exchange. Roth, I would say. Why Roth? Why not Bellow? he would counter. Roth is the sexy one, I'd say. He is real. He provokes. He's funny. Subversive. Argumentative. Fun to read. Irresistible, in fact. Maybe, Ben would say, but isn't Bellow more philosophical? More Jewish? Not at all, I would argue. Philip Roth is the one who challenges the Jewish establishment. It doesn't get more Jewish than that. So Bellow is more universal, Ben would argue, and that makes him the greater Jewish writer. His heart was set on Bellow, but his more mischievous side was seduced by Roth. This conversation could go on for ever. And it did – for years. The more I became involved in literary matters, the more he wanted to examine this basic dichotomy of Jewish literature: Bellow or Roth? The argument would usually end with Ben saying, 'Actually, I think they both have nothing on Bernard Malamud.' And sometimes I would tease him – with complete seriousness – that in fact Joseph Heller was THE ONE.

Ben himself was a sharp philosophical observer. He thought society was becoming atomised, each individual unto himself, increasingly separated from any sense of community. It was a pessimistic view of the world, and it was prescient.

Shalom and I were married on the campus of Tel Aviv University, in the beautifully lit garden of its main cafeteria (a lawn and a car park in day time). It was important to us to organise this ourselves and not to involve our parents in the logistics. Miriam, who had just turned three, wore a pretty white summer dress she called her *Hochzeitskleid* ('wedding dress'). She looked gorgeous, an angelic little blonde girl with big blue eyes. She spoke some English, but mainly German, and on each of her visits to Israel I tried to make her feel very happy and comfortable, even though she clearly missed her mother. We read stories and played a lot, I took her to the university swimming pool ... She seemed very excited about the wedding, and for me she was the central part of the new family Shalom and I were creating, although both of us were still very young: he was twenty-six, I was only twenty-two.

My parents arrived in Israel a few weeks before the wedding. They hadn't really met Shalom before. They were worried. What the hell was I doing marrying so young, they asked. They were definitely not happy about it. My father said, 'OK, he's very good-looking, and he seems very smart. But you don't know anything about him. You think you do, but you don't. And he has a young daughter. Are you sure you can love a child that's not your own?'

'Of course,' I said. 'I love her already.'

'Be careful,' my father said. 'You don't know what it's like, but I do.' I had no idea what he meant by this. Perhaps I should have asked.

The wedding catapulted my parents into an environment in which they felt very insecure. Visiting Israel and spending time with close friends and family was one thing, but to suddenly find themselves in the role of in-laws, and to have to connect with a new family they could not really communicate with (they had no common language) filled them with a sense of dread. My father dealt with it in the only way he knew how: by asserting a demand.

Israeli weddings are quite informal, and were even more so at the time, in 1977. The groom rarely wore a jacket and tie, just a nice white shirt, usually unbuttoned at the top. When my father found out he seemed shocked, and insisted that my husband-to-be show him respect by dressing formally. Shalom refused; he wanted to do it his way, and I supported him. Heated arguments ensued, all of which I had to translate, from Russian and Czech into English and back again. Shalom finally agreed to a jacket (which he intended to take off as soon as possible) but absolutely refused to wear a tie. My father threw a tantrum. My mother and Klari tried to calm him down and persuade him to let it go, but failed.

My heart stopped when I saw my parents arrive at the wedding ceremony. They were both dressed identically in what looked like uniforms: khaki trousers and T-shirts. The informality of Israeli weddings does not extend that far; people do wear their prettiest best. My parents stood out from the other guests as if they had crashed a stranger's wedding. They had done this out of protest, they said. My father had felt slighted, he told me, and wanted to show us what it felt like. I hadn't realised, until then, that as well as being deeply loving and generous, my parents were also immature. Adult teenagers. I felt let down by them. And yet, in hindsight, I find this prank subversively hilarious. In photos from my wedding my parents look great: slim, young, attractive, mischievous – if a little peevish. Like two kids misbehaving and feeling a bit bad about it, but not a whole lot. They were in their late forties and clearly not ready to be the mature and formal parents of a married daughter. Perhaps my early marriage made them a little sad.

The day before my wedding I had been relaxing alone by the university swimming pool. I was thinking about my plan not

to allow my young married status to interfere with my freedom to live as I liked – with the difference that at the end of
each day I would now go home to my husband rather than my
roommates. We had found an apartment in north Tel Aviv, on
one of the noisy main streets, minutes from my beloved beach.
I was excited.

My wedding dress was unusual. One of my friends at university was Anna, a Filipina girl whose father was a high-ranking
official at the embassy (if not the consul or ambassador himself –
I wasn't sure). One day she told me and some other friends that
her mother had just returned from a trip to the Philippines and
brought back a few hand-sewn cotton summer dresses – would
we be interested in buying them? She showed us the dresses –
there were about ten of them – but I immediately noticed only
one: a long, romantic dress made of natural cotton (more cream
than white), with a hand-crocheted bodice and sleeves. I loved
its simplicity and understated beauty. It made me feel summery
and in love. My wedding ring was similarly unusual: bought
in an antique shop rather than a jeweller's, it was a simple band
fusing old white and yellow gold. The white-gold centre was
so worn it looked almost silver. Who had worn it before me, I
wondered. Where had it come from?

Pop music – old and contemporary – from large loudspeakers
filled the quiet air around the pool. 'My Guy' – the original
Mary Wells version – came on and the lyrics suddenly connected with my mood. I was proud to be marrying a guy who
refused to give in to my father's capricious demands. This song,
a nostalgic oldie, suddenly made me feel really married. Years
later Shalom and I agreed that my father actually meant well,
and that he should have worn that tie.

'You don't write, do you?'

In the middle of my postgraduate studies in linguistics I suddenly realised I had lost all interest in its theories. The only thing that held my attention were the sentences used as data. John loves Mary. Mary loves John, who writes slowly. John, who built a house, loves Mary. John and Mary, who know Peter, live here. The house was built by John.

Such sentences, in various languages, were not meant to serve any function beyond demonstrating the abstract rules of syntax, semantics, phonology and discourse. But for me they became snippets of stories. Who was John? Who was Mary? What was it like for them to love one another? Why did he build that house, and where? Would she love him less if he hadn't? Studying linguistics had sharpened my analytic skills, but it did not make me want to become an academic. The subject of my MA thesis was the use in discourse of backward anaphora: the grammatical device of introducing a pronoun before its antecedent, i.e. the noun to which it refers. This is usually done for emphasis, or drawing attention to the topic of a sentence. I had collected many examples of such sentences and I noticed a new trend in my data gathering: instead of finding sentences from spoken usage, I was turning more and more towards literary examples, such as the opening line from *Portnoy's Complaint* by Philip Roth: 'She was so deeply embedded in my consciousness that for the first year of school I seem to have believed that each of my teachers was my mother in disguise.' In my thesis, I argued that 'she' appears before 'my mother' to make the latter the focus of the sentence and, in a sense, of the entire novel.

It was no accident that I was feeding my theories literary data; nor was it an accident that my most interesting example came from a novel by Philip Roth. In my daily life I was embedded in both Hebrew and English, but I deduced, with real pain in my heart, that my dream of becoming a writer had to be abandoned. Ben, my very literary father-in-law, unintentionally opened this wound when he casually said to me one day, 'You don't write, do you? I mean, you would have written something by now.' I was in my mid-twenties when he said this.

He could not have known that all I ever wanted was to be a writer. And I did not tell him so now, in reply to the question whose answer he chose to provide himself. My father-in-law was a gentle man who often spoke in a tentative mode, trying his ideas out on people rather than declaring them as definitive statements. Perhaps he did, in fact, want to ask me a real question about being a writer, in his indirect way, and perhaps I missed that nuance. If I could have answered truthfully I would have explained that fluency in a new language, even complete, perfect fluency, is not the same as owning that language the way one owns one's mother tongue; and that writing in a foreign language feels like walking in someone else's ill-fitting shoes. But I said none of this.

This aborted snippet of a conversation stayed with me. It made me think a great deal about my linguistic crossroads at the time. I spent several years experimenting with writing in Czech – again – and trying my hand at writing in English.

I reconnected with my Czech by returning to writing poems. This made sense: poetry, like music, inhabits a deeper, more instinctive layer of one's mind, and it felt easy, and good, to play with words without thinking too much about content. These poems turned out to be very personal and intimate. Using the language of my childhood and my adolescence transported me to that time of my life, and there (or here) I was, suddenly reliving my first love, remembering how it was to crisscross Prague's winter streets with him late at night after concerts in ancient churches or plays in avant-garde theatres, how it felt to linger by my front door because neither of us was ready to break the magic. The musty smell of old Prague stone was suddenly back, the muddied black snow, the taste of fresh snowflakes ... These snapshots of past, unforgotten experiences found their way into the impressionistic poems I was writing to preserve a part of myself I didn't want to lose for ever. I didn't want to see it as a death, even though that was exactly what it was. Typed on my old Czech typewriter I had brought with me to Israel from Hamburg, the poems were a farewell to my roots, my Czech swan song.

Not all were about my old self; the language I found again came alive for a while, and I wrote quite a few poems about my new life: about emigration, new love, and about a flight from Tel Aviv to Europe. This last poem actually appeared in the Czech émigré magazine *Obrys*, which was published in Munich. I used a pseudonym, Lenka Rellibova: a diminutive of my first name and a reference to my father's pseudonym (his last name spelled backwards) as a translator from Czech into Russian before we left Prague.

Although I was no longer seriously interested in theoretical linguistics I didn't actually drop the subject. I merely added another one, film and television. Now, instead of analysing abstract concepts, I was able to immerse myself in the exact opposite: learning how to make stories come alive on the screen.

During my interview I was asked why I wanted to study film. 'I am afraid of violent scenes in movies, and if I learn how to make them I hope I'll lose this fear.' My interviewers exchanged a few looks, clearly unimpressed. Ironically, during the entire first semester of film studies we were made to watch the very scary *Rosemary's Baby* almost every week, as a lesson in perfect filmmaking. Even after the tenth viewing, and discussing and analysing almost every shot and angle, I was as afraid to watch Polanski's masterpiece as I was at the start, and was equally affected by it.

I made two short films during this period. One was a half-hour feature about a day and night in the life of a lonely, overweight museum guard. By day he lovingly guards a huge Henry Moore sculpture of a woman; by night, he makes love to it. I asked a lonely, overweight neighbour of mine to be the star, and he very cheerfully obliged. When we were filming him leaving his house a huge noisy crowd of local boys surrounded us, mocking and teasing both the actor and the crew. I said to them, 'Do you want to be in this film? Which one of you is the leader?' One small boy declared that he was the boss, and the others didn't disagree. 'I'm putting you in charge of organising all of your friends. Make them run together from two directions, and then stop in front of the gate. And you might as well stop shouting – we're not recording any sound.' The boy turned out to be a natural director: he did exactly what I asked, transforming an unruly, aggressive crowd of young delinquents into a perfect little army of almost-silent extras. It was the best scene in the film.

My other exercise in filmmaking was a short commercial. I 'invented' a bra called Atlas, based on the idea that it holds a woman's breasts the way the Titan Atlas carried the weight of the world on his shoulders. A friend volunteered to have her breast cupped on camera by her boyfriend, a fellow film student, in a smoothly filmed combination of tracking shot and close-up. I set it to the heavenly soundtrack of Mahalia Jackson singing 'He's Got the Whole World in His Hands'. It occurred to me to offer the idea to an actual bra manufacturer – why shouldn't there be a bra called Atlas? I wrote to one of the world's leaders in lingerie, Triumph, in Munich. In reply, I was invited to present my film to a company executive at a special private screening in a Munich cinema.

My brother was living there at the time, so the trip wasn't difficult to arrange. I had visions of patenting my bra and living in carefree financial happiness ever after. The executive was a middle-aged, smoothly shaven, elegant man dressed in a pale linen suit. I – suntanned, with loose long wavy hair and in my summery best – must have looked like an exotic young woman to him. We had the chilly, classy cinema all to ourselves. I handed my 16mm film reel to the projectionist, and sat in darkness next to the German bra specialist, waiting for his verdict. As the film rolled I realised what a crazy idea this had been, and was secretly thrilled by my fearlessness. The executive shifted uncomfortably in his seat as Mahalia Jackson triumphantly sang out 'He's got the whole world in his hands' with tremendous spiritual might, and the actor's hand travelled slowly up my star's body, ending up under her breast, where it lingered.

The lights came back on. He stood up, shook my hand and said, in very Bavarian-accented German, hissing his s's: '*Sehr gewagt für ein junges Mädchen, sehr gewagt.*' Very bold for a young girl, very bold. The word *gewagt* has other, related meanings too – he may have meant racy, risqué, risky, off-colour or, simply, ambitious. Then he added, almost apologetically: 'We couldn't use it, because women don't like to associate bras with sex.'

The off-colour nature of this little adventure put me in mind of an incident a couple of years earlier, when I was still a student at Hamburg University. I had applied for a job I saw advertised on the noticeboard in my department: 'Students with foreign language skills wanted for translating film subtitles.' I was excited: this job seemed tailor-made for me. And I liked the idea of translating film captions, just as my father had done in Prague in the 1960s. He used to bring me black-and-white photo-postcards of international film stars from screenings and festivals, some of them signed. I had a crush on Virna Lisi. Perhaps the aesthetic of my bra commercial was subconsciously formed by these very womanly screen beauties of the 1960s – whose films I never saw, as I was too young.

At the mention of my knowledge, to varying degrees of competence, of German, Russian, Czech, English and French, I was immediately invited to an interview at the translation firm. The address was central, not far from the university, yet the actual door of their offices seemed hard to locate. When I finally entered I was asked to wait in a very plain reception area surrounded by milky-white glass walls, behind which there was a low-pitched buzz of some of kind of activity. I could see pale silhouettes of people moving around, and imagined films running on multiple screens as their subtitles were being translated. After a while, I began to discern that the buzz actually consisted of deep sighs, grunts and monosyllabic exclamations. Before I connected the dots in my mind and realised that the films in question were clearly pornographic, a pudgy, middle-aged bald man emerged from one of the rooms, shook my hand and said, 'We are impressed with your languages. Can you do a test for us right now?' I listened for a while longer to the huffing and puffing behind the thin partitions, wondered why they needed subtitles at all (and were they possibly recording live?), and bolted without saying goodbye.

Film studies made me interested in photography too. I joined a course at a newly formed school of photography called Camera Obscura, and began wandering around Tel Aviv with my Minolta, looking for interesting black-and-white subjects. They were everywhere: an old man rummaging in bins; a child in Jaffa wearing a Charlie's Angels T-shirt and shielding his head from a slap by his angry mother; lifelike mannequins on street corners displaying flamboyant fashions; a fruit vendor counting his day's income, ignoring my attempts to take a self-portrait in his antique mirror. Rubble growing into elegant houses, seemingly only a moment away from turning into rubble again. Endless reflections of old and new architecture in shop windows, some sparkling, some smeared with sandy dirt, blown in from the beach and during burning-hot sandstorms. With each image I connected more deeply with the city. Its language accompanied this new love, but the pictures came first.

One of my first assignments was to photograph a nude. The teacher asked us to split into pairs and pose for one another. I paired up with Yoav, a young man who seemed very serious about photography and was also quite attractive. I was only twenty-four but I had been married for almost two years by this time; I felt very safe behind the shield of my marriage: no crushes could penetrate it.

My model drove us to my apartment, where we had something to drink and then, to very soothing reggae tunes, he posed naked in different rooms. I focused on trying to shoot his body in an abstract way, without a connection to his face or personality. But later, when I developed the prints in the darkroom, I was struck by how sexual the images were. It had not been my intention. And I never returned the favour; I used my nascent pregnancy as my excuse.

This experience became the subject of my first short story written and published in English. I called it 'The Naked Nude'.

I began playing with it shortly after the situation that inspired it really occurred, but I didn't finish it until we left Israel for Canada in 1980. Boldly I sent it to England; it really surprised me when I received a brief acceptance letter from the editorial department of a small literary magazine called *Argo*, based in Oxford. The editors could not possibly have realised or imagined what this letter meant to me.

The story was written in two voices, the photographer's first-person narration and her model's more sardonic voice in brackets ('She is the kind of clumsy amateur who takes rather good pictures, but gets desperate when her film slips out of the reel in the darkroom ... I'll take pictures of her sitting in the Dead Sea. Corny purple sunset against her daring smile. I bet it won't be so daring once she's naked.'). It grew so organically from a real situation that I was able to tell it with complete fluency. I could forget about the language and just write the story. This was a real turning point.

Just before publication I changed the story's title to 'The Fraud', in reference to the narrator's refusal to keep her word. But in truth I was marking a private milestone. I felt like a fraud myself, an impostor, writing and publishing my fiction in English. My newly found literary ear and pen were hiding my foreignness. But I knew it was there, and always would be.

There had never been a moment in my entire life, since early childhood, when I didn't think I had to be a writer (although at about six I had a brief lapse when I decided I'd rather be president of my country). My diaries – written in Czech at the time – document my daily plans to write. I had many ideas, but none seemed to fit who I was, or rather who I thought I wanted to be. Then one day the diaries were suddenly in English.

Re-reading them now, I noticed something I had missed or perhaps blocked earlier, when I thought about how I became a writer in English: I was a translator before I was a writer. I translated articles and book-length manuscripts on mostly academic subjects. My father kept telling me to stop: 'You can only translate into your native language. English is not your mother tongue.' He was right. But for me the translations turned out to be an excellent teaching tool for stripping English of its foreign-language mystique and immersing myself in its syntax and vocabulary.

In 1982, when my story appeared in *Argo*, my name was printed as Jelena Biller-Lappin: my first name spelled with a J and pronounced 'Yelena', as it had been in Czech and in German, echoing the original Russian. I was still hyphenating my last name, though I would drop my maiden name soon after. The magazine described my biography thus: 'Jelena Biller-Lappin was born in 1954 and has lived in Czechoslovakia, West Germany, Israel and, currently, Canada, where she is completing a thesis in linguistics.'

My hyphenated name had appeared in another magazine, where I had published a translation from French into English of an obscure (and, to me, incomprehensible) academic article about the semiotics of the theatrical gesture. This article was found – not accidentally – by a Russian man in Moscow, who, unbeknownst to me, had been searching for traces of my existence somewhere in the world. My name and biography gave him the first hint of my married identity and my geographical whereabouts. But it would take him another twenty-five years to locate me.

V's mission was only partly accomplished by establishing contact with me. That first phone call to London would be only the beginning. He wanted more: he wanted to really know me and to prove that he knew me. We corresponded a great deal, and spoke on the phone a few times. These were long, detailed conversations, during which he tried to tell me everything I wanted and needed to know about the grandparents I never met – impressions more than facts, but they helped: my paternal grandfather's overbearing presence, my grandmother's softer nature and sadness about her many losses. Her accented Russian. 'I have read your stories,' he once told me, 'and I had to laugh, thinking, if only she knew who she really is.' He didn't want anything in return for putting me in touch with my roots, except this: a copy of this article I once translated. V said the subject matter really interested him. I promised I would try, but in the end I could not find it.

'Call it Foreign Brides'

When my husband and I left Israel for Canada in the summer of 1980 the plan was to spend a one-year sabbatical in Ottawa, where he had been offered a temporary position in the Department of Linguistics. I travelled there with two unfinished projects: a baby I was carrying, and the research I had done for my MA thesis in linguistics. The thesis would become a burden; the pregnancy and the baby sheer joy.

I flew to Canada with my father-in-law (my husband had preceded me, in order to find and set up an apartment), who also happened to be on a sabbatical that summer, in Toronto. On this journey, I saw a side of him I had never noticed before. In the airport, saying goodbye to his wife, I was struck by how hard it was for him to leave her. There was a touching tenderness and a great deal of anxiety in him at that moment. And each time we passed uniformed officials at passport control Ben was very visibly nervous. He explained to me that since childhood he hadn't been able to lose his fear of uniformed personnel in control of official papers and border crossings; the immigrant in him trembled at their sight, as if they had the power to turn him away, or worse.

I arrived in Ottawa in August, the height of summer: hot, humid, turquoise-skied, green-lawned. It looked like a picturesque, idyllic town, very pretty, spotlessly clean, not quite real. Despite being the capital city of Canada and hence suitably adorned with imposing government buildings, it seemed small, like a less-successful sibling of nearby Montreal, or the more distant Toronto – my husband's home town. In Israel, we were both immigrants; here he was on home turf. This made me feel foreign in a way that I hadn't felt before. I saw a television programme about Canadian soldiers stationed in Europe during the Second World War marrying British girls and bringing them back to Canada after the war. These war brides were disappointed to find that the men they had married overseas turned out to be very different in their home country: meek rather than strong, bland rather than exciting, ordinary rather than intriguing. I made a note in my diary: 'Write a book of stories about women living in foreign countries with their husbands, where the husbands are at home. Double whammy: marriage and being foreign. Call it Foreign Brides.' I would forget this note and only find it again almost twenty years later, after three more moves from one country to another. The idea would still fascinate me; and my first book – entitled *Foreign Brides*, as I'd originally planned – would eventually be born from it in 1999.

The book that actually made me want to write in English, or, more exactly, made me jealous that I couldn't, was a small light-blue paperback with a 1950s cover I'd picked up in a second-hand bookshop in London, on our honeymoon there in 1977, and had now brought with me to Canada. The price sticker was still on it: 12½p. Perhaps I was attracted by the bargain price, and the enticing charcoal drawing of a middle-aged man and a young woman. They are sitting at a restaurant table with a bottle of wine. The man is facing the woman but her face is turned sideways, away from both the man and the reader. The back of her elegant dress is a low-cut V-shape – one can only imagine its mirror image at the front, exposing chalk-white skin. The title of the book is *My Face for the World to See*, by Alfred Hayes. When I opened the blue paperback I read this:

> It was a party that had lasted too long; and tired of the voices, a little too animated, and the liquor, a little too available, and thinking it would be nice to be alone, thinking I'd escape, for a brief interval, those smiles which pinned you against the piano or those questions which trapped you wriggling in a chair, I went out to look at the ocean.

I have always found the books I needed in my life, at just the right time and seemingly by accident, without actually looking for them, at least not consciously. All I have to do is notice them, and something in my life changes, inner connections are made, doors open. I recognise these true moments of literary discovery by the unmistakable sense of excitement they bring, a bit like falling in love. *My Face for the World to See*, written around the time when I was born, by a British Jewish expat living much of his life in America, had me as soon as I saw the title. It promised a light touch and deep layers. It told a story of a cynical, bruised middle-aged man who inadvertently stumbles into saving a young woman from drowning herself, and by falling in love with her ends up saving himself. But I didn't know any of the story when I read that first paragraph in my literary-beginner's English. The simplicity and vividness of Hayes's writing gave me a thrill. I knew immediately: that's how it's done.

Even though I could only really understand less than half of what he wrote, it was the first English book I could feel without thinking about the meaning of each word. Each sentence instantly conjured up a situation, a world, a person's voice and character, in just a few assured, gentle brushstrokes. The process of reading fiction in a foreign language is a mysterious one: what we understand links up with what we know without understanding. I have re-read *My Face for the World to See* many times since; and each time, I found new nuances, layers, turns of phrase and beauty of prose, other profound insights disguised as casual observation. There are no extras in this story, nothing superfluous. Every moment, every sentence matters. It revealed to me the deceptively effortless simplicity of the English language, carried by gentle waves of idiom rather than weighed down by heavy syntax. I wanted to be able to do this too. After several years of resisting the unwieldiness of German, and the frustrating inaccessibility of literary Hebrew, English was an eye-opener: if I could find my way into this lightness, my dream of becoming a writer could still be saved.

After a gloriously multicoloured but very brief Indian summer Ottawa quite suddenly returned to its true identity – a mercilessly ice-cold city. But it was still pleasingly warm while I went about adjusting to the second half of my first pregnancy in this remote part of the world, without any family living close by. It had never occurred to me that this was not an easy way to live. Nor did I notice – not then – that I was repeating my mother's history: marrying and having a child far away from my parents, from any family, in a city that was foreign to them and to me too.

'The purple bead is in the bathtub'

I was napping on the living-room couch in our Ottawa apartment when my husband shook me quite forcefully in an attempt to wake me up: there was some sort of emergency. Our son Yaakov, now a year and a few months old, was screaming something Shalom did not understand, and he would not stop. I opened my eyes and listened. Then I said, still half asleep: 'The purple bead is in the bathtub.'

He stared at me in complete disbelief: 'What? How could he possibly say something that complicated?' But he walked to the bathroom and, sure enough, the purple plastic bead from a Fisher-Price set was in the bathtub, out of the baby's reach.

Yaakov had been venting his frustration in Czech, a language his father did not understand. We had agreed that it would be a natural and good thing for me to speak Czech to our son, so that he would grow up bilingual (or multilingual). Shalom's seven-year-old daughter Miriam, who split her time between living in Vienna with her mother and our home, wherever it happened to be, spoke German and English. Yaakov would speak Czech and English. What could be more natural? There was an important difference, though. My stepdaughter's

German was rooted in a real country, where she was growing up. My Czech was almost a private language; I only spoke it to my brother, mostly over the phone, and very occasionally to a few others: new Czech émigré acquaintances or, very rarely, old friends. When I visited my parents or when they came to see me they would speak Russian-accented Czech to the baby but Russian to me, so there wasn't an actual physical home for the language I was naturally introducing to my first son.

But it *was* natural: the language of my childhood was instinctively the first and only language I could speak to my baby: a Czech oasis with the newest being closest to my heart.

It was like having a secret language for just the two of us. My parents enlisted the help of friends in Czechoslovakia, who began to supply me with children's books, records, tapes and videos. Many, in fact most of them, were the material of my own childhood: the same characters, stories, poems, songs, even the same familiar actors' voices reading and performing the magical fictional world I used to inhabit when I was a child in Prague. Sometimes I felt as if motherhood was giving me a licence to go back in time.

But there was also another important reason why I taught my son to speak Czech: I wanted him to have a language in common with my parents. I had removed myself so far from them geographically and, in a sense, culturally that the only way to bridge that distance was by passing on at least one of the languages spoken in our family to my own children. Of course I chose Czech.

And yet, ultimately, I would fail. Yaakov was bilingual in English and Czech for quite a few years, until he started primary school. By then we had moved back to Israel and Hebrew became the dominant language; I felt too disconnected from Czech to enforce it. He began to reply in Hebrew when I spoke to him in Czech, and so eventually I stopped. I tried again with my second son, Yoni, who was born in Haifa, and with my daughter Shira, who was born in America. Each child arrived into a different linguistic constellation, outside and inside our home. It became harder for me to maintain my own language oasis, because it now felt like an abstraction. Gradually English, in a variety of accents (Canadian, American, British) took over, and evolved into our only family language. And so it happened that my children could no longer really communicate with my parents, despite feeling very close to them, which is a great sadness.

All my children's lives were shaped by our many moves, and for a long time I was quite blind to their effect. I'd forgotten, or perhaps suppressed, how upsetting they were in my own childhood; in an odd way they almost mirrored them. Now I found it natural to try living in a new place every few years; we did so as my husband's job took him from one university or research institution to another. As an adult Yaakov would tell me how it felt. After three-and-a-half years in Canada we brought him to Israel. In Haifa, Hebrew became his own language, and through kindergarten and several years of primary school he put down genuine roots. We then moved to America. One of the most indelible memories of his life was the dark silhouette of our plane as we took off for New York, leaving what he felt was his real home. That moment broke my little boy's heart and I didn't even know it.

Yaakov made up for it later, in his mid-twenties, by moving back to Israel from England. When he married and started his own family everyone – including his Israeli wife – expected him to speak English to his baby daughter Galia. He did, for a while; but soon he reverted to Hebrew, which felt more natural to him – thus reconnecting with the language of his own happy childhood. He wanted to end the cycle of our family's linguistic uprootings, he told me. And he has succeeded: there is no language barrier between his children and us, their grand-parents. When I speak to Galia in Hebrew I not only admire the richness and confidence of her speech, but am also deeply grateful for the fact that, unlike my parents before me, I am not a stranger in her native country.

My younger son Yoni and daughter Shira, on the other hand, are at home only in English, albeit with different accents: his has remained quite American, whereas hers is completely British. They both love living in London. My husband's native Canadian English has become our family's linguistic anchor. Despite speaking excellent Hebrew, plus some German and French, he has always remained loyal to the language and culture he grew up in. Whenever we moved from one country to another I always felt the onus of having to reinvent myself in a new environment, while Shalom seemed to continue where he left off, without showing any cracks in his identity. But maybe he just carried on without allowing himself to dwell on his feelings. He too had suffered from recurrent changes and moves as a child (within Toronto) and grew to dislike them intensely. Perhaps we were both subconsciously repeating this pattern of creating frequent displacement. Our four children, however, would all put a stop to it when they began to make their own life choices.

Fire Alarm

By the time my second Canadian winter came around I was immersed in my new life in Ottawa. I wanted to emulate the happy-looking, rosy-cheeked Canadians who seemed so cheerful no matter how cold it was. I joined a cross-country skiing class, and instead of being worried about the weather I now looked forward to forecasts of the kind of snow that was good for skiing, or skating. As his earliest childhood memory, Yaakov remembers, vividly, how I pushed his stroller in deep snow and windy weather, then turned him around and pulled him behind me to keep the wind and snow out of his face. He doesn't know that this mirrors in an uncanny way my father's memory of being pulled on a sleigh by his mother, in deep Russian winter, in the mid-1930s.

I got a part-time job in the German department at the university where Shalom was teaching linguistics. It was run by German old-timers who saw me as something of an impostor, and didn't quite trust my ability to teach their language. One of them, an older man, invited me in for an initial interview in German. He asked about my family situation, why was I in Canada, where had I lived in Germany. I told him my husband was Canadian.

'But he's not a real Canadian,' he said.

'Oh yes he is. He was born in Toronto.'

'But he's Jewish. *Ja?*'

Casual anti-Semitism doesn't always present itself as a frontal attack; it appears seemingly out of nowhere, unexpectedly making you lose your balance. By the time you have managed to regain it, the moment is gone and there seems to be nothing left for you to respond to. And yet you know it will return.

Dr M's comment left me speechless. There was so much I could have said to him, starting with who was he – clearly born and raised in Germany – to discriminate against second-generation Canadians, of any ethnicity or religion? Like most unpleasant experiences, this one taught me a valuable lesson: old European prejudice – a throwback to Germany's dark history – was easily exportable to North America, where it could still raise its ugly head even in this immigrants' haven of freedom and tolerance.

I began teaching German to mostly undergraduate Canadian students on one or two nights a week. I loved those evenings: instead of winding down after spending the day looking after the baby I would wait for Shalom to come home and then change from my home clothes into something more fun and professional-looking, and take a bus to the university in the centre of Ottawa. I felt as if my days were only just beginning on those ice-cold, dark winter evenings, when I took a break from motherhood and rejoined the adult world. One night, as I waited at my bus stop near the university, I saw a beautiful young African woman in traditional dress cross the road and walk through the deep snow, carrying a tall pile of books on her head. The books formed a still, even column, the slippery snow and ice under her feet no obstacle to her perfect balance. I wanted to be like her: strong, stable, comfortable with my own way of life, no matter where I happened to find myself.

My students were a linguistic revelation to me. Some were native speakers of French, others of English, Chinese, Arabic and other languages – and all were there to learn German. 'Our accepted method in this department is to speak only German in our classes,' a senior lecturer had instructed me unequivocally. I had learned my own foreign languages by immersion; now I was also teaching one in the same way. It was a fascinating challenge. In order to explain rules of German grammar in German to students who didn't speak a word of it I had to come up with clear abstractions combined with a natural way of communicating real-life situations as examples. It was about making grammar a natural part of a narrative I created by choosing a topic and talking about it, asking questions, involving the students in finding the answers, then asking more questions. The element of boredom disappears completely when your mind is focused entirely on understanding what's being said, and on having to respond. Taught in this way, grammar is transformed from a difficult set of rules into an almost invisible, organic part of a new way of seeing things, and of talking and writing about it. These classes were fun, and my students actually learned German – from me! It was a very satisfying experience.

After class we often lingered for a while and talked (now in English), and I became good friends with some of my students. Especially two of them: Julia, from Quebec, and James, who was from Ontario but seemed to have family links to Europe and a fascination with and knowledge of several languages. He was a keen observer of my interaction in Czech with my son, and years later he would remember how one day, while we were walking down a street, Yaakov (then aged two or three) threw a tantrum because he couldn't accept that the Czech and the English word for 'broccoli' sounded exactly the same.

I actually had a brief Czech revival in Ottawa, when I connected with a TV programme on a local cable station, produced by and for Czech expats. First I helped out by co-presenting their news, and then I saw an opportunity to slip back into my former Czech self by writing and reading my own children's stories. These programmes had an almost exclusively adult audience, so my attempt to entertain émigré Czech children was rather absurd. And, in fact, my stories had mostly adult themes and language. One was about a lonely cactus in the desert who is pricked and seduced by a rose. Of course they fall in love and marry, producing unusual-looking hybrid offspring.

There was a darker side to Ottawa, which I began to see only after our second year there, when the idyllic veneer began to peel off. We moved twice: from one apartment building to a nicer one, and then to a small terraced house with a tiny yard. The menacing undercurrent appeared shortly after our first move, out of the blue, and did not go away until we moved again.

It was a very friendly building, full of very nice neighbours of all ages. Friendly faces, friendly hellos, friendly, helpful smiles. But one of these neighbours – we never found out who – would set off the fire alarm at unpredictable times, forcing everyone to leave their homes and walk down the stairs. We lived on the sixth floor. Carrying the baby down all those flights of stairs, having dragged him out of bed and sometimes his bath, was a very unpleasant experience.

These were not exactly false alarms: the smoke was every-where. Someone had thrown burning garbage down the chute, which filled every floor of the entire building with smoke without visible fire. The drill was always the same: leave your apartment, descend on foot, avoid the lifts, congregate in the lobby or outside while waiting for the fire brigade to arrive and put out the source of the almost-fire.

At first it was only a slight annoyance. But over time, as the alarms continued, the danger and expectation of their occurrence became a genuine psychological threat. Whoever was causing it had real power over us. This perpetrator had a need to terrorise the building, and succeeded: we now lived in fear and dread of these alarms. And one wondered, which one of the seemingly very nice neighbours was actually hiding this nasty secret identity?

The method behind these fire alarms reminded me of life in a totalitarian regime: you could not really trust anyone, especially those who appeared trustworthy, and you never knew how safe you really were, or who actually controlled your safety. The invisible danger was omnipresent. It felt surreal to have this experience in Canada, the country built on more equality and freedom than any other I knew. It made me aware of the duplicity of human nature, and that it can easily swing in unexpected directions.

We never learned how to live with or adjust to the fire alarms. They never stopped, and eventually we moved away from the building. Afterwards, it occurred to me that we too may have been considered suspects by our neighbours – just like everyone else. The mistrust became absolute, and mutual.

This episode left an aftertaste of a sense of profound uncertainty: as a foreign visitor to this city – perhaps to any city? – I didn't really have a key to its true identity. I couldn't trust myself to decode what was really behind my neighbours' smiles. It could be genuine friendliness, or it could be its opposite.

Suddenly, New York

My MA thesis adviser, Tanya Reinhart, was on sabbatical in New York during our third year in Ottawa. That thesis was still hanging over my head; I had lost interest in writing it, but Tanya's sudden proximity had reawakened it. I delved back into my research in preparation for visiting her in Manhattan for a few days to discuss and finalise my ideas. It would be my first trip to New York.

Tanya was a very prominent linguist on the international academic scene, a former star student of Noam Chomsky at MIT (she always pronounced his name in the guttural Hebrew way, *Khomsky*), and one of the most colourful Tel Aviv intellectuals. She was tall, lanky, deep-voiced, with short dark hair and rimless glasses. She had a slow, deliberate way of talking, gentle but extremely assertive. In her native Hebrew she sounded slightly old-world; in English, her heavy Israeli accent was somewhat in the way of her anti-Israel views. Tanya had radical political opinions; over the years her views grew from classic communist-style subversion against Israeli government policies to outspoken accusations of Israeli crimes against Palestinians. She was as in tune with Chomsky's politics as she was with his teachings.

I had attended and loved several of her classes on linguistics and literature. She taught with a wonderful aura of intellectual experimentation and freedom, and with exceptional attentiveness to her students' voices. She listened and engaged with everyone, with both seriousness and affection. She bridged the two fields I was studying – theoretical linguistics and comparative literature – in a way that made me see that their synthesis was possible, if I chose to look for it. With Tanya, learning was a respectful sharing of insights and discussion, where mistakes and wrong paths were a natural part of the conversation. We rarely talked about politics.

Tanya Reinhart was a purely nocturnal person. She slept as long as possible during the day (she never taught in the mornings) and became active at night. When we began planning our meeting in New York she made sure to remind me that I must arrive at her apartment, where she had invited me to stay for a few days, no earlier than ten in the evening.

Noa, an Ottawa friend of mine, was driving to New York with her parents and offered to take me along. The only financial contribution they asked for was for me to cover all the refreshments along the way. Her father, she said, was addicted to Howard Johnson's restaurants, especially their burgers and ice cream. We set off from Ottawa very early in the morning and drove all day. There seemed to be a Howard Johnson's every two hours or so; I got used to the garishly cozy decor and the surprisingly satisfying meals and treats we consumed as we approached New York.

Finally it was evening and we were there, in the middle of Manhattan. I had always thought of being in New York with some trepidation. At the time it was considered to be very dangerous, and I imagined this danger to be far worse than any other city I had known till then. I was very happy to have arrived with friends, and to be able to return to Ottawa a week later with the same group of people.

Now they were about to drop me off on a street corner in the heart of New York City, somewhere near Forty-Second Street. I pretended to be absolutely fine and said thank you and goodbye and see you soon, and then they drove off and I was standing by myself on a busy corner. It was almost eleven in the evening and I was ready to feel panic.

But what I experienced took me by complete surprise. As I took in the masses of New Yorkers rushing by despite (or, as I would soon learn, because of) the late hour, as I inhaled the warm air (it was late May) and picked up snippets of conversations delivered in sharp, argumentative New York tones, I felt a deep pang of recognition. This, I knew, was familiar. This was home.

I had no explanation for this feeling, except to think – then and later – that many people felt at home in New York. Tourists, visitors, temporary job seekers, students – all came for a short while, and many stayed because it felt right. I assumed that my reaction fell into the same category. I had no connection with this city, so it couldn't possibly be home.

Tanya had instructed me to take a taxi to her place, and to make sure the driver waited until I was safely inside. 'He would do it anyway, it's part of the service.' What would he have done, I wondered, if I had been attacked somewhere between his car and the entrance to the building? Jumped in and helped? Called the police? Driven off?

The driver did wait, and I didn't even have to ask him. Tanya buzzed me inside and rode the elevator with me to the small apartment she was renting, which seemed to consist of a hallway with a kitchen-like corner, a bed and a couch all in full sight. Her face was very red. As soon as we entered, she apologised and then resumed what she had been doing: 'I'm steaming my face. Adult acne! I don't know what's going on with my skin here. It's this dirty New York air.'

When she was done she made us coffee and put some food on the table, and we talked late into the night. 'You look very new wave,' she told me. 'Do you want to go dancing?' She wanted me to have a good time, and that same night, at about two o'clock, the daughter of a New York friend of Tanya's picked me up and took me to the 'coolest New York discos'. One was a cavernous building on several floors, each level filled with different music. Once she saw that I was enjoying the sound and the atmosphere of the club the girl disappeared and I never saw her again. Like everybody there, I just danced and danced until I was inside a total music high, enveloped by a deafening cocoon of electrifying beats. Chaka Khan, Chaka Khan, everybody Chaka Khan. I talked to some people, but not very much, because what could I have said? 'I am visiting from Ottawa, that's in Canada, I have a baby and a husband, this is my first night in New York, I am here to talk to my Israeli thesis adviser about backward anaphora'? Eventually I found a taxi outside (now it was getting a little bit scary as I had no idea where in this city I was in relation to where I was going), and for the second time that night a cab driver waited until I was safely inside Tanya's building.

During this memorable New York week I visited Shalom's cousin Ruthie G (his mother's older cousin), a widow and very talented artist and dancer living in her own brownstone on a beautiful street in the West Village. One of her rooms was a gallery of her sculptures and other art. Her kitchen was an authentic throwback to the 1960s or 1970s, when she had moved to this house from her suburban home on Long Island. Ruthie was wealthy but thrifty: 'I can never take taxis! I watch the meter and feel them bleeding me dry!' A beautiful, petite woman with delicate features and a blonde ponytail, she was elegant but extremely outspoken, even harsh. After a salad lunch at her kitchen table ('Count your calories! Make a list of everything you eat!'), she took me on a long walk through the Village and other parts of Manhattan. As we walked and talked I noticed some notebooks in a pile of rubbish on the street. I stopped and picked them up – I can never not read someone's hidden stories – and found them fascinating. It was clearly a diary, written by a woman, about an unhappy love affair described in fascinating detail: 'I could have lived alone but with him the pain felt better, deeper.' After a while Ruthie said casually, 'Oh I know who that is, it's Gretchen. Everyone knew about their affair. Take it home and write a book.'

As it was my first trip, Ruthie was keen to show me some of her own personal New York landmarks. We kept walking until we reached the Upper West Side and the striking Dakota building on the corner of West Seventy-Second and Central Park West, where John Lennon had lived and where he was shot, only a few years previously. 'I used to live here too, you know,' said Ruthie. It was true: I had heard this from my husband and from my mother-in-law, who was very proud of her cousin's impressive New York credentials. She went straight up to the doorman and declared loudly, 'I used to live in the Dakota, and I'd like to show my cousin around.' He blocked her tiny frame with his bulky figure and said softly, with a smile, 'Sure you did.' Ruthie became indignant. 'You think I'm crazy? Just let me show her where I used to live. I did live here.' Once again he blocked her path, this time without saying a word. I felt very sorry for Ruthie. The doorman clearly thought she was just another mad New Yorker and could not tell, from her casual clothes and sneakers, that she was still rich enough to own not one but several apartments in the historic building.

We walked on, but Ruthie was visibly shaken. 'Everybody in this city thinks that everybody else is nuts. But it never used to matter. Now they look at you as if you don't belong.'

We went back to her house for a last drink. She asked about

my thesis but immediately interrupted what I started telling her, clearly very bored: 'But what do you really want to write? I know you're a writer.' New York seemed to be tying together some invisible strands of my life.

Haifa: A Port of Return

We had planned to spend a year in Canada, but ended up staying for longer. Still, neither Shalom nor I felt that Ottawa could ever become a permanent home for us. Each time we left, for extended trips to Europe or Israel (a long spring in Oxford, a summer in Israel, visits to Hamburg) we felt less and less inclined to return. The Ottawa winter really is a hardship, and, for us, it became a deal-breaker. After four years we decided to go back to Israel.

Shalom had a teaching job at the University of Haifa, about an hour's drive north from Tel Aviv along the Mediterranean coast. The long, almost uninterrupted line of blue sea on one side of the highway made our first exploratory trip there seem like a holiday journey, and when we reached the city and began the winding ascent to its hilly beauty, just below green-forested mountains, the feeling of moving to another European-style country was almost complete. We were headed for Ahuza, an old neighbourhood on Mount Carmel with a view of the sea below and the mountains above; wide, leafy streets and whitish-grey stuccoed houses built up or down steep levels, surrounded by tall, old trees. We didn't spend much time choosing a place to rent because the very first apartment was like a dream come true: the back view from most of its first-floor windows was towards a real wadi, as far as the eye could see. A city street in front, a green valley behind – Haifa was shaping up to be some sort of paradise. I loved it at first sight.

The sense of home was so strong that it felt almost as if our lives – our joint lives – had only just begun for real, with new roots we all shared as a family. There was a surprising sense of permanence to this move, as if it could easily become our last.

Yaakov began attending a local kindergarten, where he immediately met Yanir, a very smart little boy whose family had just returned from America, and who would become his best friend. Their friendship grew into a life of exciting games and adventures, in both Hebrew and English (many years later, as teenagers, they continued in the same vein in London, when they devised a dangerous plan to secretly climb up on our roof in the middle of the night and hook up our television aerial to our neighbours' cable; they almost succeeded . . .).

As a child in Haifa, Yaakov had the freedom to roam around with complete autonomy. After school he and many of his classmates, who were also all neighbours, would get together and simply disappear until about six o'clock in the evening, or even later. They played adventure games in the wadi, they ran around the streets in our area, the playground, and one another's apartments – with the kind of independence that would soon become unthinkable. My oldest son's childhood reminded me of my own in Prague, where I too used to explore all the open spaces, streets, my friends' homes, without constant adult supervision.

Yaakov now spoke English to his father, Czech to me, Hebrew with his friends. He began answering me only in Hebrew, and started calling me *ima* (Hebrew for 'mother') instead of *mami*, the Czech word he had previously used.

Gradually I gave up the effort to keep up this second or third language in the house, and so it disappeared. English took over.

And it took over in my professional life too. My new job was teaching English to students at the Technion, the Haifa-based Israel Institute of Technology. The aim was to improve their ability to read and write about the subjects of their study – chemistry, physics, biology, architecture – and in the process I honed my own knowledge of the language that had, by now, become second nature to me. My colleagues were, almost without exception, native speakers of English. Sometimes I had to stop and think about the miraculous fact that I had by now made English my own to such an extent that I was actually teaching it, at a high academic level, to others.

Even more important than the teaching was my friendship with one of my colleagues, a very talented writer called Sally Rosenbluth. A native of New York, she spoke almost no Hebrew, despite having lived in the country for nearly twenty years. We often got together to write exam questions for our classes. Sally was brilliant at this – her exam papers were crystal clear, appropriately challenging and always interesting to read. She obsessed about the wording of each question and sentence (I still recall a test based on the various chemical properties of garlic!) as if they were literature, and indeed I suspected that for her these exams were a substitute and a diversion from the stories and novels she was constantly planning to write. When she did write fiction, it was burnished to perfection. Yet her obsession with endless improvement was a real obstacle, and a form of painful procrastination. I learned more about the process of writing – its highs, its lows, its pitfalls, dangers and personal costs – from Sally than from any other writer I have ever known. One of her early stories of Hitchcockian psychological suspense had been adopted for television, and her first novel, *A Feast of Ashes*, had been very well received. She had known this first taste of literary success, but for the rest of her life she struggled with returning to that moment and taking it further. Sally had a mysterious love in her life (I sometimes overheard their conversations on the phone – she never seemed happy when they spoke), but otherwise was very much alone. One day she told me they had ended it, after many years. Soon after, she said, 'I met him on the street by accident and he had nothing to say to me. As if we were complete strangers.' The sadness of her life was overwhelming, like a stark, unforgiving novel.

I loved Sally's library. She had every single important work of North American and British literature, from the famous to the obscure. Sally introduced me to the writing of Barbara Pym and Rose Macaulay, among many others. In so many ways, she was my best literary education. It was from working and spending many hours with her in long conversations about books and writers that I learned how to be precise, how to avoid ambiguity, how to edit others and especially myself, and how to live with the fear of being a failed writer. The latter was so strong in her that I was afraid it could actually become contagious.

In order to be able to teach I needed part-time help with childcare. I pinned a little ad on a noticeboard at the university, and the very same evening received a call from a pleasant-sounding middle-aged lady. Her name was Yael and she was no ordinary babysitter. A very beautiful, softly spoken woman, she was an artist and a poet. Her adult daughter had recently passed away after a tragic illness, and Yael decided to cope with her pain by looking after other people's children, to 're-enter life'. She told me this almost as soon as we sat down to talk on her first visit. When she saw our book-lined walls, she immediately felt she had come to the right place, she said.

Yael became my unwavering support in Haifa, adored by the boys. But beyond that we also became very close friends, often meeting in cafés for long conversations about life, and about art. She was one of the most sensitive, psychologically gifted people I have ever known. Every conversation with Yael was a profoundly satisfying treat, like watching a fascinating film and having a close-up encounter with one of the stars. Her elderly mother, who was still alive, was a true Russian diva, a former dancer and dance teacher who was extremely demanding and narcissistic, making Yael's life very difficult in an amusing (to an outside observer) sort of way. These were stories she regaled me with; yet over the years she slowly revealed that the real hardship in her life was her marriage. Her husband was a tough man. She only began believing in herself after the age of fifty. And then she blossomed, leading her own life against the stark relief of her married one.

Yael and her husband had met in the 1940s, when they were both young fighters in the Palmach, the elite fighting force of the underground Jewish army during the period of the British Mandate in Palestine. Behind the mundane daily lives I came in contact with in Haifa there were extreme experiences that could make the stuff of books.

The most powerful of them all was the story of Dov, a taciturn elderly neighbour who was able to repair absolutely anything. His entire arsenal of tools – his livelihood – collected over many years, was in the boot of his car. One day his car was broken into and all his tools stolen. He arrived, as always, exactly on time to fix a wardrobe in our bedroom, but could only apologise, with sadness rather than anger, that he had nothing to repair it with. Then, for the first time since we knew him, he broke down and began speaking about his earlier life. He was a widower and had a grown daughter, grand-children. But he had been married before, as a young man in Latvia. One day he returned from a business trip to find that his wife and baby daughter had been murdered, along with others, by the invading German Einsatzgruppen. Dov himself survived the war and later remarried. He thought about his first family every day.

Haifa was a city rich with stories and cultures, but without the religious extremism of Jerusalem or the urban swagger of Tel Aviv. It just felt normal. Aside from its limitations (it was too small to offer a wide enough variety of jobs), it was an almost perfect fit for me and my family, a real home. Our second son, Yonatan, was born there in 1986, almost exactly six years after Yaakov's birth in Canada.

When Yoni was almost a year old I asked my mother to come and stay with us for a while so that I could go away by myself. I sometimes did this when I felt I needed to recharge my batteries after a long period of mainly looking after the kids. This time I went to London for ten days, alone, during an uncharacteristically warm month of February. I had a semi-professional reason for being there too: I wanted to do a bit of research on a subject that intrigued me.

I stayed at the Penn Club, a Quaker guesthouse in Bloomsbury, and spent most of my days at the British Library. The old British Library was like a universal church of learning: all learnable knowledge printed in books and other reading materials under one roof and catalogued in such a mysteriously simple way that browsing the index cards in those long wooden drawers was an adventure in itself. One card led to another and suddenly one had enough information to present to the librarians, who, unfazed by any requests, took a quick look and then simply said to be back in two hours, or in three, or tomorrow – and the books and papers would be waiting. Then I would sit at one of the ancient desks, imagining that, say, Karl Marx or Virginia Woolf once did the same, and study the materials I had collected.

My search wasn't completely aimless. In the 1980s, while

still living in Canada, I had become obsessed with the idea that the eighth decade of the twentieth century had similar characteristics to the eighth decade of the previous century: the same sense of time ending or running out, bringing on social panic, fear, decadence, political unrest and violence, but also innovation and artistic liberation linked to a morbid feeling of being the doomed generation. I collected quotes supporting this view from Victorian novels and diaries, and thought about writing an essay on this subject. In London, I wanted to return to this forgotten project and decided to find some real evidence to support my theory among the riches in the British Library.

Browsing those card catalogues was not dissimilar to, a couple of decades later, searching the web. I began by looking for rather vague concepts such as 'life in 1880' or 'Victorian diaries', and these opened up an interconnected world of other, completely unexpected sources. Most were books but one was entitled 'scrapbook'. I had no idea what that meant but ordered it anyway. It turned out to be my best find – in fact, it far exceeded anything I could have imagined discovering in my quest to understand what it felt like to be living in the 1880s.

The scrapbook was exactly that – an 'ordinary' woman's collection of newspaper clippings and other items relating to the execution of a young servant girl in Bury St Edmunds for the murder of her master. The clippings reflected the general public's fascination with this case. There was an air of mystery about the girl, and about the sexual nature of the detailed description of her hanging. I became so obsessed with this tale that I continued my research in another section of the library, where I had access to any number of actual newspapers from the period. The case was covered extensively, and other writings on the subject shed quite a bit of light on the conditions under which young girls from villages and remote areas were brought in as servants and were often abused in their places of work. I imagined a Victorian story of love and cruelty behind those newspaper headlines, and an era so charged with suppressed eroticism that a young girl's violent death became a titillating experience for the voyeuristic public. Death and orgasm.

About ten years later, one of the stories in my debut collection *Foreign Brides* ('Michael Farmer's Baby') would be built on my obsession with that young Victorian murderess.

I discussed all these ideas and impressions with a fascinating man I met at the Penn Club. Unlike me, a transient visitor, Ruan actually lived and worked there. Adjacent to his bedroom was another room he used as an office for his work as a psychoanalyst. I had noticed him earlier, at breakfast: a silver-haired, very good-looking elderly man (almost a Sean Connery lookalike), walking with a cane but trying not to appear to be leaning on it. He was very lively when engaged in conversation, and very quiet and thoughtful when engrossed in his books. In fact, he was almost always reading. One morning as he passed me by the door to the dining room he complimented me on my black miniskirt, green tights with black roses and black boots. He specifically commented on the combination, describing the effect it had on him. We both laughed heartily during this exchange, and I, in particular, received a reprimand from a little old English lady, also a permanent resident: 'Foreigners are always too loud,' she said. This made me laugh even harder, but Ruan became angry and accused her of being 'an objectionable racist and an idiot'.

After this episode Ruan and I always had breakfast together; and for the remainder of my stay he never again brought a book with him as we always sat together and talked and laughed. He was originally from Cornwall, a fascinating, extremely well-read man with radical views and a brilliant sense of humour. He was an anarchist and even dressed in anarchist colours, black and red. I told him about my research and my findings, and this led to an extended analysis of our times, compared to the historical period I had become immersed in. Ruan was very interested in the case of the young murderess; we had endless conversations about the psychological and sexual aspects of the story. He had three adult sons, and one evening I was invited to a very enjoyable family dinner with all of them. My lifelong friendship with Ruan was born and sealed.

We remained in touch for many years. His letters, carefully typed on his old typewriter with some handwritten corrections, were a live continuation of our conversations, and I would reread them many times. We recommended books to each other, he commented on the dire state of Thatcher's England and the stupidity of the voting public. He complained about the sounds of lovemaking emanating from the room next door to his, which was occupied by a young red-headed American woman. Some years ago, he wrote, he would have found this arousing, but now, in old age, 'it is merely a nuisance'. When I sent him a letter detailing my family's big news – our move to America, and the birth of my daughter there – he replied: 'But what of your own dreams and aspirations?'

I visited London once or twice in the following years. Each time Ruan treated me to an elegant dinner, and with each visit I saw that it was getting harder for him to move around. He was in a great deal of pain, but his spirit was as sparkling as ever, and he still wore his red anarchist socks.

Years later, I wrote to tell him that we would be moving to London from New York, and how excited I was to be able to see him more often. But by the time we settled there Ruan had passed away. His sons returned my letters to me, which he had kept carefully collected, like all his correspondence. On the envelopes I had addressed to him he had written 'Replied', along with the appropriate date.

This short trip to London from Haifa cemented something in me – something new, and something old. My old love of London and of English literature suddenly became rooted in a real connection with the city. And the new thing – maybe not exactly new, but rather renewed – was a sense of freedom: I could still accomplish everything I had always planned.

Back in Haifa I felt so at home in the multilayered city that I rediscovered my love of antiques. My favourite pastime was browsing antique shops in different parts of town. The best turned out to be just a few bus stops from where I lived, a sort of meeting point for an odd assortment of old friends who sat around with the shop owner drinking coffee, playing backgammon and talking about their respective life stories. I spent hours there asking about their antiques and considering purchases. The old furniture on display was from the time of the British Mandate, and had been imported to Palestine from Britain and other European countries. I brought some of this history into my own home – a turn-of-the-century dining table and chairs, a Victorian cabinet, a few smaller items ... The antique-shop owner, sensing my need, sold them to me for far less than the asking price.

It was my way of expressing my belief that we were, finally, living in a permanent home. Having my own antiques reminded me of the ones my family had left behind in Prague. I had never felt like buying them myself – until now, in Haifa. Dining with Shalom and our children at the elegant mahog-any table while looking out at the wild wadi below felt good: Europe (specifically England) meeting the Middle East under my own (albeit rented) roof.

Yet within a year of setting up this home with an air of

permanence we would be on the move again – for more or less the same reasons as the last time we left Israel. We worked almost five jobs between the two of us (full time and part time) and yet we were not really managing financially. Shalom had become affiliated with linguistic research at IBM (where I also spent a summer developing a dictionary for use in machine translation), and received a serious offer from a major IBM research centre in Westchester, New York. We discussed it – rather briefly – and agreed that we had to accept.

We brought most of our things to America as IBM were paying for the move, but not my beloved antiques. I sold some and gave the dining set to my best friend Orly as she moved into our apartment with her boyfriend. She has kept the antiques to this day, and still lives in the city where I tried but failed to make a permanent home for our children. It was a very near miss.

Tornado in Suburbia

IBM sent a dark limousine to pick us up from the airport when we landed at New York's John F. Kennedy airport. We were driven to a hotel in Westchester, and the very next day found ourselves in the capable hands of a real estate agent determined to find us a rental home in one of the local suburbs 'with the best schools'. I was still so naive about American discourse that I did not understand her underlying point of reference. She was speaking about nothing less than a modern-day segregation system: by 'good schools' she meant 'predominantly white'. She showed us houses for rent in whimsically named places like Valhalla, Pleasantville, Thornwood, Hawthorne, Armonk, Chappaqua. The houses we viewed were very large and made of wood – a novelty for my European eyes – and their gardens had no fences. Front doors were left unlocked and the distances between the houses were so large I couldn't really imagine ever knowing my neighbours. Almost all were surrounded by so many beautiful trees that one's privacy was complete.

We chose a house in Valhalla, at the end of a very long, steep drive. The house itself was not especially big, but its surrounding plot was impressive. The boys again had their own adventure ground, but this time, on private land.

Yaakov now became a suburban American schoolboy, travelling on a yellow school bus that stopped for him at the top of our drive. He had to undergo a quick linguistic transformation from Hebrew into English. His first, very young teacher, Miss Frank, understood his predicament and suggested that he keep a private journal. This really helped him; he felt safe in the world of his own thoughts and observations, using language to overcome the challenge of having to redefine himself in a new environment. He began writing the journal in Hebrew, gradually switching into English, which, at first, he could speak but not write. This journal is a perfect addition to our collection of family diaries, starting with the other bilingual one, in Russian and Czech, written in Prague. Yaakov's journal reads like a 1990s version of the adventures of Tom Sawyer and Huckleberry Finn: he is always getting in trouble with his teachers (or parents) for one thing or another, or into fights with his best friends (but never for long); there is a girl called Denise whom he likes or everyone else thinks he does (and she seems to really like him). He writes that he will resolve a mysterious disappearance of his poster 'with all the clues I have right here in this journal'. Every trip to New York City is recorded and illustrated.

His new Westchester friends were called Jimmy (he always spelled it 'Gimmie' in his journal), Pat and Sal (Salvatore). Most of his classmates had Italian surnames; their immigrant families had lived in Brooklyn before they moved to Westchester, many were from generations of Italian stonemasons. One afternoon Yaakov and Jimmy disappeared for hours. They had been playing in our back yard, but after a while their silence became noticeable. We began a fruitless and very worrying search along with Jimmy's parents. Several hours later the boys returned, smiling triumphantly: they had decided to walk for an hour and a half each way along local waterways and through the piping system, all the way to the Kensico Dam, a massive reservoir with spectacular stone structures, surrounded by immense woodland. Secretly I was pleased that he had done this outrageous thing: my oldest son's adventurous childhood had remained intact, despite our move to American suburbia.

In Norse mythology Valhalla is the resting place for those who die in battle. Our oddly named suburb also felt like a beautiful cemetery to me: houses enclosed by trees and vast lawns, not a soul walking down the quiet streets, not a neighbour in sight. They all seemed to be hidden in or behind their homes, built at enough distance from one another to guarantee complete privacy. American suburbia was a lonely place, I thought – not by accident, but by design.

I was already pregnant with my third child when we settled into our rented house. I kept this fact hidden when I applied for a full-time editorial job at a legal publishing company in Dobbs Ferry, a very pretty small town on the Hudson River, a thirty-minute bus ride away (I did not drive). This first American job felt like a move in the right direction. I especially liked the commute, as it got me away from the deadly quiet of my life in Valhalla. I wanted to see people – commuters, colleagues, strangers ... The company itself was a very old-fashioned family-owned but successful business. I was amused by the weekly yellow pay cheques hand-delivered to each employee in small envelopes.

Every morning a smiling middle-aged couple got on the same bus, sat down as close to the driver's seat as possible and locked their bodies in a tight embrace and a kiss, not coming up for air until they got off the bus about ten minutes later. At first, it was awkward to watch, but after a while I became used to seeing them, and when, once or twice, they didn't appear I missed their passionate yet somehow childlike presence.

Each lunch hour I left the office and went to a nearby Jewish deli for a hearty meal, always including chicken soup. My baby daughter was very well nourished *in utero*, despite my full-time work routine.

My mother arrived from Hamburg shortly before I was due to give birth, as she did for each of my children: in Canada, in Israel and now in America. On the April morning I went into labour it snowed, suddenly. By the end of the day, when my daughter Shira was born, the snow had melted completely and the sun was bright and warm. Two seasons in one day, like a celebration.

I have a photo I took from the kitchen window, of my mother sitting outside on a bench next to our wooden garden table. The baby is asleep in a blue pram; my mother is bundled up in a warm brown coat, bent over her notebook. She is writing. This is how she always wrote: in bits and pieces, short, urgent bursts of impressions and ideas she needed to record. I wish I could zoom in on this photo and read her note. What was she thinking about, how did she see this new place of ours, yet another move, yet another major, transatlantic change of location? Did she find it strange – or, rather, how strange did she find it? I was now a million conceptual miles away from any environment she was familiar with. Although, when she came home from the supermarket one day, she said that despite her basic English the staff made her feel less foreign than sales people in German shops after more than twenty years of living there. She was really aware that in this country anyone could feel American, regardless of accent or language proficiency or religion. It made me wonder: what if my parents had chosen to emigrate to the States rather than Germany when we left Prague – as so many other Czech émigrés had done at the time? Would we, as a family, have become easily integrated, and would I have had a simpler, more direct route to a new language and identity? Perhaps my mother was writing in her notebook about the wonder of having a new American-born granddaughter.

A few months after her visit my father-in-law came to stay with us for a while. On a very hot summer afternoon, while my husband was at work, the boys were running in and out of the house and Ben and I were having tea in the kitchen. I stepped out for a moment to check on my laundry, and felt a sudden, very drastic drop in temperature. At the same moment the blue sky turned black and I heard a sound almost like a train going past, coming from somewhere above. This sound instantly called up the memory of reading about a tornado in *The Wizard of Oz* – a very long time ago, in Russian. Westchester is not exactly tornado country, and no severe weather had been predicted. It just happened. Yaakov was about to go out the door when, based on pure instinct, I pulled him back inside. The very next instant one of the tallest fir trees in our back yard was lifted by its roots and dropped on the exact spot where Yaakov had been headed.

The rattling-train noise and darkened skies continued for another minute, during which we huddled in the basement. The kids' toys, a garden chair and a broom were flying through the air; through a glass door, I saw a neighbour's car briefly go up and then land again, as if it had been lifted by invisible giant hands. The most frightening sight was of the huge fir trees that were being plucked by the tornado and dropped like twigs.

When it was over we found an incredible scene outside. Our entire driveway was covered with uprooted trees, and a few had also fallen on the roof. The tornado had spared every house in our street except ours, and a neighbour's yard just around the corner. The devastation was enormous, but so was our feeling of relief: it had been a very narrow escape. Elsewhere in Westchester a woman was killed when a tree fell on her car. (Shalom, in his office only a few miles away, could not believe this had happened; it was a very localised storm.)

As we stood outside inspecting the damage, our previously invisible neighbours began arriving in large numbers. In complete silence they started clearing the driveway, breaking, cutting and moving the fallen trees and debris, and did not leave until some order had been restored and they were sure we were OK. I didn't call them – in fact, I didn't know any of them; they just came, and helped, and then disappeared again, like an army of angels. They seemed to know us, somehow, without much contact. Valhalla was a more complex suburb than I had imagined: our neighbours had quietly shown that in emergencies one was not alone there.

The tornado left a deep impression on me. Nature could kill: selectively, suddenly, for no reason whatsoever. I associate this fear with living in the faux security and comfort of an affluent New York suburb. Years later the tornado found its way into the only story in *Foreign Brides* that deals specifically with being an émigré. I called it 'Black Train'.

Pleasantville

Towards the end of our first year in Westchester County, we decided to take the plunge and settle into a home of our own. It felt surreal, but it was true: we were house-hunting in America.

Now that I knew the nature of places like Valhalla, I was determined to avoid their depressive isolation. There were several suburbs near by that were more like small towns, with everything within walking distance – shops, schools, parks, the train station. We found a lovely split-level house in Pleasantville, at the end of a cul-de-sac and surrounded by a garden. Its most beautiful feature was a brook running through the property. The boys and their friends would hold on to a long tree branch to swing over it. Another proper swing was suspended from an oak tree near the front of the house.

My children's Westchester childhood was now a complete paradise. Shalom's job appeared to be solid. But I was, once again, without a professional anchor, aside from some freelance editing.

Nevertheless I was happy, and ready to return to my old dreams. It was time. I joined an urban writers' colony in New

York City called the Writers Room. Once I became a member I was able to go there and write at any time of the day or night. Most of the writers were actually living in the city, some even around the corner in the Village. But they too needed a small space of their own to work on their books. For me, the commute from Westchester to Manhattan became a lifeline to the kind of place I had always preferred: noise, people, the buzz of activity that did not directly involve me but made me want to develop my thoughts into something others may want to read. The Writers Room was an oasis of silence in the midst of city noise – in New York! I could hardly believe my utterly unexpected luck. My house was so close to the city where I was most excited to find myself writing.

But as I began working on some stories and ideas for a novel I felt a surprising need to first pay my final dues to the two languages, and countries, I had left behind by collecting and editing the writing of others. A small independent publisher, Catbird Press, liked my idea for two anthologies.

In 1994, I edited *Jewish Voices, German Words*, an anthology of fiction and essays by young Jewish authors who had been raised in post-war Germany and Austria. (One of the contributors was my brother, who had by then just published his first book of stories, *Wenn ich einmal reich und tot bin* (*One Day When I'm Rich and Dead*).

Then, to collect material for my Czech anthology, I travelled to Prague in 1996, for the first time since I left, in order to properly research and reconnect with the new Czech literary scene. My aim was to find current Czech writing for translation into English – which I would edit. I was very curious to find out what had happened to Czech literature during my exile.

In *The Prague Orgy*, the epilogue to his Zuckerman trilogy, Philip Roth paints a picture of Czech life during what turned out to be the interregnum between two revolutions – the

Prague Spring of 1968 and the Velvet Revolution in November 1989. Roth's narrator, the American Jewish author Nathan Zuckerman, is fascinated by the existence of a rich literary culture under siege, where major authors are silenced by the regime and forced to survive on menial jobs: 'I imagine Styron washing glasses in a Penn Station barroom, Susan Sontag wrapping buns at a Broadway bakery, Gore Vidal bicycling salamis to school lunchrooms in Queens – I look at the filthy floor and see myself sweeping it.' I was excited by Roth's juxtaposition of the two literary worlds I felt close to.

The new Prague I saw in the 1990s was, similarly, a city of surreal juxtapositions; in the process of both clinging to its pre-invasion cultural past and embracing whatever the new freedom would bring – both good and bad. I walked down the once so familiar streets and found them as estranged from my memories as the streets in my émigré dreams. I noticed that nightclubs and bars with strange names had sprung up in otherwise completely residential buildings, random foreign bodies in tune with the new spirit of laissez-faire. This was why I gave my second anthology a rather odd title: *Daylight in Nightclub Inferno: Czech Fiction from the Post-Kundera Generation.*

I looked for writers whose work had begun to emerge after the Velvet Revolution. Unlike my German anthology, this one was a personal quest. One of the authors placed her fiction in my old neighbourhood, in the streets around the church that had been the dominant landmark of my childhood. Was I trying to compensate for a fraction of my own loss? I knew that, had I stayed in Prague, I would have wanted to be one of the authors included in this anthology, not its editor.

Both anthologies helped me close the chapter of my life where, as a writer, I was still tapping in the dark. I thought of it as pre-writing: a process of growing into my chosen language (English), and my home (New York). As I returned to writing, attempting my first collection of stories, I sometimes wondered: would my first book define and identify me as an American writer?

But, as always, things did not go according to plan. Within four years the situation at the IBM research centre where my husband was working changed dramatically – for the worse. Along with many of his colleagues, Shalom found himself in a very precarious situation and had to think of alternatives. After a period of job interviews he ended up with two options: another software research company, based in Boston, or a return to academia at the University of London's School of Oriental and African Studies. Together we chose London. To get back to Europe – to be geographically closer to both our sets of parents – seemed like a very good idea.

Suddenly, London

Our family was now an amalgam of our joint wanderings. The boys had already been uprooted several times; for Shira, it would be her first. My stepdaughter also chose London for her university studies, and she would end up living there permanently, in several years' time. The move to London would turn out to be our last. It was, surprisingly, like coming home.

Ironically, the deal for the house I chose for us almost fell through because of a beautiful old tree outside its fence; its roots had grown so strong and deep they were undermining the foundations. The tree had to be cut down. De-rooted, this house became our solid home. The children would grow up there, leave on their own personal journeys, and always return. When we moved in the garden was so overgrown with knee-deep weeds that a passionate gardener friend felt forced to declare 'Nothing good will ever grow here.' He was wrong: from year to year – and despite our successive dogs' attempts to subvert our efforts – we cultivated our private corner of London land until it gave us flowering beauty, soft grass, fruit-bearing pear and apple trees, and even a corner of fragrant mint and rosemary. I remembered a letter my grandmother wrote in the year before she died, describing in detail her plans for sowing all sorts of berry plants in the garden of their small dacha near Moscow – in preparation for our next visit, which never happened ... I copied the list of all the varieties of berries she mentions and planted them in memory of my grandmother. I think she would have liked the idea – her berries in London! – and maybe even found it funny. The strawberries, blackberries and raspberries are English enough, but the blackcurrants make me think of another garden and another era: my grandparents' in Russia, living on the brink of fateful disasters but always with joy.

I made two fortuitous yet unrelated professional discoveries. By assisting, for a few months, an eminent literary scout I discovered a delightful profession I never knew existed. The work seemed tailor-made to some of my literary whims and guilty pleasures: it basically consisted of reading novels in various languages and getting paid for it. The second happy accident was answering an ad for the editorship of a magazine called the *Jewish Quarterly*. I had never heard of it, but editing a literary magazine was something I had played at since my childhood, and here was a chance to do it for real.

This part-time job completely took over my life for about four years. I tried to create a kind of Jewish *New Yorker*, on a tiny budget. It was not an easy time, but it was a very exciting one: working with leading journalists, historians, critics, novelists, poets and playwrights from around the world was a dream come true. Unfortunately the financial constraints became too severe for me to continue, but the thrilling taste of editorial involvement with interesting authors will stay with me for ever. After spending a few years 'just writing' – fiction, investigative journalism – I found that I missed working with writers on their books. So I returned to editorial work, and to scouting, this time for my own publishing clients in various countries. It turned out to be the best way of making sense of my own linguistic trajectory: international book fairs, especially Frankfurt, make me feel like a happy chameleon, darting here and there between languages and cultures and feeling at home with so many different ones. My umbrella of foreignness is not even remotely a stigma, or a complicated fact. On the contrary: otherness and individuality are literature's heartbeat.

London turned out to be the place where I could finally return to my old idea of stories about women who follow their husbands to countries that are not their own. This first book was set all over the world – Germany, Russia, Prague, Israel, New York, Beirut, London … But my second, *The Nose*, was in many ways a novel about my new home town. And not just the city we know, but also the hidden London, with its abandoned Tube stations, ghosts of a shadowy past. Perhaps I already sensed something about my own hidden, but unforgotten, history.

'With love, Pa'

I had been settled in London for almost ten years when the phone call from Moscow dramatically disturbed my inner equilibrium. As much as I tried to pretend that its revelation would make no real difference to my life, it most certainly did. It caused a mixture of confusion and excitement, and, over time, raised many questions.

My first instinct was to call Hans Keilson, the German Jewish writer and psychiatrist who had fled Nazi Germany for Holland in the 1930s. In his nineties now, he was a wise and very funny man who had a uniquely sensitive insight into every aspect of the human condition. I had sought his expertise two years earlier, when I was writing an investigative piece for *Granta* magazine about Binjamin Wilkomirski, the author of *Fragments*, which turned out to be a fake account of a Holocaust childhood by a Swiss man named Bruno Dössekker. Dr Keilson had worked closely with child Holocaust survivors in the Netherlands, and helped me understand their psychology. (It was also during this time that I realised he was a wonderful but forgotten novelist, and began bringing his work to the attention of publishers around the world. Eventually, after another decade, this led to a triumph for him: Farrar, Straus and Giroux published two of his early works to great critical acclaim, and the author's great joy and disbelief: he was by now over a hundred years old, and suddenly in print again.)

I rang Hans Keilson and told him what had happened; as far as I could tell, if the Russian relative had not discovered me I would never have known who I really was. So I asked him: how should I respond to what my parents had done?

His reply surprised me. He said, 'Your parents are wonderful, wonderful people. They did the right thing by not telling you. They wanted your life to be simple and full of love. And they succeeded. You need to thank them.'

Although I was not quite ready to leave it at that – not yet – this insight really helped me. I could accept the fact that my parents were very young when they decided to create a family without my biological father's presence in my life. And now that I knew Joseph existed I couldn't wait to meet him. 'I would like to be a fly on the wall during that meeting,' my father said when I told him I would see Joseph in New York. It was the only time he would ever refer to him, to his actual physical existence, so directly.

I flew to New York from London about a week after V's phone call, on a journalism assignment. Joseph drove in from New Jersey to see me at my Manhattan hotel. After a couple of nervous calls about parking facilities he finally knocked on my door. When I opened it I saw a tall, very blue-eyed older man who did not look unfamiliar. He came bearing gifts: butterfly fridge magnets, Venetian glass figurines, a bottle of expensive cognac. He explained each present: the colourful butterflies were to amuse my children; the two figurines – one big, one smaller – represented him and me, 'finally reunited'; and the cognac was for us to open and drink 'in memory of your grandfather, who loved it'. Joseph revered my maternal grandfather and had very fond memories of playing cards and drinking quality alcohol with him. 'Your grandmother Zelda, on the other hand, really disliked me, and couldn't hide her feelings.'

Our conversation was in Russian, as it had been on the phone when he first rang me. He still had that very slight stutter, which made him sound shy.

'Ask me anything you want,' he said with a warm smile. 'Anything you want to know about the past – I will answer.'

This was tender music to my ears. At that moment all I really needed to hear was his way of telling the story of my birth, his way of completing the missing pieces of the puzzle, his voice telling me what it meant to him to have lost me. In truth, I wanted to feel more than I wanted to know, to test my emotions for this man who was a stranger yet also – well, not a stranger at all. In this he didn't disappoint. He spoke about his feelings for me as a baby, of how he trusted my mother to take good care of me and respected her decision to take me to Prague with her new husband, and how he always honoured his promise to stay out of the picture so as not to complicate matters. I was placated: my absence from his life had caused pain but not forgetting. He had always kept me in his heart, he said, and thought of me often. When he came across my mother's published photo of me (quite by accident, he said – but I wondered: perhaps not quite by accident?), in which I am sitting laughing on a park bench, my new father fast asleep on my shoulder, he was delighted, and showed the picture to everyone with pride. This was a photo my mother had submitted to a competition entitled Photographers for Peace, demonstrating that in peace times, a father can be blissfully asleep while his daughter plays. She had won a prize.

He had come alone. He did not invite me to his home. Nor did he explain (beyond reiterating the commitment he had made to my mother) why he had made no effort to find me in all those years. Later I found out that he was very angry at the relative who contacted me. This made no sense to me: if he was really so pleased to see me, why would he be mad at the man who made it happen? Eventually, this relative would also tell me that it was my paternal grandmother who had made him promise that he would look for me. She thought it was wrong of her son to allow me to disappear from his – and their family's – life. And yet, according to my mother, my paternal grandparents never tried to contact her parents in Moscow to enquire about me, or to ask to see me when I visited from Prague – or even before I left.

I met Joseph on a number of occasions during my subsequent trips to New York. Each time – even during my first one – he phoned me daily at my hotel, asking in a very worried tone of voice whether I was safe. He seemed to be genuinely concerned. Yet I sensed such neurotic overprotectiveness in his anxiety that I thought, with relief, how lucky I was to have been raised without it.

We corresponded by email quite often, a few sentences here and there, about his family, about mine. He sent me photos he had taken (he was an amateur photographer, especially interested in colourful, abstract, phantasmagoric fractals), photos of himself at a shooting range, a newspaper article about an actress whom he thought looked like my mother when he knew her (dark hair, sparkling eyes, strong eyebrows). He spoke and wrote very kindly about my parents, sent them his warmest regards and expressed his gratitude for how well they had raised me. He read and enjoyed my books, and commented on them. He read them in the original English and this made me sad – sad for my father, who doesn't speak or read English, and who could only ever read my writing in German translation. It was indescribably ironic to me that Joseph shared my main language – English, the language in which I was a writer, and which dominated my personal domain too. But when we met we always spoke Russian. When we talked about books we discovered we had similar tastes, but also that we each wanted to plug some gaps in the other's reading. I gave him *Good as Gold* by Joseph Heller; he undertook to send me the entire Nero Wolfe series by Rex Stout, book after book. A new volume arrived every few weeks, until I had at least a dozen of them. I devoured them all and became addicted to the world of the genius, eccentric New York immigrant detective and his sexy, sarcastic sidekick Archie Goodwin. In one or two of the paperbacks was written, in a neat hand, 'With love, Pa.'

Joseph also corresponded, occasionally, with my children, especially Yaakov and Shira. I had told them about his existence shortly after I found out myself, though each one separately. Yaakov was somewhat interested yet quite philosophical about it; he saw it as a new fact in my life, not his. I took Shira to a shopping mall for the occasion, and told her, carefully, while we were having lunch in a restaurant. I tried to explain the whole story without shocking her, and indeed she didn't seem shocked at all. In fact, like me, she was rather intrigued. Her emails with Joseph were funny; he wrote her little poems about Zak, our dog, and other amusing notes. He seemed to be very aware of each of my children's personalities and talents. Yet he never tried to come to London and actually meet them, or invite them to America. He and his family had been based in New Jersey since the mid-1970s, and his son was now living in Brooklyn; we could all have easily been in touch when we lived in Westchester – so close. Perhaps our paths did cross accidentally; we would have had no idea.

In fact, a very eerie coincidence did occur. His son, my half-brother Y, happened to be booked on the same flight as me, on my return journey after the first meeting with Joseph.

We had made our respective bookings long before. We could have been random fellow passengers, strangers – yet we were actually brother and sister, and ended up sitting next to each other. Y was angry at his father for not telling him he had a sister: 'I always thought I was an only child, and really wanted a sibling. I wish I had known I had an older sister.' And my brother Maxim, it later turned out, had also felt betrayed by our parents' secret, as its revelation changed our family's history for him too. So I was not the only person who was affected by their silence. Secrets always create echoes.

Yoni was the only one of my children who resisted the idea of having 'another grandfather' and felt that this new father figure in my life was a betrayal of his own loyalty to my father. He has never really got over the disappointing fact that all the qualities he so admired and identified with in my father – from his cool dress sense to his strong personality and generous nature – were not, as it now turned out, a part of his own genetic inheritance. Regardless of my children's individual responses to Joseph, I was relieved to just tell them the truth, without burdening them, and myself, with having something to hide. And I thought that my parents could easily have done the same with me. Why on earth hadn't they, and how could they have lived with such a huge untruth for so long? Despite Hans Keilson's wise interpretation of their secrecy as an act of kindness, I never stopped wishing the truth had been revealed to me by my parents themselves, rather than a stranger. That too would have been an act of love, albeit a difficult one after all those years.

Shalom was very interested in my story at first, and supportive of my need to figure out this new branch of my family tree. But as I began learning more and more about it, and tried to share with him what I knew, he said I had developed an obsession, and refused to indulge it. At some point I stopped, or tried to. But it was difficult not to share it all with him.

Joseph claimed to be completely open with me and anxious to satisfy my curiosity on any subject, yet he never told me that by finding him I also found a very large extended family. His father had been one of about a dozen siblings; except for him, and a brother and two sisters who had never left Russia when the family emigrated in 1914, all had lived full lives in the United States, and their children and grandchildren were in active, affectionate contact with one another. Eventually, I began this journey all by myself.

The Other Side

Soon after his first phone call, V sent me an email in quite convoluted English explaining my family history. His basic facts were not wrong: names and dates of birth of my biological father, his parents and sister; my grandfather's undercover work; the dates of their moves. He tried to write a little genealogical summary for me, to help me orient myself in the new family I was about to become acquainted with. He himself had lost all his family, and he wanted his daughter V to know hers. 'You are her first cousin. It's an important tie.' He also explained that it had been, in fact, one of my mother's relatives in Moscow, an academic he knew through work, who had pointed him in the right direction. Eventually he rang my mother in Hamburg and asked for my number in London. She gave it to him, without asking why. Perhaps, after all those years of hiding her big secret, she needed to be relieved of it.

At first I took the information he had given me for granted, as an accurate summary. But over time, especially when Joseph pointed out some discrepancies, as well as the fact that V was not exactly a reliable narrator of events he had not himself witnessed, I decided to conduct my own research. Investigative journalism – especially into stories based on interesting deceit – had been my favourite kind of writing for some time; to apply my curiosity to my own family history would be doubly exciting.

An internet check of my grandfather's name (Leon Minster) quickly led to information in the National Archives in London about his intelligence work in Shanghai in 1934, and then, step by step, detail after detail, the life of the Minster family emerged as a result of my systematic searching on various online genealogy tools, and in all available literature and archives – including, very helpfully, the FBI archives, obtainable under the Freedom of Information Act.

I suddenly found myself not only knowing my biological father's identity, but also first sketching, then colouring in, every inch and detail of his – and therefore my – family history. And the history led, very quickly, to the present. History is the hidden map of who, where and how we are today. Within a few days of discovering my grandfather's name on the front page of a Connecticut newspaper from August 1951 I had learned the married name of one of his many sisters. Other articles mentioned the name of her son, and her other sisters. Various local community events were announced and described, and I was beginning to see a picture of my great-aunts' and a great-uncle's lives over many decades. Even my great-grandfather was mentioned in connection with a synagogue service. One by one the hidden family began to emerge from the shadows of the distant past, morphing into people whose names were in telephone directories. I located one relative, who led me to others. Many others. A flurry of emails and telephone calls later, I suddenly found myself warmly welcomed into a large family I had never known existed. Politely curious about the circumstances of my birth and parentage, my new cousins – twice removed, or more, or less – opened up a whole new world to me. The fascinating thing was that it brought me right back to the original old world we had all come from: Russia and the Ukraine.

My father Joseph was born not in Russia but in Brooklyn, New York. I could trace his parents' registered presence there until the mid-1930s. Every US census until 1930 provided me with relevant information about both my grandparents and their families. I found their exact addresses, professions, the names of their neighbours ... The fact that they owned a radio. The languages they spoke, read and wrote: English, Russian, Yiddish. Each time a document yielded an address I immediately searched for it on Google Maps and Google Street View, to check if that particular house was still standing. In many cases the Brooklyn buildings looked old enough to have been there in the 1930s; others had been replaced by car parks. The virtual reality of Street View was not an abstraction for me, but a tool enabling me to really see, with my own eyes, the continuity of my ancestors' actual physical timeline: they lived here, then here, then here, then here ...

While poring over my new archives, I couldn't resist the urge to virtually travel from my desk in London not only to these New York addresses I didn't know, but also to all my own, real homes. First in Moscow, then in Prague. Then in Hamburg, followed by Tel Aviv and Haifa. In Ottawa and in Westchester. Every house I have ever lived in continued to exist after I moved on, and now I was able to see it: this window, that balcony, this door and that view ... Street View triggered concrete memories that were suddenly no longer dreamlike, but could be checked and verified against the image on my computer screen. The narrative reconstruction of my life was no longer an exercise in playing with notions of time and place: it was rooted in real places, linked to real time. The Google-photographed clouds in the sky above my school in Ostrovní Street were soothingly familiar, as if they had remained stationary, unmoved by winds, weather and time, since my last days in Prague.

I became a little intoxicated with this freedom to roam the past and the present simultaneously. I located Selidovo, the tiny Ukrainian village that was the home of the Minster family for many mostly happy years before my paternal great-grandparents left for America in 1914. I found many photographs linked to the internet map: someone had literally walked from one end of the village to another and captured, then posted, the views in numerous detailed images. I sensed its stillness, the quiet beauty of its fields and trees and river, and saw one or two dilapidated buildings that seemed to fit the description I had read in family lore of the type of house my great-grandfather owned ('a grey three-room, one-storey masonry structure'). One of my great-aunts, Gertrude, had written short but detailed narratives in dreamy, literary prose about growing up in Selidovka. They were precise memories, sweetened by time and distance, of moments and events dating back to the beginning of the twentieth century: her two older sisters' large weddings, with the entire village, Jews and Gentiles, in attendance; her father physically throwing out a paedophile Hebrew-school teacher; her mother's kitchen and pantry, overflowing with colourful meats, grains, fruits, vegetables, herring, pickles, eggs – all fresh. Another great-aunt, Vera, had recounted her own memories to a grandson, Jonathan, who turned their conversations into an essay written in the 1980s, combining oral history with historical research to impressive effect. Apparently unaware of the seismic political changes in her native Russia in the early years of the twentieth century, Vera's mind retained fairy-tale cameos of her young self in a vanished time and place. Among the fragrant white-blossoming acacia trees outside the family home, and in a neighbouring cherry orchard, she would lose herself in reverie while reading and memorising Pushkin's poetry, reluctant to go back inside when called by her mother. She told of a family sleigh ride, of the house always full of children eating, laughing, singing, playing the guitar. She painted a detailed portrait of the family, and especially her imposing father Samuel David – 'part father, part folk hero':

> He looked very striking: blue eyes, curly, black hair, a red beard and rosy cheeks. His Yiddish was mixed with Hebrew, and with the peasants he spoke only Ukrainian. He had a beautiful friendly smile that captured everyone's attention. And a very trusting face. If you met him once, you trusted him and he trusted you. And he used to be cheated out of his last nickel over and over and over again. My mother was very reserved. But for father a mensch is a mensch, a man is a man, you can always talk to a man. He was a leader of the community. He wasn't educated like some, he wasn't a Hebrew teacher. But he was a born leader and a born independent thinker and I and my brothers, too, we all adored him.

She described the inside of the house in such detail, room by room, corner to corner, that a photographically accurate depiction could easily be made of it by someone with the ability to draw by ear, in the manner of a police artist creating a facial composite. In fact, Vera's descriptions could be used to draw not only the house but also its inhabitants – my great-grandparents and their fourteen children, one of whom was my paternal grandfather. In America he was called Leon; in the Soviet Union, Grigori; but in the Tsarist Russia of his childhood his given name was Israel. I learned this only from the passenger lists I found for the family's journey to America in July 1914, on a ship called, ironically, the *Czar*. I don't know what the family called him at home in Selidovka because he hardly appears in Vera's account, except when she refers to her brothers collectively as 'the boys'. In fact, it is almost as if he had been erased from the family record – or had done so himself. And yet, for me, Leon's life is the key to my own beginnings.

Based on this written account of my relatives' transmitted memories, and my own exchanges with newly discovered American relatives, I now have an almost seamless portrait of the family I never met, and from whose history I had been excised. Jewish law is wise to postulate that Jewishness is transmitted via the mother; the reasoning is that it is never certain who the father is. But in my case Jewishness was not in question: both my fathers were fully Jewish and, if one looked far enough, their roots were not even that dissimilar or geographically far removed.

The sentimentalised East European Jewish roots kitsch is a commercialised blend, in various art forms, of *Fiddler on the Roof* and Chagall-style tableaux, a sepia view of life in pre-revolutionary Russia as a set of idyllic scenes depicting Jews as confined and reduced to an endlessly mournful existence punctuated by Yiddish song and dance. Despite living in restricted areas and by limited means as a resented and often mortally persecuted minority, the life of East European Jewry was far from sad, bland or uniform. It was rich and multifaceted, covering the entire gamut from the ultra-orthodox to the secular, politically diverse, intellectually and artistically vibrant, both simple and sophisticated. Its literature (in Hebrew and Yiddish) was the precursor of American Jewish writing in its subversive questioning and breaking of taboos and the culturally normative status quo.

My great-aunt Vera's memories of my father's family – those who lived in the Ukraine and immigrated to Connecticut – end on a whimsical note: 'Well, that's it. Everything will fly like a dream. And that's our life,' she says, first in Hebrew, then in

English. But there was nothing dreamlike about her meticulous, realistic portrayal of how that family lived and who they were. They left only days before the outbreak of the First World War, and a few years before the revolution. Those two world-transforming events occurred without their presence or participation. Yet I often wonder whether my grandfather might have caught the revolutionary bug as a teenager, while still at home, and whether this led to his later political involvement with Soviet military intelligence. Had the family stayed, perhaps they too would have changed at the forced speed of revolutionary light.

In his daughters' accounts of him, my great-grandfather Samuel David cuts an almost mythical figure that would not be out of place in a Western. There is not a trace of shtetl Jewishness about him: he is the self-assured, optimistic, self-reliantly prosperous owner of a local oil mill and three houses, and apparently a successful horse trader. The family history reads almost like life down on the ranch somewhere in Texas ... He has the respect of the local Ukrainian population, invites the entire *dorf* to an annual New Year's Eve party, the family speak Ukrainian and Russian as well as Yiddish. They love to sing and will for ever remember the local folk songs. There are guns in the house for self-protection, but they are rarely used. Except once, when the ripple of the pogroms approaches Selidovka and the father happens to be away, as he often is, travelling on business. The entire family is relocated to a friendly peasant's home while the oldest brother guards the house, gun in hand. The pogrom passed the village by; the fear and readiness to protect themselves remained. Perhaps the first germ of the idea to escape Russia's dangers and leave for America was born then, and brought to active fruition a few years later, when the oldest son was drafted into the Tsar's army – and was rescued from the place of his service and smuggled abroad by the father and another brother.

The Ellis Island records list the arrival in New York of my great-grandmother Temma, with nine of her children, on a ship sailing from Latvia. Her husband and two older sons had arrived a few months earlier via a more circuitous route. For a long time I could not find any trace of their arrival in New York – and then I did. On a passenger list of a ship arriving from Bremen, Germany, were two brothers: my young great-uncles. Their father was already in New York. I was told a family story of Temma's first shocked sighting of her husband upon disembarking at New York after many months' separation: he had shaved off his majestic red beard. She thought this meant he had converted to Christianity. In fact, he remained true to his religious beliefs and became a stalwart member of his Connecticut synagogue. But in other respects, I can't help but think his strong spirit was broken in America. Having arrived with a small fortune earned and saved from his flourishing business in Russia, he placed it all in a New York bank, which went under shortly after. He lost everything. My great-grandfather's arrival in the American promised land was in ironic, stark counterpoint to his life in the old country: a man who, in Russia, fed a family of fifteen with his intelligence and know-how, and without any education, suddenly became an old man (though not yet in years) dependent on his children's support. From roaming the Russian countryside in any weather conditions, in pursuit of deals and contacts, returning home with money, food and a mood of cheerful excitement, he quickly turned into an elderly paterfamilias living in placid suburbia. But had they stayed, his and the family's future would most likely have been a sinister one: after the revolution their businesses would have been expropriated or destroyed, they would have faced dire poverty, starvation during the war, and, like many other Ukrainian Jews, the prospect of being murdered by the Nazis. So a bit of boredom and maybe even depression in American suburbia was not too high a price to pay for the family's life in freedom and, eventually, prosperity.

The only occupation Samuel David attempted in his new home was that of a matchmaker, which is an honourable service in the Jewish community, a mitzvah usually performed by women. Perhaps it was simply an extension of his considerable charm and amiable communication skills, his genuine interest in people. His own married life, like much else about him, could be the stuff of a dark romantic novel. He had married two sisters. The first, Masha, died shortly after giving birth to their third child – the boy who would eventually become the young man whose military draft in 1914 triggered the family's exodus. After a while (not a very long while, it must be said), the widower found the task of juggling children, an infant and his business too much, and asked his in-laws for help. They offered him a younger sister as a mother for the semi-orphans, and a wife. 'Does she want me?' he asked. She said no, she didn't want him. But the parents decided otherwise. 'She will marry you,' they said. 'It's God's will.'

Family lore has it that Temma, the younger sister, was in love with a young man, but it was unthinkable for her to disobey her parents. So she married her brother-in-law, and the bed in which her sister had given birth and died was now hers. Year after year new babies arrived, until the final count of fourteen (including both sisters' offspring). For a while I wasn't sure – I was wondering whether my great-grandmother might have been the forgotten older sister (forgotten because it had become a family taboo to remember that there had been two mothers, and that some of the siblings were also first cousins), and that I would never know where she was buried. Somehow this mattered. But calculations and comparisons of dates of birth definitely confirmed that my great-grandmother was the much younger Temma. If she had not given up her first, real love and refused to marry her brother-in-law, the chain of events that eventually led to my birth in Moscow would not have taken place. I know exactly where she and her husband, my paternal great-grandparents, are buried in Connecticut. Both died in the 1940s. They must have wondered what happened to one of their sons – my grandfather – who left New York in 1934 with his wife and two small children. Did they know that he and his family ended up back in Russia? What would they have made of this reversal of Samuel David's optimistic odyssey from oppression in their old country to freedom in America? If they knew, they must have been perplexed, to say the least. Or, more likely, angry.

I have two striking portrait photographs of my paternal great-grandparents in their younger middle age. They are in colour, possibly retouched. Temma has an open, pleasant, but unsmiling face, dark hair and dark eyes, a high forehead and straight brows; she looks dignified and competent, a woman in charge of her own domain. Samuel David's blue eyes (a strong genetic trait in the family), dark hair and red beard give him a dramatic and strong-willed look. My great-aunt Vera revealed enough about their background and character in the accounts she gave to her grandson to make them feel familiar to me, these strangers whose genes I carry. Both came from so-called Jewish colonies – small, very poor agricultural settlements in rural Ukraine given to Jews by government decree. They could work the land but could not own it. After reading the names of these colonies in my cousin's historical account, and learning my great-grandmother's maiden name, a Google search (or rather on Yandex, the Russian search engine) led me to a volume from 1890, published when the colonies still existed. The book contained all the vital statistics: depictions of the dwellings, how many souls per house, even the names of the families. The name of my great-grandmother's father was among them. I also found another, contemporary source in English, listing all the exact locations and data regarding the Jewish colonies in Ekaterinoslav (the name of the wider area), along with the information that they were all demolished in the 1950s as unprofitable – and because the Jewish population was no longer there. One source listed the names of men shot to death in one of the colonies by a paramilitary nationalistic group, around the time of the October Revolution. Several men from my great-grandmother's very large family were on that list. It is most likely that she never found out. It felt odd to realise that I, the misplaced, forgotten, invisible, denied and almost accidentally found again great-granddaughter, was now the meticulous family historian, digging up facts that had become buried under more than a century of political upheavals and lost family connections.

Samuel David originally came from another such colony in the same area. All were founded on basic agriculture, and all had Jewish schools. Education was paramount, as it ever was in the poorest of Jewish communities anywhere. But my great-grandfather was not as interested in his studies as his mother had wanted him to be. As a young boy he had one passion: his pigeons. Vera's voice tells it best, in her own slightly Yiddish inflection:

He loved pigeons. From one or two birds, he raised them to several. And they nested and used to fly all over and come back and nest on his roof again. But his mother felt, and rightly so, that he gave them too much time, the time he should have been sitting over books, especially the Chumesh, the Hebrew religious texts. But he always was busy with his birds. He had trained them so well that he would put food in his mouth and they would eat it from there. His face grew soft when he told the story.

Well, anyways, his mother finally decided to get rid of this preoccupation. So one day she sent him to bring water home, as always, and when he came back, he found the pigeons already slain and salted and ready to be cooked, probably eight or ten of them. I don't know how she caught them. How could my grandmother have climbed on the roof of the house and caught them? Or maybe she enticed them to come in.

Vera continues:

Samuel David said he felt the first bouts of revenge and rage and he kicked over the bucket of water and spilled it over the kitchen. Water enough probably to last a day. And, of course, he didn't eat the pigeons. Well, he said that from then on, he just couldn't look at his mother. He had such a feeling of animosity. But did she achieve her aims? I don't think so. Whether she made a scholar out of him, I don't know. Because at fifteen or sixteen, he had already left home . . .

If I wrote a novel or screenplay about this family's history it would begin with this scene of Samuel David as a boy, lovingly tending his pigeons. Forgetting all around him: his parents, siblings, the poor colony, the hard work, the deadly boring studies. He would be visibly entranced by the pigeons' freedom to fly where they pleased, and grateful they always returned to him. His overworked mother's scolding voice trailing in the distance. A close-up of a bird eating out of the boy's mouth. The intimacy so palpable it would be almost uncomfortable to watch. Cut to his mother talking in hushed, angry tones to his father. She wants the boy to study his Torah. Enough with the dirty birds. The father is trying to calm her down, but her frown is deep, her lips a thin, hard line. Her eyes sad. She knows what to do. Cut to the boy walking the dusty distance to the well on a hot sunny day, to bring water in two heavy buckets, one pigeon flying along. Cut to him entering his mother's low-ceilinged, dark kitchen, pails of water still in his hands; a close-up of a pan with a couple of skinned birds ready to be roasted. Feathers underfoot. The boy's horrified face. Then the rage, the violently spilled water, the boy's tears kept hard in his eyes: his mother just made him into a man, an angry man. Cut to the boy alone on the roof. Day turns into night. He stares at the starry skies and now he knows: he will leave, soon, alone, and be as free as the birds his mother sacrificed.

In actual fact, Samuel David didn't roam too far from his birthplace when he married his first wife. His mother ended up living with his brother Tevye (yes, I had a great-uncle called Tevye – my only concession to *Fiddler on the Roof* ...) in one of the Selidovka houses belonging to Samuel David, next door to his own. So the rupture was not complete, his filial duty was done despite the rage he could never forget or forgive. But she did not live in his house, and the fact that he told the story to his children himself, with all the details, and not once but often, proves that the boy's pain lived on in the man.

Interestingly, his daughters were better educated than his sons, most of whom had to start working after their basic Hebrew schooling was complete. The girls, on the other hand, finished Russian high school and were immersed in Russian language, literature and music for the rest of their lives. As my great-aunt Vera says to my cousin, 'I wish you could learn Russian so I could recite Pushkin with you in the original. You would be thrilled with the beauty of the language. It's like music ... You read Russian literature, prose and poetry, and you also thrill to the poetry of the language. I recite it all the time, at night, in the morning and in my sleep ...' She spoke about their remote home village – a mere speck on any map – as having windows to the wider world: 'The mail, which came three times a week, connected Selidovka to news and literature. Jewish bards also came through. They were like a walking newspaper, they'd give you the news of relatives and friends in other places and meanwhile have a place to sleep over.' She was proud of her father's forward thinking about education for women, and the fact that he became 'the first on his block to own a gramophone. We had all the contemporary songs and music. And we used to subscribe to newspapers, like *Novoye Slovo* [New Word] and *Novyi Mir* [New World] from Harkov and Ekaterinoslav. With one of the newspapers came a bonus gift: all the classics in translation. All the Scandinavian writers, Knut Hamsun, Ibsen. Then Jack London and many more.'

The chronology and logic of fate should have dictated that the great-granddaughter of Samuel David – i.e. me – would be far removed from the thrills of the Russian language, and would find Vera's praise of Russian quaint and charming, more exotic than comprehensible. And yet it turns out I find it completely natural, because of Russian being my first language, and one whose poetry I love. When Samuel David said to his family in Yiddish one day in 1914, '*Nu, wasses zein de einde?*' ('What will be the end of it?'), adding 'They'll take the boys away,' and they agreed and said 'Let's go to America,' that should have been that: a Russian Jewish family emigrates, changing the narrative of their lives to escape from the bad to the good, from danger to safety, from oppression to freedom, and, without yet knowing it, from mass murder to survival and prosperity. Almost all of Samuel David's children married in America and had children and grandchildren and great-grandchildren. Not long after their arrival, but presumably following the loss of family savings, Vera recalls how 'we would sit on the porch – mother, father, and I – and we would see the boys walking up the street, and my father would say, "You see this, Vera? – *De zeis Voira?* – that's what I achieved, that my sons should be safe from the Russian bullets. These are my riches.'"

Except that one of his sons put an unexpected twist in the narrative by choosing to reconnect with Russia, now the Soviet Union. Leon's decision to do so is the greatest mystery of my unlived life, the life that ultimately led back to Moscow. A naturalised American since 1919, my grandfather had served in the US military as a very young man, worked at various menial jobs, dabbled in radio and photography. The economic depression hit him hard, like everyone else. Yet something deeper occurred to him and in him, something that I will never know and understand, that I can only guess at. As early as 1926 he secretly went back to Moscow and joined the Comintern, becoming a New York-based officer of the GRU. I found his name on many passenger ships sailing between Europe and New York; these must have been the return legs of his journeys to Russia. When he married my grandmother Bessie in 1928 he was already a fully active, if rather minor, member of the Soviet spying apparatus in the United States. Did she know? She must have done – if not immediately, then soon enough, when she chose to join him on the foreign assignment that was to lead them back to Moscow, permanently.

Had my grandfather not, one fine day, decided that the Communist International was the answer to the world's problems, it is safe to say that I would never have been born. I find this truly hilarious. I wish I had known him: I would have told him this in person. I also would have told him how I managed to find so many traces of his activities and his life – all I had to do was be curious, and search. Thanks to the available documentation I have learned more about his clandestine itinerary and his life as an undercover officer of the GRU than he would have imagined a granddaughter he saw only once, as an infant, could possibly know. The only part that still remains almost entirely under wraps (at least to me) is the Soviet side of his history with the GRU, which would include a detailed account of his work in Spain; except for one mention on a published list of (mostly distinguished) officers, I have not been able to research those archives. But outside of the USSR, I was able to confirm that in New York, Leon Minster was part of a network under Manfred Stern, known later in Spain as General Kleber. My grandfather was in Spain in 1936–7 (sent from the Soviet Union). I have a smiley photo of him feeding pigeons in a Spanish square – perhaps a brief respite from more serious activities.

I also know – because family members who spoke to him when he was living in Moscow have told me – that in later years he was torn between pride and disappointment. 'If people knew how much we achieved they would appreciate us more,' he would say, alluding quite openly to his work as an agent. Yet he also regretted the implications of the path he had chosen, eventually grasping that rather than bringing up his children in a country where Jews were free, the Soviet Union was on a par with Nazi Germany when it came to persecuting innocent people – including Jews.

I am mystified by Leon's decision to choose his loyalty to the Soviet Union over his new homeland, the United States. There is no question that the two were irreconcilable, and that his view of the world transcended mere countries: he must have believed in communism as a struggle for worldwide social justice, and against nascent, yet increasingly powerful, fascism. I have so many questions for this Russian American grandfather of mine who died in 1968 and is buried in Moscow. But this past belongs to others, not to me. It connects with mine, but there is a thin line between knowing enough and knowing too much. Sometimes I feel I am in danger of crossing it.

Yasha, the brother who stayed in Russia when the family left in 1914, ultimately reconnected with his long-lost siblings in the 1970s, when he sent a long, sad letter to them via a friend, in Russian. My cousin quotes from it at length in his history of the family, though the original may be lost. These lines capture not only their story, but also, indirectly, mine:

Amidjan, Uzbekistan
Rosh Hashanah, 1976

Dear Family,

To those I do not know, to all of you together, I greet you with the New Year. I wish you, from the bottom of my heart, many happy years and a good life, until 120 years . . .

Early one morning, the year the First World War began, we all said goodbye to each other at the Chaplino station. Not all of you were brave: the only ones who weren't sleeping were my mother Temma and my sisters M and V. We had the last kisses, the last walk, the last – although not the last – tears. Everyone seems to have felt we would not see each other again, and maybe we will never see each other again . . .

. . . We once lived together under one roof in our father's home. To write now is not hard – how to write, what to write, this is the question . . .

When I read this letter I felt included in the Minster family history: those farewells, separations and new beginnings had, ultimately, affected my own life. Of all my new relatives I have met so far, I feel closest to Linda, a cousin once removed. We had a rendezvous in Venice, and she visited me in London. Her father was my grandfather's younger brother. We have exactly the same sense of humour and share an obsession with researching family history via archival documents, which we put to the test almost every week during long telephone conversations between London and Philadelphia.

Linda and I often marvel at the poetic justice of our reunion; she has said that my grandparents would be delighted to know that I have resurfaced and rejoined their side of the family – as would her parents. But above all, she and I are happy about it because we have so much fun, and we have love for each other. She once said to me, 'Thank you for finding us.'

'Oolong and so-long'

If my grandfather's parents and siblings really didn't know the whereabouts of their son and his family, or really thought they were dead, they could have asked the FBI, who had reports from someone returning from Moscow. This person described my grandfather as bitterly disappointed about life in the Soviet Union, especially for Jews. Although the reliability of secret service archives is as questionable as their purpose, they do, nevertheless, throw an interesting light on the era in which they were compiled.

Each delivery from the FBI archives arrived as a surprise: just as I thought I could not possibly receive any more material, they seemed to have given the green light to more uncensored pages. The best surprise was a CD-ROM with file photographs of my grandparents and a few other relatives. Sadly, the photo they had of Joseph as a baby was not approved for release.

My favourite item of all the documents I discovered while researching my grandfather's (minor) cloak-and-dagger story of espionage was this letter, which was found in their apartment in Shanghai, after their hurried departure in 1935:

Mortimer Lippmann, M.D.
320 New York Avenue
Corner Union Street
Brooklyn, N.Y.
May 14, 1935

My dear Mr. and Mrs Minster & Family:

Very happy to have the family letter, which arrived this day, May 13, 1935. It appeared that all the little medicines, that you took along came in handy, but that the illnesses amounted to practically nothing.

Some day will start digging at 320 New York Avenue, because upon looking at the globe find that Shanghai is at the same altitude and latitude but on the other side of the world. Proceeding at the rate of several feet a day, when not busy should reach my destination shortly, with a surprise visit. Therefore, do not become frightened, if you see a man suddenly sticking his head out of the ground before you. This is no joke. I really mean it.

One becomes very tired of the same sameness every day and to be very frank with you, never saw what a sore throat looks like in a yellow man, I wonder, what they do, when the patient's liver does not work and he becomes yellow. Perhaps, then he is all washed up. In that case no ticket, no shirt.

Having 1,827&9/10 English in me after tracing my family tree, makes me a drinker of tea. No where in the world can one get a better cup of tea than in China. Hence this brings me to my letter, having to say in the brand of the Chinese tea, oolong and so-long until I hear from you again. With lots of luck to you all, I am,

Very truly yours,
Mortimer Lippmann (signed)

I assumed that the amusingly named sender of the above letter – Mortimer Lippmann, M.D. – was most likely a fictitious character, or the name of a real person used as a cover, and the letter itself almost certainly written in code, or perhaps as a code. I found it in a file in the National Archives containing about fifty pages of records kept on my grandfather by the British secret service. MI5, via the Shanghai Municipal Police, watched him in Shanghai in 1934 and 1935, and combined forces with American intelligence in the 1950s to interpret his history in relation to several post-war and McCarthy-era hearings and depositions about communist spies and sympathisers, and in relation to what was happening in Japan and China in the years leading up to the Second World War. The files contain many errors, but also some very interesting information.

We now live in a time of forgetting, but also of remembering. Our era – the early twenty-first century – seems to be built on transience: letters and postcards have been replaced by emails, the many digital photographs we take almost constantly are rarely printed out, often disappearing into forgotten computer files rather than finding a permanent place in tangible family albums; printed books may be on their way out, coexisting with or replaced by electronic readers we don't quite know whether to love or hate. We rely on our computers and on our smart devices to be our memory, and when they are lost or irreversibly broken we never really know how much of our life has disappeared with them. Perhaps because I belong to the post-war generation my life, despite many geographic transmutations, is almost entirely documented on paper, in the form of letters, notes, photographs, school records and much else. Some of my relatives have also done their bit for the physical survival of our family memories. An Armenian cousin on my mother's side has written a family chronicle. A great-uncle, also on my mother's side, recorded a taped account of his knowledge of the family's history, going back almost two hundred years. My mother has written a memoir and autobiographical fiction. ('I don't know how to make anything up,' she often says.) My brother has written a sort of memoir, which he describes, a bit defensively, as a 'self-portrait'.

When I set out to retrace my life along the fault lines of its languages, I did not expect to find actual archival material to illustrate my many wanderings and linguistic incarnations. As an investigative journalist I have spent months and even years researching my subjects and their histories. Writing about myself would, I thought, be a refreshingly light exercise in comparison: I know what I know, all I have to do is figure out how it all connects into a coherent narrative. My diaries, letters and photos would help where my memory might fail.

But a strange thing happens when you are examining your own personal archive. In spite of it all being about you and by you, and hence so intimately familiar it instantly brings back long-forgotten moments, you also find yourself reading it with the kind of careful attention you would give to the documenta-tion of a complete stranger's life. All those mini-narratives need to be thoroughly examined, understood and interpreted; all the photos placed in their right context and read for the stories they tell; all the fragments reassembled, like the pieces of a broken mirror. Painstakingly glued together, they will, you believe, once again reflect the true you: the person that disappeared deep inside who you are today.

When who you are today turns out to be a composite not only of the history you know but also a fragile construct based on secrets and lies, the process of piecing yourself together out of such flimsy smithereens becomes more complicated still. The surprise of knowing, since February 2002, that my biological father was an American-born Jew raised in Moscow had worn off by the time I began working on my memoir. By then I had met Joseph several times, as well as his son (my half-brother) and some of his grandchildren, and I was in fairly regular email contact with him and in telephone contact with his sister, my Aunt R. Then one day, not long after Barack Obama became president, the extended honeymoon period was over: I was suddenly cut off from my newly found father and it was all Obama's fault.

I noticed that, one day, Joseph's emails simply stopped. They were never very frequent, but they had been caring and amusing, and constituted a form of conversation, which I cherished. We never really discussed politics, even though it was clear that we would not be likely to vote for the same political party had we been living in the same country. In the manner of most émigrés from the former Soviet Union, he had a natural distrust of everything that represented socialism to any degree. Our political differences never really bothered me – until the day he included me in a group email that mocked Barack Obama in an offensive manner. I objected, and asked that he never send me that sort of stuff again. He apologised, but things began to cool off. Clearly Joseph had come to the conclusion that I wasn't entirely worthy of his trust. The American spectrum of contemporary politics, with its sharp divisions into liberals and Tea Party conservatives, suddenly materialised at the very centre of our private domain.

I continued to speak on the phone to my aunt, even though most of our conversations ended in shouting matches. Her political views were, if anything, even more extreme than her brother's. We talked in Russian; I loved her dirty jokes and her witty, idiomatic, clever banter. But gradually she developed the habit of bringing the topic of Obama's birth certificate into every conversation, and accused him of 'not being an American patriot'. 'One second – let me just turn Rush Limbaugh down so I can hear you,' she would say, and then, after chatting amicably about illnesses, diets and random but to me always fascinating memories of her childhood, she would suddenly declare: 'Obama is a communist. And you too. You're a fucking liberal.'

I did not really mind being described as a 'fucking liberal' by R – I already knew she had similarly dismissed a great number of my newly found relatives, most of whom were politically moderate; I was in great company. But one day, I asked her point blank:

'Is that the reason Joseph has stopped communicating with me? Is it really because I like Obama?' She replied, cautiously, that this was only part of the reason.

'What's the rest of it?'

'He's paranoid,' she said. 'But he tends to be right. He thinks you're trying to find out too much about our parents, and write about it. They wouldn't like it.'

Although this claim was not exactly false – I was, at this time, already starting to develop a lot of interest in my grand-parents' history – the entire premise of this conversation was surreal and absurd. My grandfather, for his own reasons, had been an active communist. My biological father's and his sis-ter's passionately anti-liberal stance was rooted in an emotional response to a lifetime of politics playing a destructive role in their family dynamics. This did not surprise me; but what did upset me was the head-in-the-American-sand approach to their father's – my grandfather's – adventurous history. There was a sense of past danger and of fear, which was still acute; a whiff of secrets in the family closet, to be left alone and untouched, not disturbed by my curiosity. I was, after all, a virtual stranger, an intruder, forcefully entering the family fortress and shaking its well-concealed foundations. But I was also the forgotten child, discovering the family after five decades of living (very happily, it has to be said) in complete ignorance of my biological roots on my father's side. I wanted to really know his family, even if he didn't. I felt a sadness for the grandparents I never knew, and I wondered: had I been missed at all? Did my absence make any difference to their lives?

'Your grandparents wouldn't have wanted you to dig around in their past,' R told me on the phone one night, in a tense voice. I thought about what she said, and reached exactly the opposite conclusion. I decided that they would have wanted me to know who they were and how their lives had turned out. After all, when my mother was dating Joseph she often heard his parents' past being spoken about with pride, as an achievement: his military intelligence work in China, in Spain ... And if they didn't want me to know? Well, too bad. I wanted it. I was sick of the politics of secrecy, of all the enforced silences. The traumas and tragedies of twentieth-century history generated an abyss of silence within many families, on both sides of the Atlantic and on different sides of the political spectrum. I really do believe it's time to open the books, understand what happened and how our relatives lived, and live our own lives not in the shadow of lies and secrets but in the healing light of truth. Out in the open, the myths surrounding those secrets fall apart, and what remains is the only thing that really matters: the stories we inherit.

And so, in this spirit of granddaughterly defiance, I immersed myself in thorough, systematic research of the story of Leon Minster and Bessie Kahan, my grandparents. To find out all the facts, beyond the selective morsels of information volunteered by Joseph and my aunt, I needed historical sources. These turned out to be plentiful. His actions and movements were recorded by the secret and security services of various countries: the FBI, the Shanghai Municipal Police, MI5 and the (still) inaccessible Soviet archives.

I wasn't really surprised to find his name in books, in

academic studies and in various historical sources. What was unexpected was the depth and degree to which his observers tried to penetrate his family history, including an attempt to put together a complete family tree. It was here that I learned about some of the many siblings on my grandfather's side, and ultimately was able to trace their descendants in many corners of the United States.

The National Archives revealed a substantial fraction of a much bigger file. But I found a great deal more than I had originally bargained for. Leafing through pages upon pages, I actually gasped when I suddenly saw photographs of my grandparents in their thirties, along with samples of their signatures. Bessie looked extremely familiar, and I could see some of my own features in her almost-smiling round face. My grandfather looked vaguely comical and also imposing; I could see him playing an extra in a *Godfather*-style movie. Both had classically Jewish, East European faces, and that added to the element of intimacy. The grainy copies of these passport photos, probably from the 1930s, made my grandparents more real to me than the stories I had heard or read about them. Suddenly, here they were. I just wanted to hug them.

My odyssey of following up on all the clues the secret service had so thoughtfully collected for my perusal was only just beginning, and in time I would feel satisfied that I filled that gap in my identity and finally knew the American side of my roots. The events of the first half of the twentieth century and my grandparents' participation in them had all led to the constellation that brought together my Russian Jewish/Armenian mother and American Russian Jewish father in Moscow, and hence to my birth there. Yet I remained most fascinated by the letter from Mortimer Lippmann, M.D.

I read it as, most likely, a warning to leave Shanghai due to an imminent danger. The references to 'yellow' were probably a way of communicating that courage was needed to deal with what was about to happen. The apparently random numbers specifying the writer's degree of 'Englishness' and erroneous statement about latitude were clearly the real code or information imparted via the letter; impossible to crack now, though an expert I consulted did try. But beyond the letter's real aim, I was amused by its humorous prose, the random accumulation of funny facts – from tea to digging one's way from Brooklyn to Shanghai, and comments on the boredom of the medical practice. Above all, this letter addressed to my grandparents in Shanghai was the very last physical trace of their, and their children's, presence in the West, as Americans. This was the cut-off point, after which they would disappear in the Soviet Union and begin a new life under different, assigned names and identities. Mortimer Lippmann's letter was like every other trace I had of their existence: cryptic, pithy, funny, with hints of adventure, danger, mystery and even romance. It fired my imagination and my desire to keep on digging, like its author, from one end of the world to the other, hoping to find something of myself in the lives of my unknown ancestors.

Several years after my discovery of the Shanghai letter I decided to run the name 'Mortimer Lippmann' through ancestry.com, the way I had done for my own relatives. For my grandfather it had led me to many documents such as his military record – he had served in the American army at the age of nineteen.

Dr Lippmann's identity turned out to be entirely genuine. Here was his exact address, confirmed. His employment as physician – confirmed. Even his signature matched the handwriting in the letter addressed to my grandparents. Mortimer Lippmann was clearly just a friend, and the letter had contained no code, just a humorous way of writing a note to friends.

I liked this result even better than my fanciful conclusion.

My grandparents' lives may have been dramatic and subversive, but they were also rooted in normalcy. If I had been lucky enough to meet my grandmother Bessie I would have brought her this letter she had never received, and we would have talked about the time when, as a young mother with two children, she had followed her husband to Shanghai from New York in 1934, only to be forced to flee to Russia soon after. She never saw her parents and brothers again.

Chain

Had I known both sets of my grandparents in Moscow I would have been exposed to (American) English and Yiddish, which Joseph's parents spoke to each other. My grandmother's private telephone book (each page scanned and emailed to me by V, in another dedicated attempt to connect me with my past) clearly shows that English was the language she clung to and never gave up as her own. Almost every page has a few words written in English – notes about office opening times, some names are in Latin letters rather than in Cyrillic, a few personal comments and reminders: 'First Aid' – 'Matches – door' – 'said to call up tomorrow'. I found my mother's and my other grandmother's names and work telephone numbers in that book, the only physical link I have of my two family histories visibly intersecting, ink on paper. On one of the pages my grandmother wrote down three tentative versions of an English word, playing with it, trying to get to the right sound:

inhom
inhomogeous
inhomo

My guess is that in the 1950s or 1960s, when she wrote this down, she was trying to come up with the correct term for unhomogenised milk, a food label that may not have existed before she left America in the 1930s. Or perhaps it did, and she had momentarily forgotten how to say it and was experimenting with the options. These notes were a little window into her linguistic perfectionism: looking for the right form of an English word by writing it down. I hope she got there in the end, because her final 'inhomo' wasn't anywhere close ... My aunt told me that my grandmother loved dictionaries. So do I: I can actually get lost in reading a dictionary or thesaurus. Those final gleaming crystals of verbal precision are the results of wading through so many layers of uncertainty, errors, semantic confusion. But it is the search itself that excites me, and here I had a tiny bit of evidence that my grandmother shared that passion.

Her doodles, present on every page of the address book, also remind me of my own: geometric shapes growing into quite complex structures when they are repeated and combined; copying the printed words – Name, Patronymic, Last Name – and traced over and over in various pens and pencils. The book itself, 'For Telephone Numbers', has a dark blue cover, with its price on the back: 7 roubles 10 kopeks. I don't know whether it was her only one, but it went back to the 1950s and perhaps earlier. Had I not, ultimately, acquired English yet retained my Russian, my grandmother's phone book would have been almost completely unintelligible to me. But as it is, all its elements are crystal clear. Had I known her, I would have been so very curious about her otherness, the different languages spoken in her Moscow home, the mysterious past and connections they conjured up, the faraway world she came from. It's the same curiosity I am feeling now, the longing to really know the grandparents I never met, and their story.

But how much would she have revealed to me? Most likely, very little. I would have come up against a wall of tense silence and paranoia, of hints at a lost youth and forbidden subjects. My mother was shown one photo of my grandmother's many brothers, the family she left in America. She never knew anything about my grandfather's family. His service in Soviet military intelligence was alluded to with pride, but he had retired – or rather, was dismissed – long ago, and made do with simple manual jobs, such as working in a dusty printing press warehouse (which ultimately severely undermined his health). My grandmother was the family's breadwinner in Moscow, using her editorial and language skills for work in English-language radio programming and translation, among other things. I can imagine how her English sounded, having heard many Jewish Brooklynites of her generation – Russian-born, Yiddish- and Russian-speaking, raised in New York – but I don't know what her Russian was like. I heard from my mother that it wasn't fully grammatical, that she made mistakes and had an accent. Having returned to the homeland she never adapted to her old-new mother tongue with perfect fluency. My grandmother's real mother tongues were English and Yiddish. My grandfather's Russian was more fluent than hers, I am told. As for his English, I imagine it must have had some of the same abrupt, gruff cadences I heard in Joseph's American speech. Had I known my grandparents, I wonder if they would have let me in on the secret of their real names.

My younger cousin V, R's only daughter, grew up hearing English in her Moscow childhood. In fact, her first word was 'tiger', after her favourite toy. Would I have known some English as a child in Russia, had I heard it spoken by my biological father and his family? It's a tantalising thought.

My mother's parents are buried in Moscow. I have not been

back there since 1963, the year my grandmother died. I have never seen their graves, except in photographs.

My paternal grandfather is buried in Moscow too. V – the relative who had first told me about my other family's existence – once emailed me directions to his grave: 'Turn left at Sacharov's grave and you'll come to the Jewish section. He is there. The inscription is in English.'

Follow the Languages

I am a reluctant memoirist. My curiosity about the lives of others is endless; my need to reveal anything about my own almost non-existent. But when I found out that my life story was, in fact, rooted in a web of invisible connections, I became interested in unearthing the buried threads linking them all. In my case, the well-known saying 'follow the money' could be replaced with 'follow the languages', as each led to another world. To explore them all, and to understand how they became intertwined, would be to reveal the narrative pattern of my life. It felt more like a series of concentric circles than a linear narrative, each circle encompassing (almost invisibly) the people whose lives had shaped and affected mine. I became so involved in analysing this narrative habitat I almost forgot my main reason for visiting it: to unearth all the secrets my parents and grandparents had erected around our lives like a wall of concrete. My own life was somewhere behind that wall, in the shadow, almost as a shadow, of others.

Without my presence their stories were literally all over the place, without an arc to hold them together, and without an interpreter to explain their meaning. This, it turned out, was my role. My cosmopolitan life was not just my personal slice of multicultural chaos; it gave me the tools to translate the past into the present. I can more than understand all the strands in my complex family make-up: I can feel them too. That's what language really is: a way to feel reality in a certain way, distinct from others. If I could gather all my key relatives, dead or alive, in one room, lock the door and make them talk to each other I would be the only person who could really explain every single one of them to the others, let alone understand their various languages.

In my mother's memoir, there is a sentence which struck me as the quintessence of all our wanderings: 'Each new emigration had been anticipated by the preceding one.' My migrating lifestyle has not been an exact replica of my mother's history, but it certainly has roots in her experience.

The purpose of wandering is to find a place one can call home, if not for the current then for the next generation. It has not worked out that way in my family. Each new home turned out to be only an illusion of permanence. Some of those illusions were better than others; some became surprisingly long-lasting. A lifetime is not so many years for a person to play with; when you move, or rather, as is often the case, flee from place to place, country to country, language to language, you are constantly rewriting the narrative of your life.

Perhaps my life could be described as five languages in search of an author: born into Russian; transposed into Czech, then German; introduced to Hebrew; and finally adopted by English. Notice the passive mode I just used (without thinking about it) to define these moves and mutations, from one linguistic haven to another. It is very seductive, and comforting, to believe that fate gives us very little freedom to make our own choices. Émigrés like to see themselves as victims of circumstance, of higher forces that deprive them of the chance to live their lives as originally planned – had that war, revolution, financial disaster or nasty neighbour not prevented them from staying in the country of their birth. As a multiple émigré myself, I have come to resent this sentimental, self-pitying, teary-eyed view of what is, of course, a genuine loss.

In the only story I have ever written on the subject, 'Black Train' in *Foreign Brides*, a family is forced to emigrate from post-invasion Prague not for political reasons but because the mother, a well-known actress, suffers an attack of diarrhoea at a drunken New Year's Eve party. Despite this non-heroic cause of their exile, my characters' experience of it is genuinely painful. I summarised it in one short paragraph and was very surprised to find it quoted in almost every review of the book:

> All émigrés have the same basic story to tell: there is that small death when they leave their home country, there is that short-lived euphoria when it looks like they've been blessed with a chance to rewrite their script in a free society, and then comes the life-long sadness once they realize that they have made an irreversible choice to cut themselves off from their roots. They can appear successful and lead exciting lives – but they will always feel like second-class citizens, wherever they are. And that huge void inside will never, ever be filled.

Foreign Brides was meant to be a (mostly humorous) take on foreignness and marriage, but my critics correctly identified the real core of it as the rootlessness of exile: an abyss rather than an amusing gap in one's life. In the same story there was a shy little sentence, which is the leitmotif for this memoir: 'We knew that as time went by, our native language would ossify, and our painstakingly acquired English would always feel like snow falling on ice-cold skin.'

Immigrants – all immigrants, not just writers – are familiar with this pattern. Their mother tongue survives as a link to their home (both far away and close, if they choose to function primarily within the confines of a new community in their host country), but it does, indeed, ossify and become a relic from their past, even if they speak it daily. Some exiled writers continue to write in their native language even while geographically separated from its source. W. G. Sebald was a case in point: despite moving to England his writing language remained German. Elias Canetti also wrote in German (not his first language) while living in England. Vladimir Nabokov was an émigré Russian writer in Paris, publishing his novels, though not his poetry, under a pseudonym, before moving to the United States and becoming an American writer in English. Joseph Conrad, a Polish émigré, is considered one of the best writers in English literature.

Similarly, Milan Kundera initially wrote in Czech after immigrating to Paris, before adopting French for his later novels. In one of his essays, he says:

> When I finished *The Farewell Party*, at the very start of the 1970s, I considered my career as a writer over. It was under the Russian occupation and my wife and I had other worries. It wasn't until we had been in France a year – and thanks to France – that, after six years of a total interruption, I began to write again.

Is Kundera still a great Czech novelist, now that he is using French? (He says that he considers himself a French writer – but would his readers agree?) I heard a recording of Susan Sontag introducing Nabokov at a reading in New York in 1964, saying that she 'hopes she can claim him as our, American writer'. Mr Nabokov didn't respond, at least not audibly; I wonder if he nodded or smiled at the time, aware of the complexity of

Sontag's claim. Nabokov, described in his *New York Times* obituary as 'the arguably best English stylist since Joyce', confessed in the last version of his memoir *Speak, Memory*, in a chapter written under the guise of a review of his own book, 'as an English-writing author, Nabokov has always felt insecure'.

I too have my own story of embracing English as the language in which I finally decided to write, after a journey through four others. An event that took place some years ago triggered the original idea for this book. I was on a panel at the Literarisches Colloquium Berlin in February 2000, where my brother and I had been invited to speak about the experience of being writers in exile. The moderator was looking to add another writer or journalist, to 'thematically' complete the constellation. I suggested that he ask W. G. (Max) Sebald, whose trajectory as a writer was in interesting counterpoint to my brother's and my own. To our great delight, he agreed. I treasure the recording of this conversation in German, which reveals Sebald at his best – wise, modest, witty, thoughtful and utterly without pretence. He was surprisingly cheerful that evening, I remember, having just had some very good news from his agent about a deal made for his books, and feeling financial relief for the first time in his writing life. He was very relaxed, his usual slight gloom was gone, and he seemed to find the conversation refreshingly non-highbrow (contrary to our host's expectations and attempts to steer it in that direction). He seemed entertained by my brother's provocative attacks on the German literary and media establishment, and my pithy replies to 'profound' questions ('When do you think in German?' 'Never.'). He was self-deprecating about his own German, saying that he 'never lost his local dialect'. Had he moved to a serious place like Hanover or Hamburg, his German would have evolved, he said. But because he left for England it remained as it was – implying that there was an archaic quality to his native language. In his own way, he considered it to have ossified, or frozen.

The moderator, Denis Scheck, asked us interesting questions. If language defines one's identity, who are we? Am I a British writer? Is my brother a German novelist? What language do we think in? Nabokov's name came up often (it seems that he believed that the human brain thinks and dreams in images rather than verbal constructs) throughout the entire discussion, an omnipresent authority on the subject of being a writer in exile. The moderator was curious: what language do you dream in?

Actually, this is a question often asked of multilingual people. The simple answer is that dreams do not follow predictable linguistic patterns. I can easily assign a language to a person who doesn't speak it, putting, say, Czech words in my Canadian husband's mouth if the mysterious workings of my dream call for it. I once had a pretty mystical dream which was all silent except for a few words spoken in Hebrew by a kind of Greek chorus. Recently I had a vivid dream I would have loved to discuss with Mr Nabokov. In this dream I was typing a Czech text on an old typewriter. In fact, I wasn't even typing: I was simply thinking complete, perfectly coherent and fully formed Czech sentences, and they were coming out of the typewriter as a neat paragraph, all in one go. It was a boring piece of dry literary criticism, but I remember being pleased with it. I could read every word.

So I was dreaming in both images and language, although one could argue that the Czech sentences, being a piece of readable (and thinkable) material, did constitute an image, at least in part. This was a dream very clearly related to my recent purchase of an antique Czech typewriter, which I had picked up in a junk shop during a stay in Prague.

I went there to confront the physical relics of my loss, and to re-establish its evidence. To re-trigger and replenish old memories, which may have suffered some discolouration over time. I very consciously retraced my childhood and early adolescence. I walked between my old homes and schools, paying close attention to every house, milestone and corner. I even entered my old school, which was empty for the summer holidays. Long-buried incidents and feelings came flooding back, until it was almost unbearable to stay there and I fled to a nearby café, which catered to a rich touristy or American expat clientele. Nothing could have brought me back to my real, post-exile world faster than the ridiculously high price of my cup of coffee – and the very young waitress who addressed me in English at first, assuming that I was a tourist. In a deeply painful and deeply ironic sense I was exactly that.

Everyone leaves a childhood behind and moves on into the world of adulthood. For émigrés the difference is that the lost childhood is more lost, not just a memory but a wound, because, no matter how happy it may have been, it represents – as I said in my story – a kind of death. As a writer, I died when my parents decided to emigrate, and I knew it. And then came the miracle of being reborn in English.

English is not my mother tongue, not even remotely. It is, in fact, something far more valuable: a language I was lucky enough to be able to choose, after not finding a home in any of my other linguistic shelters. It is a borrowed language, a gift and a treasure. Had it not come my way, at just the right moment in my life, I would have lived, truly, bereft. No one would have known this – I would have settled on another profession, possibly a far more useful one, and my lack of an inner anchor would have been masked by some measure of professional success in a job not defined by writing. Would it have mattered? God, yes.

When I walk my dog in the medieval forest near my home in

north London I look down at the tangle of tree roots under my feet and am instantly transported to my childhood in Prague. We were always warned not to step over the *bludný kořen*, a mythical tree root that had the power to make you wander for ever, never finding your way back. I must have stepped over it many, many times.

Epilogue

A few months before he passed away in September 2012, Joseph emailed me, asking for the contact details of the new relatives I discovered in America. He was curious. This interest was a surprise: he had not seemed keen to be in touch with them earlier, though he did meet some of them when he first arrived in America from the Soviet Union in the 1970s.

I was very sad to hear about his death. Not because I had ever really felt a father–daughter relationship with him, but because he was a genuine link to one half of my hidden origins. My renewed connection with him had opened the way for me to explore the past that was hardly mine, and yet I had to uncover it in order to feel at peace. Joseph himself remained a distant presence, but there were moments of tenderness, especially in his writing to me, that hinted at the pain he had never come to terms with, by giving me up.

On a recent visit to my parents, after watching yet another episode of a Russian matchmaking programme followed by a classy German *Krimi*, I was overcome by the need to end our charade. One awkward word triggered another and I was suddenly crying and talking about the unmentionable: my biological father. Before my father's anger gathered speed I told them that Joseph had died. And that I needed to talk to them freely. I went into high Russian emotional gear: 'I love you very much and I know you love me, but how can that be really true if you don't want to know what I've been going through? Enough secrets. How can you have lived with it for so long?' I said more than that. I said everything.

I could see that my father was genuinely upset, and surprised that I had felt so much pain. Something shifted; when we said goodnight and hugged I wished I could rewind time and tell my young parents not to bother with all those secrets: I could deal with the truth. And yet, even as I thought this I almost understood why they had. Perhaps they had been right to raise me in a secure cocoon, without external complications. And after all the years of trying to piece together all the sides of my identity I now knew: none of that other history meant anything compared to the real life and love I had shared with my parents. Our arguments, no matter how heated, have always dissolved into laughter. Even on this difficult evening, my father eventually relaxed and seemed willing, once again, to remember and talk about something from his past.

'So how come you arrived in Prague by plane in 1947? Wasn't it an expensive way to travel at the time, especially for a kid?'

'My father insisted. He tried to hide my passport to stop me from leaving, but eventually gave in because I was so determined to go live with my brothers in Prague. So he paid for the best way to do it.'

'What was it like on the plane? Was it full?'

'No! It was just me and Dolores Ibárruri.'

'Who??'

'Don't you know who she was? She was a famous Spanish communist. She lived in Russia then.'

So my teenaged father had shared a plane ride from Moscow to Prague with Dolores Ibárruri, a communist heroine of the Spanish Civil War, but also, as I later found out, a ruthless politician. Somehow, this never before mentioned – or remembered – tableau was a hilarious icing on the complex cake of all his silences. And immediately after mentioning her, he refused to elaborate any further – as always.

My father fell very seriously ill during one of my parents' visits to Prague. I stayed with my mother while he was in hospital in a medically induced coma following surgery. We visited him twice a day, and perhaps for the first time in my entire life I saw their passionate relationship in its pure form. Her strength, support and devotion was indescribably powerful; he, in brief moments of responsiveness, inhaled her love like oxygen. It saved his life.

My mother insisted on taking public transport to the hospital – buses and trams. 'I need to observe other people, how they live. It distracts me,' she said. Other passengers, noticing the tiny, beautiful woman in her eighties who was so full of young smiles and laughter, could not have possibly guessed that she was on her way to visiting her critically ill husband. As always, she faced life unafraid, and without drama.

As the tram lurched through the crowded streets my mother pointed out her personal landmarks: 'This is the hospital where Maxim was born. I sat on that bench just before we went inside . . . '

My mother often says, 'My life is like a novel. I'm really keen to know how it will end!' Perhaps she shaped my life like a novel too, giving me my story but hiding its inner truth, so that I could find it myself.

Acknowledgements

I owe much gratitude to all those who helped, listened, advised (for and against), engaged in endless conversations and endured all my revisions. This short memoir needed a long gestation period.

Clare Alexander was the first agent to work with me on forming the germ of an idea, the proposal that became the book. I am grateful for her early insight and support.

Rebecca Carter is more than my agent today. She has the passion of a true literary mentor. Her warmth, loyalty and editorial wisdom sustained me during a very difficult period. Thank you, Rebecca, for laughing and crying in all the right places.

My deepest thanks belong to Lennie Goodings, my truly wonderful editor at Virago, for her infinite patience, strength and brilliant insight. I will cherish her pencilled notes for ever, as a reminder of how editing should be done: with a firm hand, but also with love.

I also owe a big thank you to Zoe Gullen, a copyeditor par excellence, for her very sharp and also very sensitive eye.

To Jon Gray, my favourite designer in the world: thank you for this perfect cover, created to the soundtrack of Serge

Gainsbourg singing 'La valse des officiers' in Russian, learned phonetically from his mother.

I am grateful for so many interesting conversations with my relatives, and to family archivists whose written or oral accounts I was able to draw on, on all sides of my family: my great-uncle Alyosha Cachmachcev and my cousin Jonathan Rosenblum. I am also grateful to my cousin (twice removed) Linda Minster Silverman, who talked to me, endlessly and mostly long-distance, about everything that was, and everything that might have been.

The documents I received from FBI archives, and others I discovered in the National Archives, were invaluable in helping me piece together my grandparents' history. I am also grateful to the London Library for helping me work on historical microfiche data from British Police Archives in Shanghai. I am extremely grateful to Boris Volodarsky for his historical expertise on Soviet military intelligence.

I thank my mother Rada Biller for all the stories she told me, and for those she wrote so beautifully in her books. I thank my father Semjon Biller for all the stories I know he couldn't tell, but sort of did anyway.

I thank my brother Maxim for always, always listening, and asking all the right, difficult questions.

And to my family – my husband Shalom, my children Miriam, Yaakov, Yoni and Shira, my grandchildren Galia and Noam, Zohar, Ela and Omri: I thank you for being who you are, and I love you all. Keep talking.

Credits

149–50   Gabriel Laub, 'The Way to the Mainland', from
          Home Country: Narrated Landscapes (Munich: World
          Wide Fund for Nature and Pro Futura, 1994).

156   Introduction to Elena Lappin (ed.), *Jewish Voices,
          German Words: Growing Up Jewish in Postwar Germany
          and Austria* (North Haven: Catbird Press, 1994).

209   Alfred Hayes, *My Face for the World to See* (1958;
          London: Arrow, 1960).

265ff.   Extracts from Jonathan Rosenblum, 'Two Songs
          of the Nightingale (Reflections of a Ukrainian
          Jew)', History Independent Study, Northwestern
          University, Evanston, Illinois, 1986. Reproduced by
          kind permission of the author.

280   From KV 2/2962, 1934–1954, The National
          Archives.

295   'Black Train', from Elena Lappin, *Foreign Brides*
          (London: Picador, 2000).

296   'Part Six: Works and Spiders', from Milan Kundera
          (trans. Linda Asher), *Testaments Betrayed: An Essay in
          Nine Parts* (London: HarperCollins, 1995).